Critical Theory and World Politics

Andrew Linklater has been one of the most innovative thinkers in international relations for over twenty-five years. The introductory chapter and eleven essays in this volume provide an overview of the distinctive approach to critical international relations theory that he has been developing during this period. They reflect on the following areas of inquiry:

- the 'problem of community' which is concerned with the relationship between the obligations that political communities have to their members and the duties they have to the rest of the human race
- the 'problem of citizenship' which results from ongoing debates about whether the achievements of national citizenship can be repeated on a worldwide scale
- the 'problem of harm' which revolves around the sociological question of how far human societies have made progress in creating global mechanisms that protect all persons from unnecessary suffering.

These essays provide a unique approach to the state, citizenship and humanity that will interest researchers and students in international relations, political theory, historical sociology and cognate areas of inquiry.

Andrew Linklater is Woodrow Wilson Professor of International Politics at the University of Wales, Aberystwyth. His main publications and research interests have been concerned with the changing nature of political community, the significance of critical theory for international relations and the problem of harm in world politics.

Critical Theory and World Politics

Citizenship, sovereignty and humanity

Andrew Linklater

LONDON AND NEW YORK

First published 2007 by Routledge
2 Park Square, Milton Park, Abingdon, Oxon OX14 4RN

Simultaneously published in the USA and Canada
by Routledge
270 Madison Avenue, New York, NY 10016

Routledge is an imprint of the Taylor & Francis Group, an informa business

Typeset in Times New Roman by Prepress Projects Ltd, Perth, Scotland
Printed and bound in Great Britain by Antony Rowe Ltd, Chippenham, Wiltshire

British Library Cataloguing in Publication Data
A catalogue record for this book is available from the British Library

Library of Congress Cataloging in Publication Data
Linklater, Andrew.
Critical international relations theory : citizenship, state and humanity / Andrew Linklater
p. cm.
Includes bibliographical references and index.
1. World citizenship. 2. International relations. 3. Critical theory. I. Title
JZ1320.4.L56 2007
327.101–dc22
2007006060

ISBN 10: 0–415–39929–7 (hbk)
ISBN 10: 0–415–39930–0 (pbk)
ISBN 10: 0–203–96090–4 (ebk)

IBSN 13: 978–0-415–39929–6 (hbk)
ISBN 13: 978–0-415–39930–2 (pbk)
ISBN 13: 978–0–203–96090–5 (ebk)

Contents

Acknowledgments

The papers that are reprinted in this volume as chapters appeared between 1982 and 2007, the majority in the last ten years. They have been selected to highlight the development of a critical approach to world politics that has its origins in the analysis of theoretical accounts of the relationship between the obligations that fellow citizens have to each other and the obligations they have as members of the human race. The volume is in three parts. Part I consists of three chapters which consider various theoretical considerations of political community and moral obligation. Part II comprises four chapters which analyse several approaches to uncoupling citizenship from the sovereign state and linking it with cosmopolitan political theory and practice. Part III consists of four chapters which endeavour to take the previous discussion forward by laying the foundations for a sociology of states-systems. This ongoing project has two aims: to analyse dominant attitudes to harm and suffering in different historical eras and, reflecting the themes discussed in Parts I and II, to consider the prospects for extending community and solidarity in the context of increasing human interconnectedness.

Each chapter has been revised to clarify points, to reduce repetition and to introduce material that brings out the connections between the various chapters with the aim of adding coherence to the volume as a whole. The introduction provides an overview of the linkages between the problems of community, citizenship and harm, reflecting current interests, which are explained in Chapters 10 and 11, in building new links between international relations, figurational sociology and world historical approaches.

Many debts have been incurred in the course of preparing this volume for publication. My first debt is to Craig Fowlie at Routledge, who proposed this collection, and to Craig and Natalja Mortensen, who oversaw the various stages of its production. I am grateful to Routledge for the opportunity to put this volume together and for the invitation to take stock of an evolving project which has sought to build connections between international relations and the cognate fields of political theory and historical sociology. Richard Devetak and Richard Shapcott provided invaluable advice on which papers to include in this volume and on their organization. Richard Devetak and Toni Erskine made insightful comments on the introduction. Thanks go to Jack Donnelly for solving a crucial problem.

I am grateful to the following journals and publishers for permission to reprint the chapters in this collection: *The Review of International Studies* and Cambridge University Press for 'Men and citizens in international relations', 1981; 7: 23–37, and 'Towards a sociology of global morals with an emancipatory intent', which was published in January 2007; *Alternatives* for 'The problem of community in international relations', 1990; xv: 135–53 (from *Alternatives: Global, Local, Political.* © *Alternatives.* Used with permission of the World Order Models Project and Lynne Rienner Publishers Inc.); Cambridge University Press for 'The achievements of critical theory', in S. Smith, K. Booth and M. Zalewski (eds) *International Theory: Positivism and Beyond*, Cambridge: Cambridge University Press, 1996: 279–98; Allen and Unwin for 'What is a good international citizen?', in P. Keal (ed.) *Ethics and Foreign Policy*, Sydney, 1992: ch. 2 (see www.allenandunwin.com.au); United Nations University Press for 'The good international citizen and the Kosovo crisis', in A. Schnabel and R. Thakur (eds) *Kosovo and the Challenge of Humanitarian Intervention: Selective Indignation, Collective Action and Good International Citizenship*, Tokyo, 2000: ch. 30; Sage for 'Cosmopolitan citizenship', in E.F. Isin and B.S. Turner (eds) *Handbook of Citizenship Studies*, 2002: 317–32; *European Journal of International Relations* for 'Citizenship and sovereignty in the post-Westphalian age', 1996; 2(1): 77–103; *International Political Science Review* for 'Citizenship humanity and cosmopolitan harm conventions', 2001; 22(3): 261–77; *International Affairs* for 'The problem of harm in world politics: implications for a sociology of states-systems', 2002; 78(2): 319–38 (this article first appeared in *International Affairs* (London) and is reproduced with permission); and, finally, *International Politics* for 'Norbert Elias, the civilizing process and international relations', 2004; 41(1): 3–35.

Introduction

The chapters in this collection are united by a particular interest in the ties that bind together the members of political communities and simultaneously separate them from the remainder of the human race. They are especially concerned with bounded communities, which are a problem for themselves in that they exhibit unease when efforts to protect security and other interests lead to excessive force, cruel and humiliating behaviour, negligence and other ways of infringing moral principles that grant all human beings equal moral standing. They are linked by a specific interest in the relationship between the duties that individuals have to one another as citizens of separate states and the obligations they have to all other persons as members of humanity.

The unrivalled destructiveness of the modern instruments of violence, the need to control global linkages that place vulnerable peoples at the mercy of world-wide economic forces and the urgency of reducing levels of environmental harm, which may yet make the planet uninhabitable, have made the relationship between the sovereign states' conception of its rights against, and duties to, the rest of humanity more important than ever. They have made the relationship between 'community' and 'cosmopolis' one of the central ethical and political questions of the time.

Immediate security needs, whether actual or perceived, often lead human beings to think only from the standpoint of their particular community. But over recent decades, human beings have become entangled in global relationships that force them to reflect on the moral consequences of economic and other linkages with 'distant strangers'; they have become exposed to greater pressures to detach themselves from the immediate needs of their particular ways of life in order to reflect on the possible fate of the entire species. These are unprecedented challenges although they reflect the much older phenomenon of whether the species can develop 'modes of thought appropriate for larger and larger human groupings'.[1] Current levels of global interconnectedness have posed the question of how norms and institutions can be constructed that will not only deal with the age-old question of how separate communities can coexist with the minimum of force but also solve the problems of satisfying the basic needs of millions of fellow human beings and protecting the physical environment on which all life depends.

Human communities have been pressed into close contact in what is a relatively recent stage in the social and political evolution of the species; in consequence, societies have come under increased pressure to reflect on whether there are universal moral and political principles that can enable them to live together peacefully. The broad contours of world history reveal why a global consensus on basic norms has been so difficult to achieve. From the earliest recorded phases of human history, the survival of social groups has depended on particularistic loyalties that have often displayed suspicion of, and hostility towards, adversaries and widespread moral indifference to the interests of the other members of humanity. Unparalleled levels of human interconnectedness have therefore been superimposed on the much older phenomenon of powerful emotional ties to particularistic communities. Arguably, the central question in the study of globalization revolves around the issue of how the relationship between these dimensions of social and political life will develop over the coming decades and centuries.[2]

As suggested earlier, global connections have developed to the point at which the awareness of economic and other links with 'distant strangers' has become a central feature of everyday life. Repeated images of 'distant suffering' invite large numbers of people to think more deeply about the relationship between the obligations they have to their communities and the duties they have to other human beings. Modern societies are therefore faced with the question of whether the bounded loyalties that have been central to the survival of social groups for millennia are now an impediment to the establishment of global political institutions with responsibility for managing the social, environmental and other effects of unprecedented levels of human interconnectedness. They are also acutely aware that there are no guarantees that separate communities can develop more cosmopolitan forms of identification or even agree on the moral and political principles that might regulate their increasing interdependence.

Modern societies are no different from their predecessors in believing that the loss of national lives in warfare is more 'grievable' than the death of foreigners, although some of their members lament this condition of moral favouritism and look forward to a world in which universalistic moral beliefs determine collective responses to global problems.[3] The moral standing of the ties that bind persons together in specific communities and divorce them from other social groups is the issue at stake in the tension between these different responses to 'distant suffering'. This is not a new problem by any means. In many historical eras, societies have considered how the obligations that insiders have to one another should be related to the duties they have as participants in wider social and political networks or as members of the same species. A comparison of different states-systems suggests that this normative issue has been most prominent in the modern international system for the plain reason that the universalistic moral dispositions that have been inherited from the medieval world have ensured that bounded political communities are a problem for themselves. This is especially evident in Western theoretical and practical debates about the relationship between the duties of citizenship and the duties of humanity.

One of the most influential essays on international relations theory four dec-

ades ago maintained that political philosophy and the study of international relations had been largely insulated from each other in the history of Western political
thought. The former had concentrated on lofty questions about the idea of the
'good life' within the state, the latter on the most basic questions of 'survival' in
the condition of anarchy.[4] The general orientation of the following chapters has
its origins in a rather different conception of Western intellectual development.
During the seventeenth and eighteenth centuries, major theorists of the sovereign
state and international law did not make a sharp distinction between 'internal' and
'external' spheres of inquiry in the course of reflecting on what they regarded as
the central normative problem in international relations: that is to say, considering
how the obligations that human beings possessed in the original state of nature
stand in relation to the duties they have come to possess as citizens of sovereign
political communities (see Chapter 1).[5] This concern with the relationship between citizenship and humanity (which is described as the problem of community
in the first part of this volume) has been at the heart of international political
theory ever since.

The problem of community raises various normative, sociological and practical or 'praxeological' questions about the state and humanity. These questions are
concerned respectively with the philosophical analysis of the rights and duties
of sovereign states, with the political forces that have the effect of reproducing
bounded communities and the pressures that encourage cosmopolitan orientations, and with the practical matter of how separate societies should respond to
human rights violations and other pressing global concerns (see Chapter 2). All
these questions are offshoots of classic theoretical disputes about the problem of
'man' and 'citizen' in international relations. They are a product of the tensions
that exist because societies deal with foreigners, who are deemed to be the moral
equals of co-nationals in some respects (for example by having certain human
rights in common) but are denied most of the entitlements that the members of
particular societies may have conferred on each other.

The problem of community raises important but under-researched empirical
questions about how far the members of particular communities in different historical eras sympathized with the victims of suffering in other societies and how
far they believed that all peoples have a universal moral obligation to avoid causing each other unnecessary harm. It is worth pausing to consider these matters
in more detail before explaining how the problem of community is linked with
two other broad themes in the chapters below: the problem of citizenship and the
problem of harm.

Incomplete as it is, the anthropological record indicates that many early societies were frequently at war, whether in the form of low-scale ritualized violence or
in organized attempts to weaken or destroy other groups. Only the most isolated
social groups appear to have enjoyed the enviable condition of a lasting peace.[6]
Attitudes to force have usually been the dominant factor in deciding how the
problem of community has been 'solved' in the different phases of human history.
Clearly, warfare often prevents the extension of sympathy and solidarity across
borders; at times, it cancels such sentiments entirely. But most societies have had

internal and external reasons for wishing to control violence in international affairs: internal reasons because of the need to ensure that decisions to relax the
usual restraints on force do not leave members exposed to excessive violence at
the hands of returning warriors; external reasons because pragmatic concerns,
including the high value attached to commerce, urge the search for a solution to
violent conflict or because religious norms or secular standpoints that affirm the
equal standing of all persons have provided ethical reasons for endeavouring to
limit force.

The tension between immediate security needs and moral or religious scruples
is obviously far from being resolved – and may never be resolved – but the centrality of violence in human history should not detract attention from collective
political efforts to control force in the relations between organized groups that
stretch back to the earliest historical records. This is one reason for wishing to
locate the problem of community in the broadest possible historical context. The
motive for developing new links between world history, historical sociology and
international relations arises from the absence of a systematic inquiry into the
extent to which different states-systems created 'cosmopolitan harm conventions'
(conventions that are designed to protect all persons from indefensible harm irrespective of their citizenship, nationality, race, religion, gender, and so forth).
One purpose of the proposed area of inquiry is to understand what the modern
states-system may have achieved, and might yet accomplish, in the way of overcoming forms of xenophobia, group egoism and moral indifference to the interest
of outsiders, which have been the norm for millennia (see Chapters 8–10).

It is instructive to consider how the theoretical disputes over the relative importance of the ties of citizenship and humanity gave rise to these sociological
questions. The differences between Vattel's claim that there was not the same
need for a world society as for a society of individuals and Kant's contention
that increasing levels of global interconnectedness made cosmopolitan political
communities essential are especially relevant in this context. What has been described as Kant's 'Copernican Revolution' in political thought was a response to
the continued lawlessness of international relations in the Age of Reason and to
the inadequacies of self-regarding sovereign states in the emerging era of closer
global economic and political interdependence.[7] The rational ordering of the modern political condition could be accomplished by expanding the rule of law to
ensure that all human beings would be treated as equal members of a 'universal
kingdom of ends'. When compared with Vattel's rather static account of the state
and humanity, Kant's approach stands out for its emphasis on the need for cosmopolitan orientations to the moral problems that are the inevitable consequence of
rising levels of global interdependence.

Kant's decision to place the problem of community in a world historical framework of analysis that was concerned with the development of humanity from the
beginning of time made him the first great theorist of the international relations
of modernity. There are clear links between Kant's approach to the problem of
community and Marx's similarly world historical argument for transforming the
relationship between the nation and the cosmopolis in the context of global capi-

talism; and there are evident connections with Elias's reflections on the need for modes of sociological inquiry that move beyond the methodological nationalism of analysing societies in isolation from each other in order to analyse largely uncontrolled global processes. Despite their very different positions on the relationships between normative purpose and sociological inquiry (which need not detain us here), all three approaches to the global politics of modernity display the same broad historical interest. They have a common desire to understand how very long-term patterns of change have entangled various societies in global economic, political, military and economic processes that they only partly control. This shared interest in understanding the processes that affect humanity as a whole was combined with a specific interest in the relationship between the material expressions of growing global interconnectedness and the relative influence of national and cosmopolitan forms of identification.

This preoccupation with considering the problem of community and rethinking the relationship between citizenship and humanity in the light of uncontrolled global processes is the link to considering the significance of critical social theory for the study of international relations in Chapters 2 and 3 and 8–11. Frankfurt School social theorists sought to free the materialist interpretation of history from the theoretical and political liabilities of economic reductionism, while at the same time preserving Marx's claim that the fundamental political question is how human beings can control more of their history under conditions of their own choosing.[8] Reflecting this theme, Chapters 2 and 3 in this volume introduce the claim that the classic normative questions arising from the problem of community should be linked with the critical theoretical claim that political inquiry has an emancipatory purpose. The task is to highlight surplus social constraints and to identify the possibilities for new political relations that are immanent within actual communities.

Habermas's contribution to the development of the critical theoretical project has focused on the cosmopolitan possibilities that are said to have been inherent in ordinary communication since the appearance of the earliest human societies. His discourse theory of morality has stressed the practical possibility of creating dialogic relations which embody the ethical ideal that all human beings have an equal right to participate in making any decisions that may affect them. It is immaterial from this standpoint whether such decisions are taken within the societies to which affected persons belong or are made in distant places where they are denied voice and representation. The emphasis on equal moral entitlements to participate in the relevant decision-making processes, and the parallel stress on equal rights to shape deliberative outcomes, are invaluable for contemporary reflections on ideal ethical responses to the vulnerability of persons to both proximate and remote sources of harm. This emphasis should be a critical element of any ethic that aims to promote the humane governance of global economic and political interdependence.

Whether deliberative ideals can be realized is a complex and contentious matter that requires some remarks on the second theme with which this volume is concerned, namely the question of whether the 'contours' that lead from national to world citizenship 'are already becoming visible'.[9] Many political projects with the goal of advancing cosmopolitan ideals (whether by defending transfers of wealth from rich to poor or by supporting international criminal law to ensure restitution for the victims of war crimes or human rights abuses) have defended one or other version of 'post-national' citizenship. It is important to ask why the idea of citizenship has been pressed into the service of contemporary cosmopolitan projects in this way. At first glance, a concept that immediately invokes fundamental moral distinctions between 'insiders' and 'outsiders' would seem to be an unlikely resource for developing viable projects of this kind and for rallying support for them.

Over approximately the last two centuries, citizenship has been linked with the idea of the nation and inextricably connected with bounded political communities governed by state monopoly powers that have responsibility for protecting the interests of co-nationals and not for advancing a more inclusive conception of global welfare. Its exclusionary nature has never been unproblematic however. Theories of the state and international relations in the seventeenth and eighteenth centuries remain significant for current debates because they cast light on the difficulties that modern cultures have had with the idea of national citizenship. They also elucidate why theorists from Kant to Habermas, in addition to numerous political movements, have found one or other ideal of post-national citizenship so attractive.

The theories of state sovereignty and international relations in the centuries in question combined a natural law approach to ethical universalism with a strong defence of bounded associations. One of their postulates was that human purposes are much the same everywhere. The universal law of nature recognized shared vulnerabilities by claiming that each person in the original state of nature had the same moral right to live in freedom from unnecessary harm. The formation of sovereign states was designed to provide legal safeguards from violent harm on a scale that was practically possible. Freedom from harm was to be guaranteed by citizens' rights, which only the state could protect. The belief that rights to security could not be defended in any other way was a principal reason for the triumph of the sovereign state over the different forms of political association that competed for influence in early modern Europe. Territorial states appeared to solve the problem of scale in that the most viable were large enough to defend themselves from external threats but also sufficiently compact to be administered from a central point. As a result of this success, the most powerful nation-states proved capable of creating and governing global empires that were unprecedented in the history of the species. The legitimacy of the European nation-state, and the reason why non-European societies wished to establish independent sovereign powers on their soil, are inextricably linked with its unusual political capabilities and unrivalled global reach.

Human societies have yet to enter the 'post-Westphalian' era in the sense of surrendering crucial powers to substate and transnational political authorities that are the object of strong popular loyalties; however, public confidence in sovereign institutions has declined in recent times, as doubts about the ability of states to solve the problem of environmental degradation clearly reveal. One consequence of the lowering of public expectations is that many political discourses have turned to visions of 'post-national' citizenship to make the case that individuals should take personal responsibility for that part of the world that they can affect (notions of environmental citizenship, fair trade, ethical tourism and socially responsible investment illustrate this trend). The idea of good international citizenship has been coined to stress the responsibilities that states have for the world at large (Chapter 4). In a more radical step, some conceptions of post-national citizenship envisage new forms of political community in which state powers are shared with 'higher' and 'lower' authorities and where traditional 'national' loyalties yield significant ground to more local and cosmopolitan attachments (see Chapter 6).

It is useful to consider these developments in connection with older concerns about the supposed achievements of national citizenship, such as Rousseau's claim that individuals became 'enemies of the rest of humankind' when they departed from the natural condition to establish sovereign states and Kant's contention that the 'same unsociableness' that led human beings to form states created the need for a 'cosmopolitan condition of general political security' that would protect the rights of everyone. Kant did not object to the territorial state as such but problematized the ethical code that shaped the way in which sovereign powers are exercised. Kant's idea of world citizenship may now seem tame because it was limited to duties of hospitality to strangers, but his argument that human beings are obliged to enter into a civil condition with everyone they can possibly harm has radical implications for world order. This dimension of his political theory envisaged a central role for international and cosmopolitan law so that the achievements of citizenship would be projected beyond national borders. The establishment of appropriate global legal and political arrangements, supported by commitments to world citizenship, would ensure that all persons would be protected from unnecessary harm. All subsequent visions of post-national forms of citizenship are indebted to this crucial ethical ideal.

Considered from this angle, it is hardly surprising that the idea of citizenship has been pressed into the service of cosmopolitan political theory and practice. At least three reasons exist for this development. They include, first, the belief that citizenship involves moral responsibilities to ensure that others enjoy the benefits of belonging to the same moral community; second, the idea that citizenship gives force to basic rights to freedom and security, which all human beings should possess; and third, the contention that citizenship embodies the right to participate in the public sphere, which is one of the main achievements of modernity.

Accounts of post-national citizenship aim to project one or more of these ideals into the traditionally inhospitable realm of international politics. Cosmopolitan citizenship and good international citizenship stress the need for compassion towards all other members of the human race, for assuming personal or collective responsibility for, among other things, the global environment, and, in some formulations, for risking the lives of co-nationals in military efforts to end or prevent serious human rights violations abroad. Concepts of world citizenship have stressed that basic human rights should be protected by international criminal law.

Several political theorists have added that national citizenship will lose much of its value unless it is uncoupled in some measure from nation-states and grafted on to supranational political institutions. That vision of the 'supranationalization' of citizenship through the establishment of worldwide democratic structures envisages radical global political innovations that may take centuries to realize, if indeed they can be realized at all. All such notions of post-national citizenship argue for a profound shift in the relative influence of traditional solidarities and cosmopolitan forms of identification (see Chapters 6 and 7).

Several critics of such visions protest that democratic structures and welfare systems can be realized only within bounded national communities. They argue that efforts to supranationalize citizenship are destined to fail because there is no common culture or shared nationality to support the global equivalent of demanding civic responsibilities. Many opponents of the view that cosmopolitan citizenship requires humanitarian intervention to stop human rights abuses have maintained that the end result is most likely to be a new form of imperialism, assuming (which many doubt) that national citizens are prepared to accept the human and other costs that long-term commitments to rebuild war-torn societies invariably entail. The critics have drawn attention to the risk that scarce political resources will be squandered on efforts to create new forms of community and citizenship when the central task is to consolidate existing nation-states and to assist in creating stable political structures in societies that do not possess the institutions that the citizens of secure liberal democracies usually take for granted (see Chapter 7).

Debates will continue about whether the defence of territorial sovereignty and national citizenship lends legitimacy to the nation-state at the very point when the main challenge is to embody ancient ideas about the universal community of humankind in more powerful regional and global organizations; and disputes about 'humanitarian war' will persist regarding the political ramifications of using violence to try to alter the relationship between duties to the state and duties to humanity (see Chapters 5 and 6). Critics of world citizenship have stressed the impossibility of creating global political arrangements when nation-states are the main focal point of popular loyalties and when there is little public interest in launching experiments in developing alternative forms of community and citizenship. However, the chapters in the second part of this volume defend the claim that the humane governance of global interconnectedness, now and in the future, will require stronger cosmopolitan moral orientations coupled with radical institutional innovations. On this argument, various conceptions of post-national citizenship provide valuable moral resources for weaning the human species away from particularistic attachments that thwart collective efforts to control global processes in conformity with the ideals of the Enlightenment.

The last few paragraphs have shown how the analysis of the 'problem of community' evolved into an inquiry into the 'problem of citizenship'; the next part of the discussion explains how this turned into the analysis of the 'problem of harm'. Carr's argument for new forms of political community in post-Second World War Europe provided the initial impetus for wishing to steer the critical theory of international relations in this direction.[10] His approach, which was indebted to the writings of Marx and Marxism, stressed the desirability of new international planning arrangements that would protect the security interests of the citizens of European states: not only freedom from physical violence but also levels of economic security that unregulated market forces had dashed in the interwar years. Central to the discussion was a belief in an epochal change that confronted human beings with new modalities of harm. To the traditional harms associated with military conflict it had become essential to add the more recent phenomenon of 'transnational harm', which was the result of uncontrolled global economic forces. For Carr, the central issue in the post-war years was how to replace sovereign nation-states with forms of political community that would have responsibility for reducing the harmful consequences of higher levels of human interdependence.

The notion of epochal change that can be found in Marx's prescient reflections on capitalist globalization, as well as in Carr's writings, invites the analysis of the problem of harm in world politics and, within that framework, the more specific investigation of how far cosmopolitan harm conventions have influenced the evolution of different states-systems (Chapter 8). A few preliminary comments about harm conventions in all social systems may be useful before taking the discussion further. All viable communities have such conventions that define what constitutes harm or injury and which distinguish between acceptable harm, such as official systems of punishment, and proscribed harm, such as murder, theft, deceit, and so forth. This generalization also holds for societies of states. An attempt to develop the 'sociology of states-systems', which was outlined in Wight's essays, must aim to ascertain how far different societies of states introduced international harm conventions in order to limit violence and maintain order. It must also endeavour to establish how far they created cosmopolitan harm conventions, which had the more specific objective of protecting all persons from unnecessary pain and suffering (Chapter 9). This approach can explore whether the modern states-system has made progress over the course of its development in embedding cosmopolitan harm conventions in the global constitution. It can also investigate the larger issue of whether or not it is meaningful to claim that modern international society has advanced beyond its predecessors in making such conventions more central to attempts to steer the future development of humanity.

It is useful to reformulate the problem of community in the light of this focus on harm and harm conventions: the issue then becomes how loyalties to particular societies can be influenced by cosmopolitan orientations so that communities cause as little harm as possible to outsiders. This concern with harm draws on ancient ethical themes. As a result of Stoic influences, a major strand of Western moral and political thought has maintained that the duty to avoid unnecessary harm to any other person is the most basic human obligation. Observing this ethical principle is one way of creating a condition in which the obligations that bind citizens together in particular communities do not clash with their moral duties to other members of humanity.[11] The political significance of the rules of war in many different states-systems raises a more general point in this regard. Widespread acceptance of the need for rules to protect combatants and non-combatants from unnecessary suffering reveals that successful experiments in creating cosmopolitan harm conventions have usually been the product of a broad intersocietal consensus about the undesirability of elementary forms of physical and mental suffering. Success in this domain has been anchored in widely shared conceptions of undesirable harm rather than in some common conception of the good (on which societies have famously disagreed).

Arguably, the most basic forms of solidarity between strangers can be derived from the observation that human beings are mentally and physically vulnerable in similar ways because of their shared biological inheritance (see Chapter 11). Common vulnerabilities, which have been intelligible to human societies across the boundaries of time and place, provide the most accessible route to a cosmopolitan ethic; and yet the historical record is unambiguous that the idea of common humanity, which can be grounded in such similarities, has never determined how the constituent political parts of the human race have conducted their external affairs. One of the purposes of a sociology of states-systems is to examine the extent to which common humanity made some impact on the dominant ideas about how the species should be organized. One aim is to consider how far these distinctive forms of universal political organization have been the site for collective learning processes that have revealed how bounded communities can coexist with the minimum of pain, injury and other forms of suffering. One task is to try to understand what these global political arrangements have contributed to the development of the 'species power' for steering human affairs so that they do not burden individuals anywhere with unnecessary harm (see Chapters 9–11).

Whether the modern society of states has made (or is likely to make) progress in creating cosmopolitan harm conventions that protect all individuals from senseless suffering requires some final comments about the significance of Elias's account of the 'civilizing process' for international relations (see Chapters 10 and 11). In Elias's particular sense of the term, the civilizing process refers to the development over approximately five centuries of the modern European belief in having left behind the savagery of earlier times and having moved beyond the barbarism of neighbouring places. The idea of civilization was employed to explain the development of these European self-images and not to endorse them. The 'civilizing process' was the core concept around which Elias organized the analysis of changing social attitudes to violence and suffering and associated shifts in the operation of such basic emotions as embarrassment, shame and disgust over the centuries in question. The inquiry proceeded from the assumption that all human societies have civilizing processes as all face similar problems of learning how their members can satisfy basic needs without killing, injuring, demeaning and in other ways harming each other repeatedly in the course of pursuing their ends. Applying this approach to international relations, the question of whether the modern states-system has progressed beyond its predecessors or over its own life cycle is concerned with how far a global civilizing process has helped to tame the harm that the constituent political parts do to one another in the course of satisfying basic security, economic, cultural and other needs. For its part, the comparative analysis of states-systems is the sphere of inquiry in which Sociology and International Relations can come together to examine global civilizing processes in different historical eras.

These themes can be usefully connected with the main points that have been made during the discussion of the problems of community and citizenship. The development of modern citizenship was connected with the rise of the city and with related notions of civility and civilization; it has furnished the citizens of bounded communities with the legal and political resources with which to oppose what has come to be regarded as senseless suffering and unnecessary harm. The tension between 'man' and 'citizen' has been predicated on the assumption that the individual's moral obligations are not exhausted by duties to the state but must allow scope for at least some cosmopolitan responsibilities. The belief that certain duties transcend citizenship and emanate from common humanity announces the hope that a global ethic will come to have a greater civilizing effect on the conduct of international relations. Visions of post-national forms of citizenship can be regarded as critical to the project of extending the civilizing process so that all persons, and not just those who happen to live together in the same sovereign state, are free from unnecessary harm. Those visions, therefore, aspire to replicate the achievements of domestic civility at the higher level of the global political order.

Whether the human race and its constituent societies will ever solve the problems of community, citizenship and harm in the manner suggested in this collection is a purely speculative matter. On the available archaeological evidence, the first human societies approximately two hundred to two hundred and fifty thousand years ago consisted of a few dozen members – which was the upper limit the natural environment could sustain. In the course of very long-term patterns of change, human beings overcame these limits, as theorists from Kant to Elias have stressed. The development of more expansive social systems followed in conjunction with the increased ability to subject natural processes to their collective will. When reflecting on what the human species might yet achieve at the level of world order, it is useful to remember that settled agricultural communities emerged quite recently in human history, probably around ten to eleven thousand years ago at the start of the Holocene period. Complex urban settlements are products of the last five millennia of human development. Considered from this angle, modern territorial concentrations of power with global reach, and the mastery of natural forces that has accompanied them, are very recent developments indeed. To highlight the scale of the change, it is worth remembering that the Ancient Greek international system consisted of approximately seven hundred city-states with very limited global power. In a very short period of time, the modern states-system has come to revolve around two hundred independent political communities which, individually and collectively, exercise dominion over the entire planet and include the whole species.

The global architecture of modern social and political life – the existence of a universal international society linking sovereign states and embracing the whole of humanity – emerged then in what is still an early stage in the social and political evolution of the species. Human beings have only recently become enmeshed in high levels of global interconnectedness. They are still in the process of learning how to adapt their ways of life to this condition and how to create cosmopolitan conventions that keep pace with accelerating interdependence. It has been suggested that the four or so billion years in which human life may be sustainable on earth (assuming that the sun is about half-way through its lifespan and that humanity survives well into the future) may give human societies enough time to work out how to coexist peacefully and how to 'make their life together more pleasant, more meaningful and worthwhile'.[12] That period may make it possible for the species to bring global connections under the dominion of cosmopolitan principles that assert the right of all human beings to pursue their vision of a decent life in collaboration with others. This was the ethical idea that informed Kant's doctrine of perpetual peace and Marx's vision of universal communism. Despite world-weariness with utopian experiments and widespread disenchantment with the belief that political action can secure universal emancipation, it is premature to abandon the quest to embed cosmopolitan moral ideals in the organization of world society. The problems of community, citizenship and harm deserve to have a central place in the critical theory of international relations for these reasons.

Part I
The problem of community

1 'Men and citizens' in international relations

Since Rousseau political theorists have had frequent recourse to a contrast between the fragmented nature of modern social and political life and the allegedly
more communitarian character of the Greek polis. At the heart of this opposition
was the belief that the polis represented a condition of unsurpassable harmony
in which citizens identified freely and spontaneously with political institutions.
Compared with their ancient counterparts, modern citizens exhibited a lower level
of identification with the public world and a stronger resolution to advance their
separate interests and to pursue private conceptions of the good. Nevertheless, the
disintegration of the polis was not depicted in the language of unqualified loss.
History had not been an entirely unmitigated fall, because the individual's claim
to scrutinize the law of the polis on rational grounds involved a significant advance in human self-consciousness. The positive aspect of its decline was found
in the transcendence of a parochial culture in which neither the right of individual
freedom nor the principle of human equality had been recognized. The modern
world had lost the spontaneous form of community enjoyed by the ancients but it
surpassed that world in its understanding and expression of freedom (Hegel 1956:
252–3 and Hegel 1952: paras 260–1, esp. additions; see also Plant 1973: ch. 1 and
Taylor 1975: chs 14–15).

Much is made in the writings of Hegel of the necessity of integrating the
ancient ideal of community with the modern principle of individuality. Indeed,
for Rousseau, Hegel and the early Marx the modern political problem is how to
make good citizens out of modern individuals, out of persons who are no longer
spontaneously citizens (O'Malley 1970: introduction, esp. pp. xi–lxiii). This
problematic relationship between 'man' and 'citizen' combines with an equally
important, if less discussed, political problem: how should human beings relate
the obligations they acquire as humans with the obligations they acquire as citizens of bounded political communities? Again, Hegel's account of the experience
of Greece is important. Within the polis, only citizens lived properly human lives;
neither slaves nor the citizens of other states were thought to have equal moral
worth. Moreover, the citizen's integration into the life of the polis involved an
unquestioning acceptance of the roles and responsibilities of membership. This
'immediate' identification dissolved on account of the individual's claim to

criticize the life of the polis in accordance with principles of universal reason. A new type of moral consciousness challenged both the exclusiveness of the polis and the supremacy of its civic obligations. Later, it made possible the claim to belong to two societies: the natural society of one's birth and the universal society embracing all persons by virtue of reason (Colletti 1973: ch. 12; Taylor 1975: pp. 385, 395–7). The distinction between 'men' and 'citizens' created an important problem for international political theory: the problem of how to reconcile the actual diversity and division of political communities with the newly discovered belief in the universality of human nature.

The conflict between citizenship and humanity is fundamental to the experience of the modern states-system. This is so because the emergence of moral and religious individualism or universalism divided the Western experience of morality between two dominant perspectives (see Walsh 1972). According to one conception of moral life, the individual understands morality as 'an affair internal to a particular community' (Walsh 1972: 19); the separate community is the source of concrete ethical life and the main object of political loyalty; the states-system is the inevitable product of the species' division into a variety of particularistic social moralities; the idea of humanity, lacking expression in the roles and responsibilities of a form of life, exerts little or no constraint upon the relations between states. According to the second conception, 'the moral law binds men as men and not as members of any particular community' (Walsh 1972: 19); individuals may employ their rational faculties to determine the rights and duties that necessarily govern them all; the state, moreover, is an incomplete moral community, too limited to satisfy the individual's sense of wider moral responsibilities, and the states-system is an obstacle to the institutional expression of the human race.[1]

The earliest systematic writings on the modern states-system displayed deep tensions between these moral traditions (Pufendorf 1927, 1934a, 1934b; Vattel 1964). In the history of modern international thought these works comprise the first stage in the understanding of the relationship between humanity and citizenship. As human beings, it was argued, moral agents have duties to one another that are prior to the formation of separate states; as citizens they acquire specific obligations that they share with fellow members of bounded political associations. As political obligations are superimposed on primordial moral ones, individuals have to decide their relative claims on them. For the classical writers of the states-system 'the services of humanity' ought to survive the establishment of any 'special bond with some particular society' (Pufendorf 1934a: 242); they claimed that 'no convention or special agreement can release [men] from the obligation . . . to fulfil the duties of humanity to outsiders', a responsibility now assumed by the state and its rulers (Vattel 1964: 5–6). The classical writings assumed that states could deftly balance the obligations that individuals incurred as human beings with the obligations they have as the citizens of particular societies.

A second stage in the history of international thought highlighted an endemic weakness in these proposed solutions to the problem of relating two types of moral experience. Classical theory itself conceded that the processes of establishing special bonds within states were concluded without contractors conforming with their natural duties.[2] Rousseau and Kant made the important claim that universal ethical obligations were compromised by forms of competition and conflict that were inherent in a world of sovereign states. The species' condition was transformed totally by the experience of living in and among states. It was necessary now for individuals to behave merely as citizens and to ignore the ties of humanity. Thus, for Rousseau each one of us is 'in the civil state as regards our fellow citizens, but in the state of nature as regards the rest of the world; we have taken all kinds of precautions against private wars only to kindle national wars a thousand times more terrible; and . . . in joining a particular group of men, we have really declared ourselves the enemy of the human race' (Rousseau 1970: 132). The states of Europe exhibited 'glaring contradictions' between 'our fair speeches and our abominable acts, the boundless humanity of our maxims and the boundless cruelty of our deeds' (Rousseau 1970: 135–6). Extending this theme, Kant wrote that 'the same unsociableness which forced men into (a Commonwealth) becomes again the cause of each Commonwealth assuming the attitude of uncontrolled freedom in its external relations'; citizenship provided individuals with the security that facilitated the development of a kingdom of ends within the state while jeopardizing the goal of a kingdom of ends at the global level (Kant 1970a: 183). In this way, the contradiction between citizenship and humanity came to be regarded as the key ethical problem of international relations.

Insofar as there has been an impetus for Western political theorists to reflect upon the relations between states, it has been provided by this dichotomy. Theorists have confronted not a world of politics the 'recurrence and repetition' of which is alien to a discourse concerned with order and progress but a world of moral tensions, and their first business has been to discover a means of understanding and overcoming them. This ambition underwent a radically new development when, building on ideas that originated in the late eighteenth century, theorists inaugurated a new phase in the history of international thought. Underlying this departure was the historicist assault upon both the supposed uniformity of human nature and the alleged timelessness of universal ethical principles. The focus upon the diversity and incommensurability of moral systems was combined with a critique of that realm of human obligation that had been presumed to be in conflict with the ties that bind national citizens (Berlin 1976: xxiii; see also 'Herder and the Enlightenment' in the same volume; and Stern 1962: ch. 6).

Whether defensive or critical of the 'man–citizen' dichotomy, it is unsurprising that theorists of international relations made it their principal concern. Its pre-eminence corresponds with the view that 'the need for philosophy arises when the unifying power has disappeared from the life of man' (Marcuse 1969: 36). However, what must be at issue since the emergence of historicism, and relativism, is the validity of arguments that seek to defend the claim that the experience of living in and among modern states exhibits unresolved tensions. To consider this problem further, and to specify what turns upon it, I propose to analyse three conceptions of the 'man–citizen' dichotomy. Two of these perspectives have been mentioned – modern natural law and historicism. To these shall be added a third perspective that focuses on the historical development of the species' capacity for self-determination.

The rights and duties of citizens

The dichotomy between citizenship and humanity appears in the earliest theories of the modern states-system. These writings reflected a broader movement in European culture, the rise of individualism, and its particular expression in political theory, the substitution of an 'ascending' for a 'descending' conception of government (see Ullman 1961: 24). Contractarianism was incorporated into these theories to account for political obligations and to justify the primacy of obligations to fellow citizens. Civil society was conceived as the outcome of individual negotiation. Individuals surrendered their inherent, absolute rights to obtain a condition of civility conducive to their 'utility' (Pufendorf 1934a: 103; Vattel 1964: 9a–10a). Because of their natural equality and liberty, society could be constructed only through free, individual exchanges of equivalent benefits; reciprocity made social life possible and consent gave force to obligation. As a society of individuals was more necessary than a society of states, and since a universal political association was unobtainable anyway, contracts were concluded not by the whole of humanity collectively but separately within emergent political groups (Pufendorf 1934a: 274; Vattel 1964: 5–6). Individuals left the state of nature by granting each other determinate rights and duties, the rights and duties of citizens. Between their respective political associations, however, the state of nature continued to exist. As individuals were not parties to contracts with outsiders they were free from specific international moral responsibilities. States, moreover, had binding or 'perfect' obligations to those who had consented to their establishment, but not to other persons. By such compacts, individuals specified the ultimate obligations of citizenship within associations, the sovereignty of which expressed the necessarily bounded character of moral and political life.

Classical theorists did not presume that the states-system consisted solely of insulated moral enclaves, however. Had they done so the individual would have possessed a unified moral experience. On this assumption the state would have been the sole moral constituency and the states-system would have been an unproblematic form of world political organization. That these conclusions were avoided was a function of the belief that states were artefacts superimposed upon a primordial moral community coextensive with humankind. Classical theorists sought the theoretical integration of contractarianism and moral universalism. They developed that tradition of thought that originated in one of 'the most decisive change[s] in political thinking', a change that 'came some time between the days of Aristotle and Cicero, and proclaimed the moral equality of men' (Carlyle 1930: 7–11). The doctrine that human reason was endowed with the capacity to apprehend non-contractual, immutable moral principles inherent in the nature of things became part of the dualistic foundations of modern international theory. Thus, 'the universal society of the human race' arose as a 'necessary result of man's nature' (Vattel 1964: 5–6). There was an obligation upon 'the race of men' to cultivate 'a friendly society' because of 'nature's will' that all persons are 'kinsmen' (Pufendorf 1934b: 212). On account of this primordial and universal moral community, obligations to citizens could not constitute the outer parameter of the individual's moral experience; and vertical divisions between states, correspondingly, could not be the sole, defining characteristics of the states-system.

The attempt to mediate between two distinct philosophical traditions made it impossible for those early theories to develop a coherent account of the modern system of states. Their failure is manifest in their discussion of the character of sovereign rights and the principles of statecraft. Ascertained within contractarianism, the constitutive principles of the states-system are rough reproductions of the principles of conduct observed by individuals within the original state of nature (Pufendorf 1927: 90; Vattel 1964: 7). The sovereign's right to promote the interests of his association, by force if necessary, is analogous to the right of self-help that existed prior to the creation of society. States must possess these rights until and unless they consent to their amendment or surrender. But, from a perspective inclined to highlight the unifying capacity of human reason, the attempt to endorse these absolute, vertical divisions between communities is unjustified. It commits the error of forming 'a plan of geographical morality, by which the duties of men in public and private situations are not governed by their relation to the great Governor of the Universe or by their relations to humankind, but by climates, degrees of longitude, parallels not of life, but of latitudes' (Burke, cited in Bredvold and Ross 1970: 17). Such a 'plan of geographical morality' violates the existence of a universal moral constituency upholding the rights and duties that bind all persons together in a world society. The ethical state cannot regard its rights and responsibilities as constituted by the transactions between its individual members alone; the former cannot emanate from a pact that excludes all but future citizens, and the rights and duties of insiders and outsiders must be harmonized. Indeed, as Fichte observed, to avoid being 'in contradiction with the concept of right, a commonwealth . . . must embrace the whole globe, or at least, must contain the possibility of uniting the whole of mankind' (Fichte 1869: 215). The dual foundations of classical theory advanced competing ways of ascertaining the scope of the individual's moral sensibilities and their implications for the organization of international society.

Sharply opposed accounts of the morality of statecraft emerge from these diverse philosophical bases. Here, a familiar dichotomy between private and public ethics arises alongside the 'man–citizen' division. On the contractarian account, the principle of reciprocity facilitates the emergence of a society of states, but the reason for states is a constraint upon the level of sociability that can be exhibited in their external relations. Because of the structure of political obligation, states cannot allow that international obligations are permanently binding nor can they dismiss out of hand any act of duplicity or violence outlawed within domestic society. Because duties between human beings cannot be extended indefinitely into the space between states, moral and political experience is bifurcated into the distinct realms of private and public ethics. This bifurcation is an inevitable product of the compact that the sovereign, as trustee for the welfare of the community, must sometimes deny the validity of principles that are normally observed in the conduct of purely private relations. This dichotomy is not objectively given in the anarchic nature of the states-system but depends on the prior decision to confine the principal moral constituency to the boundaries of the political association. On account of the apparent rationality of this decision, morality can be neatly divided into two realms without disturbing the unity of citizens' moral lives.

Nevertheless, if the states-system is an artefact superimposed upon a pre-existent world morality then the legitimacy of this division must be questioned. Considered alongside the belief in universal reason, the separation between private and public ethics is a reflection of the incomplete, one-sided nature of moral life. Artificial boundaries between states create an indefensible tension at the heart of the individual's moral experience, whether apprehended or not. What is at issue, therefore, is the existence of particularistic social moralities that centre the individual's moral sensibilities on the immediate, political group. Against this practice, moral universalism asserts that a person should be concerned with 'the all-encompassing sphere of cosmopolitan sentiment' (Kant 1964: 140); moreover, the moral self-consciousness of individuals and societies ought to develop to the point at which 'a violation of right in one place of the earth is felt all over it' (Kant, cited in Forsyth *et al.* 1970: 216). The sovereign should not be party to a division between the principles of domestic and international political life; and, as moral agents, sovereigns should honour obligations to collaborate to control the states-system so that 'it may be brought into conformity with natural right' (Kant 1970b: 228–9). On this account, the attempt to weave universal moral principles into the affairs of states holds the key to overcoming the tension between the obligations of men and citizens.

Two conceptions of moral obligation were embedded in the classical reflections on the Western states-system. But the corresponding visions of world political organization were not made explicit and the internal contradictions of the argument were suppressed. Typical of these writings was the tendency to relax the force of obligations to humanity. Pufendorf and Vattel both relied on the argument that these obligations possess an essentially indeterminate status. Pufendorf (1927: 48) argued that it is only within civil societies that human beings have ascertained the precise composition of the rights and duties that should bind them together; the social contract established what they could not be certain of on the basis of the natural law alone. Vattel (1964: 7–8) stated that the content of the natural law is imprecise, that it lends itself to varying interpretations, and that states should therefore generally refrain from judging each other's conduct. Obligations to citizens are determinate; obligations to other human beings are not. However, neither Pufendorf nor Vattel wished to deny the realm of human obligation with its supposedly civilizing effects on the relations between states. Perhaps the implication to draw is that the states-system is as rational a form of world political organization as human beings can establish prior to making obligations to humanity more concrete at some (improbable) future point. But, in neither writer's work is there a suggestion that the states-system exhibits only an imperfect or qualified form of rationality. Indeed, the roles and responsibilities of members of sovereign states appear to pre-suppose the absolute rationality of the state and the finality of the states-system. Although 'the services of humanity' survived the formation of special political arrangements, citizens were urged to hold 'nothing dearer' than the 'welfare and safety' of the state; similarly, sovereigns were required to comply with the imperative that 'the welfare of the people is the supreme law' (Pufendorf 1927: 121, 144). 'No convention or special agreement' could cancel 'the duties of humanity', but a constitutive principle of the state-system declared that 'the liberty of a Nation would remain incomplete if other Nations presumed to inspect and control its conduct' (Vattel 1964: 5). The attempt to legitimize these propositions reveals that, at best, classical theory equivocated between contractarianism and universalism.

The principal merit of Kant's political philosophy was its attempt to overcome the inadequacies of earlier international relations theory. In contrast to 'the miserable comforters' (Grotius, Pufendorf and Vattel), Kant aimed to take the principle of equality seriously as a principle of international relations (Kant 1970b: 211; Gallie 1978: ch. 2). The main features of his conception of world politics are sufficiently well known to make recapitulation unnecessary here. In short, the approach sought to establish the absoluteness of reason and to overcome the division between contractarianism and universalism (Murphy 1970: 110–1). Nevertheless, the dominant trends in social and political thought did not coincide with Kant's individualistic foundation for a world ethic; they ran counter to doctrines that supposed there was a distinction to be made between the norms of particular times and places and the values supplied by an overarching reason. Romanticism, for instance, criticized two key elements in the traditional contractarian theories of society and politics as exemplified in the writings of Pufendorf and Vattel: first, the belief that human arrangements were artefacts through which humans sought to satisfy pre-social needs; and, second, the belief that individuals possessed, irrespective of their cultural or temporal location, the same set of rational capacities (Lovejoy 1941). The second of these criticisms was presumed by later writers to undercut Kant's critique of the states-system.[3] Irrespective of the accuracy of this point, the impact of romanticism was to transform the basis on which traditional international relations theories had rested.

The historicist theory of international relations

Employing the romanticist critique of individualism and rationalism, historicism claimed that human capacities were inseparable from the forms of life in which they developed. By claiming that ethical capabilities were similarly dependent, it was thought possible to subvert the belief in a universal moral constituency required by transcendent reason. The latter worldview was predicated upon the wrongful abstraction of individuals from their social and historical contexts. Individuals, it was argued, were not human beings first and French or German afterwards (Treitschke 1915: 127–8). Only in the West had thinkers become preoccupied with analysing the human condition as it might have been prior to the appearance of different social and political practices (Treitschke 1915). The discourse that aimed to depict the natural characteristics of early humans simply underlined its cultural limitations; invariably, present day social categories were projected on to the thought and action of 'natural man'. Culture's unavoidable and irreducible qualities were no more evident than in the theorist's ambition to transcend them.

It was therefore argued that the primordial fact about humanity is the existence of cultural individualities. Individuals are not undifferentiated members of a humanity that might one day attain political unification but participants in the diverse communities of 'intellect and spirit' which have developed in history (Sterling 1958; Aron 1966: 585–91). The function of states was not to maximize the pre-social requirements of their members but to preserve and enhance the cultures for which they were responsible. Human existence involved cultural pluralism and the necessity of recognizing divisions between sovereign states. But, if there is no moral law that is transcultural, on what basis can international political theory be developed and what possibilities are there for reasoning about the relations between states? Historicists believed that they had established that a theory of obligations to humanity was problematic; the aspiration to specify universal moral duties immediately privileged values that were dominant within a few cultures. But the rejection of transcultural or suprahistorical values was not a denial, it was supposed, of a genuinely international political theory. Historicism took humanity to be neither an essence shared by all persons nor a set of innate natural tendencies but the totality of diverse and often incommensurable cultural configurations.[4] Humanity was revealed in the various forms of life that had developed in radically different cultural contexts. No single culture could manifest the totality of human possibilities; and since every state had a significant role to play in preserving and unfolding human capacities, separate states did not detract from, but enhanced, humanity.

A unique discussion of the presuppositions of a states-system emerged alongside this account of humanity. Each culture had the right of access to its own political form under the rubric that institutional differentiation was required by cultural pluralism. For the historicist, the state has obligations to enhance its variant on humanity, and moral consciousness need not appear in the form of a tension between 'internal' and 'external' ethical requirements. Horizontal moral ties between individual members of world society are deemed illusory; what is objectively necessary is the division of the species between bounded political communities (Sterling 1958; Aron 1966). Unlike classical theory, however, these propositions could be advanced without being vulnerable to Kant's charge of failing inexcusably to apply principles of natural right to the 'wasteland' between states. Historicism had sought to overcome that dichotomy between the state and humanity which had produced internal contradictions in rationalist theories of international relations. By reducing individualism and cosmopolitanism to mere abstractions, historicism sought to overcome the age-old separation between man and citizen.

The historicist critique of modern natural law theory may appear to be unanswerable, but historicism cannot avoid generating its own set of internal contradictions. Rather then dwell on the familiar argument that historicist reasoning is self-refuting,[5] it is important to identify some problems in its attempt to characterize the relationship between culture and humanity.

In order to do this, I shall assume the existence of two cultures that are founded on mutually exclusive principles of international relations. While one culture accepts the historicist's claim that all cultural configurations help to manifest humanity, and acknowledges obligations to other states on this basis, the other confines obligations simply to relations between members of its own, allegedly superior cultural formation. The historicist argument is that each culture is necessary in order to manifest the diverse range of human possibilities. This observation has a highly specific meaning in the circumstances described because these cultures negate rather than complement one another: they reveal the species' capacity to express itself in wholly antagonistic forms of life. To make a different assertion it would be necessary to choose between these cultures on the grounds that one expressed human potentialities more adequately than the other.

Although this point resurrects that very dichotomy that historicism was summoned to deny, it is a division that historicists cannot avoid. For if we consider the relations between these cultures, on what basis can the first assert that the other should recognize its contribution to human capabilities, and on what basis can it claim that the other should recognize its rightful existence as a sovereign state? It is not possible for the first society to appeal to the presumed equal validity of cultures. For on that very basis its opponent may claim that its denial of obligations to outsiders is a legitimate expression of cultural difference. While historicist reasoning appeared to believe that a principle of the equal validity of cultures was coincidental with a principle that cultures should treat each other as moral equals, it is evident that these propositions are not logically connected. At this point the historicist argument is confronted with a clear choice: either the first principle is advocated with the consequence that there is no longer a defence for the states-system; or the latter principle is advocated at the expense of regarding various cultural systems as equally valid. As the historicists made the decision to advocate the second principle, they reintroduced the dichotomy that was found in classical theory. In brief, to assert the value of the principle of the equal treatment of cultures in the face of a claim to reject it is to resurrect a division between concrete cultures and the moral principles that transcend them and to invite consideration of what is best for humanity.

Rather than claim that an ethnocentric culture should acknowledge that all cultures possess equal moral status, the historicist might move to a relativist position. This development would involve affirming the equal validity of all cultural systems, including their different conceptions of international relations. It is assumed that one 'can turn to history as an indefinitely rich compendia of life styles, all of which stand in external relation to one another so that in choosing or rejecting any one I make no comment on the others' (O'Brien 1975: 68). Here, the relativist wishes to endorse two incompatible propositions: first, that there are no transcultural criteria that facilitate the rational ordering of cultures; and, second, that a society that takes a relativist position has reasonable grounds for rejecting cultures predicated on principles that are antagonistic to relativism. Accordingly, neither historicism nor relativism can bridge the gap between humanity and citizenship without self-contradiction. But if these doctrines are inconsistent, and if natural law doctrine succumbs to the criticism that its account of humanity ignores cultural diversity and historical change, what is to be made of the division between 'men' and 'citizens'?

The philosophers of history

Let us return to the historicist position and begin with the observation that historicism may be made the object of a critique similar to the one it directed at the theory of natural law. If the latter abstracted individuals from historically evolving cultures, the former abstracted cultures from the wider forms of human experience (including, for example, social interaction with nature) through which the evolution of human capacities takes place (Colletti 1972: 39). To take this further, it is important to consider the philosophers of history with their focus upon the formation and development of the human species itself. What relativism and historicism omitted was consideration of the manner in which unique human powers were developed through the multidimensional aspects of the social world. Within the theory of history there was an attempt to establish a hierarchy of human capacities through a consideration of humanity's place in the worlds of society and nature. This endeavour has major implications for understanding the nature of the dichotomy between 'man' and 'citizen'.

Philosophical historians sought to give an account of the nature and potentialities of historical subjects. Their principal contention was that history was made possible by the existence of creatures that were free. To be free, on this account, was not to be beyond the jurisdiction of the law, to be unconstrained as in the state of nature of the modern natural lawyers, but to have the capacity to initiate action. The human species was unique by participating in a historical dimension made possible by the capacity for freedom and agency. Uniqueness stemmed not just from this power but also from the related potentiality for collective learning and development. The species was not static but underwent radical transformation in the course of positing and acting on freely determined ends. Philosophers of history wished to highlight the evolution of species-powers and parallel forms of collective self-consciousness. In brief, they sought to understand the historical processes that made it possible for individuals to transcend their locales by identifying and sympathizing with all members of the human race.

The a priori of history was the existence of a being that was capable of transcending, at least in part, the world of natural determination. What had to be discerned were those characteristics that explained the emergence of a non-natural being. Unsurprisingly, this ambition was realized by analysing humanity's early immersion in, or interaction with, nature. Theorists of history followed Rousseau's conjecture that early humans were natural beings with the latent capacity for free action and self-advancement. Kant regarded humanity as that unique part

of nature in an earlier age which possessed the latent faculties of reason and imagination that allowed the establishment of non-natural ends; Hegel emphasized
the distinctive capacity for self-consciousness and for expressing the dominant
forms of social self-consciousness in a world of increasing freedom; Marx regarded labour as the instrument whereby non-natural ends and the self-creation of
the species were made possible (Hegel 1952: para. 4, addition; Kant 1963: 55–6;
Marx 1977c: 39; Rousseau 1968: 170). What history revealed and developed was
the species' ability to enlarge these distinctive powers. It showed human beings in
a world of their own making, 'a second nature', in which gradual expression was
given to unique potentialities (Hegel 1952: para. 4).

This understanding of humans as dynamic, self-constituting beings took issue
with natural law doctrines and historicism alike. The former were wrong to assume
that the right ends for humans were fixed independently of history, given in nature
or pre-determined by a divine being.[6] The belief in the immutability of human
nature and in unchanging rational faculties, which was revealed in the natural law
discussion of individuals in their original state, overlooked processes of historical
transformation. Natural law doctrines abstracted human beings from the forma-
tive role of concrete ensembles of changing social relations (Hegel 1952: para.
145; Marx 1977a). Medieval natural law theories, with their conception of the
universe as a system of interdependent parts, each possessing its distinctive telos,
had confused natural and normative orders. Laws of nature derived their validity
from their existence alone, whereas laws of social conduct depended for their
validity upon some level of human endorsement. The focus upon long-term historical processes gave rise to a division between the repetitive physical world and
the potentially progressive world of history (Hegel 1952: addition to the preface;
Hegel 1956: 54). Historicists, moreover, might be accused of having failed to give
an account of the formation and development of unique species-powers, including
the capacity for identification with, and concern for, all other human beings.

The species' capacity for rational self-determination was held to be capable
of extension in two respects. First, human societies could expand their rational
powers and, second, they could enlarge the sphere of their operation. What was
open to humans as historical beings was the ability to enlarge freedom through
ever-increasing rational control of the self and its environment. Through the
medium of history, human beings could come to grasp the higher purposes and
possibilities of free beings along with a more refined awareness of the conditions
that were necessary for their realization. Gradually, they could gain a form of self-
knowledge that was always theirs potentially but that was actualized only within
the more advanced social and political arrangements. As the creation of a world
of self-determining beings was a gradual historical process it was inconceivable
that all cultures could be conceived to be equally valid. They could be judged by
the extent to which their members understood and expressed the potentiality for
collective self-determination – for making more of their history under conditions
of their own choosing (see Marx 1977b: 300) and for making world history in
accordance with stronger cosmopolitan attachments.

Philosophical historians proposed, therefore, a theory of 'historical periodization', which would reveal the main stages in the movement to higher levels of ethical and political self-consciousness. The urge to place different societies on a scale of ascending types is exhibited both in Hegel's analysis of world historical peoples and in Marx's consideration of various forms of socially organized production (Hobsbawm 1964: introduction; Evans 1975: 72–9). It was this aspect of philosophical history that Kant commended to the theorists of international society. A 'minor motive' for constructing a universal history was the issue of what various societies had contributed to the growth of world citizenship (Kant 1970a: 191). In brief, the possibility arose of placing different political associations, or systems of states, on a hierarchy of forms in accordance with their proximity to a condition in which the idea of rational self-determination is extended into the world of international relations. The execution of this purpose suffered on account of the general disrepute that came to surround philosophical history in the English-speaking world at the beginning of the last century. In the writings of T.H. Green (1916: ch. IIIb), however, there was an insightful attempt to integrate philosophical history and the study of the relations between states. What requires attention, moreover, in the context of the present discussion, is the manner in which the division between 'man' and 'citizen' can be located in a theory of the historical formation of distinctive human powers and capabilities.

Following Kant, Green maintained that in the course of their history human beings refined their moral capacities. The deepening and broadening of moral obligations revealed the growth of the potentiality for (collective) rational self-determination. In early societies, rights and duties were attached to persons only as members. A common good was recognized within such societies 'while beyond the particular community the range of obligation [was] not understood to extend' (Green: 1916: 238). The nature of human development was revealed in the ability to recognize 'an ever-widening conception of the range of persons between whom the common good is common' (Green 1916: 237). The culmination of this growth of freedom was contained in the understanding that fundamental obligations were not confined simply to relations between citizens, or to relations between sovereigns and subjects, but ought to extend to all relations between human beings as equal persons. The highest forms of moral consciousness involved identification with 'a universal society co-extensive with mankind itself' – the highest level of social integration the institutions of which could regulate the relations between humanity's constituent parts (Green 1916: 239–40).

For Kant and Green, the ideal political environment would reflect the unique capacity to live in a world governed by moral principles that all persons freely imposed on themselves. The species would transcend nature and express its capacity for self-determination most perfectly when it managed the totality of political relations with recourse to self-imposed, universal moral obligations. To use Kantian terminology, the species would realize its potentiality for combining individuality and cosmopolitanism only in a condition in which all persons were equal co-legislators in a universal kingdom of ends. Accordingly, a cosmopolitan culture occupied a higher place on a scale of social types than one in which moral sensibilities were concentrated exclusively on insiders. A states-system in which

societies aim to establish institutions which express their belief that human beings have 'a claim upon human society as a whole' (Green 1966: 157–8) was
more adequate than one in which particularistic social moralities were thought
to have absolute validity. On this basis, philosophical historians sought to criticize plans of 'geographical morality' without succumbing to the objection that
they superimposed an abstracted, static morality on diverse societies. While they
acknowledged the historical importance of cultural individualities, they did not
draw back from positing the existence of transcultural criteria for evaluating human conduct. They sought to derive ethical criteria from long-term processes of
change. In so doing, they thought it possible to regard particularistic moralities as
forms of human understanding that would be transcended as humans grasped the
nature of their capacity for collective self-determination.[7]

Philosophical historians implicitly rejected the options of ethical absolutism
and relativism; immanent within their writings was the belief that these are sides
of a false antinomy. What is true of general social and political principles may be
taken to be true of the division between humanity and citizenship. This dichotomy
is not a feature of an idiosyncratic and relative moral code, nor is it a conflict
between a particularistic social morality and the requirements of an immutable
ahistorical ethic. Although the dichotomy may arise only within particular cultures at specific points in their evolution, its significance is much deeper. However
cast, it expresses a conflict within the experience of the states-system. But, when
characterized adequately, the conflict reveals dissatisfaction of a specific kind,
namely with the impediments upon human freedom that issue from the character
of sovereign states and the constitutive principles of the international system.

Here there is a parallel with the division between 'man' and 'citizen' that was so
important within Hegel's account of the character of ancient and modern politics.
The emergence of individualism within Greek society represented dissatisfaction
with the parochial nature of social and political life. The Greek's challenge to
a traditional and customary morality expressed the aspiration to live in a social
world that embodied individual reason (Hegel 1956: 251–3). Social and political
morality was not simply 'an affair internal to a particular community', it had to
express the subject's particular sense of the nature of rational conduct. If this
freer social world was to exist, Hegel argued, the individual's estrangement from
the customary morality of the polis was essential.[8] It was necessary to realize
a higher understanding of self-determination than was found in those cultures
in which members thought their social relations rested on natural sanctions or
obeyed moral obligations blindly and spontaneously. It was this demand for a
higher level of self-determination, expressed in the contrast between 'man' and
'citizen', that was subversive of Greek political life. Nevertheless, individualism
itself could not provide, on Hegel's account, a sufficient condition for the existence of a free social world. Individualism, especially when it was the rationale for
the pursuit of private interests, became an obstacle to the development of a social
environment subject to collective control. The product of individualism was a
condition in which individuals were subjected increasingly to impersonal laws
operating within their societies (Hegel 1956: 317–18). To reach a higher level of

self-determination, it was necessary to allow agents to pursue their separate objectives while being integrated within an ethical state that expressed the capacity for collective self-determination. In this way the reconciliation of the opposition between humanity and citizenship, which had been necessary to progress beyond the parochialism of Greece, could be effected.

Philosophical history provides the resources for characterizing the division between 'man' and 'citizen' in international relations in a similar way. The modern state may offer its citizens freedoms unavailable to members of earlier forms of association; it may make available greater opportunities for individual self-determination and for taking part in the process of controlling the immediate social and political environment. Nevertheless, states separately only imperfectly realize the human capacity for collective self-determination. The possession of citizenship alone is not sufficient to enable the individual to participate in the control of the wider political environment. As Rousseau observed, the citizen's ability to live an autonomous life within states is limited severely by the disruptive power of international events. Refuge from a form of heteronomy, which had its source outside the state, could be found only in autarchic states (Hoffmann 1965: 63). Furthermore, as Kant also observed, the world of sovereign states appears to be a world of necessary conflict and competition. Accordingly, theorists have claimed that, compared with domestic politics, international politics are 'less susceptible of a progressivist interpretation'; the anarchic nature of the states-system is presumed to subject states to impersonal laws and to limit their ability to engage in moral conduct (Wight 1966a: 26). However, it is important not to locate resistance to change only in the states-system, thus imputing the character of bounded political communities to their supposedly natural environment. As the discussion of contractarianism sought to show, the fact that states pursue their particularistic interests and insist upon their sovereign rights, and the fact that they conduct their external affairs on the basis of a separation between the principles of domestic and international political life, is a function of the nature of the state as a particular ensemble of rights and obligations. Those patterns of behaviour are implicit in the character of the sovereign state itself, implicit in forms of political community that assume the priority of obligations to fellow citizens.

As a result of this phenomenon the conflict between citizenship and humanity acquires fundamental importance in both the theory and the practice of international relations. For, as we have seen, what the existence of a realm of human obligation does is challenge the state as a particularistic moral community that generates heteronomous relations in its external affairs. It may be suggested that the form of estrangement that is exhibited in the division between human beings and citizens is as necessary in the experience of the world of states as it was in the life of the Greek polis. It may be regarded as a division that is integral to the movement from attempting to realize autonomy in the relations within states to attempting to realize autonomy in the relations between them.

The actualization of a higher form of international political life requires that radical critique of the state that historicism was unable to supply and modern natural law theory was unwilling to undertake. We have raised the possibility that the idea of humanity may provide this function if it is reconstituted within a theory of history which is able to avoid the inadequacies that were endemic in traditional and modern theories of natural law. It may well be that the existence of a moral community more inclusive than the state can be defended only on the basis of the species' capacity for collective self-determination. If this is indeed so, it may be contended that only within an international political association, which aims at maximizing human freedom, can the species express its unique capabilities while recapturing morally integrated lives.

2 The problem of community in international relations

This chapter considers the problem of community in international relations. It begins with some brief observations about the nature of state formation in early modern Europe and proceeds to discuss key philosophical, sociological and practical questions that have been central to international political thought ever since.

In their different ways, these questions are concerned with the character of moral inclusion and exclusion in social and political life. The recurrent philosophical questions have been concerned with whether or not there is any rationale for the state's inclusion of citizens and exclusion of non-citizens from the moral community. The main sociological questions have focused on whether or not the dominant principles of inclusion and exclusion in the international states-system are changing. Questions of practice have raised the issue of whether foreign policy should work within the customary principles of inclusion and exclusion, which privilege the interests of co-nationals, or should advance 'higher' cosmopolitan commitments. Various schools of thought have sought to answer one or more of these questions, but no single perspective has answered all three systematically and successfully. This chapter sketches the manner in which a critical approach to international relations can develop a distinctive approach to the issues raised above; at the same time it suggests some new directions for critical international relations theory.

The argument is developed in five parts. It begins with a discussion of the philosophical, sociological and practical problems that have long been central to the study of international relations. Part two claims that a critical solution to these problems should recover the political project initiated by Kant and Marx. Part three considers some criticisms of ethical universalism and suggests how the defence of a universal community can be developed. Part four suggests some new directions for the sociology of international relations. It argues for empirical analyses of the ways in which the interactions between different forms of social learning have structured the relations between 'insiders' and 'outsiders' in various states-systems and civilizations. Part five identifies some universalistic themes in contemporary international relations which have grown in importance in the more recent conduct of foreign policy.

The problem of community in the modern states-system

The modern European state emerged within the confines of a single civilization united by the normative and religious power of Christendom. During its rise the state sought to free itself from the moral and religious shackles of the medieval world. But while pursuing this aim, the state was aware of the dangers of totally undermining earlier notions of international order. Over time, the principles of sovereign equality and non-intervention, as well as the practice of diplomacy and interstate collaboration to maintain the balance of power, became the constitutive elements of the modern society of states. Independent political communities constructed the language of international society for the explicit purpose of maintaining order. Their aim was to enjoy the benefits of preserving an international society without incurring the risk that individual citizens would challenge the state's legitimacy by proclaiming their allegiance to a cosmopolitan ethic. Even so, the idea of a community of humankind has been one theme that the modern state has never been able to silence entirely. An earlier notion of a cosmopolitan morality that could be involved in criticizing states or in supporting a vision of a unified world society survived the transition from the medieval international order to the modern society of states.

The questions that have been central to the Western theory and practice of international relations since the emergence of the states-system fall into three main types – the philosophical, the practical and the sociological. It is important to make a few observations about each, as they are the central questions for a critical theory of international relations.

The recurrent philosophical questions in modern international relations theory have considered the grounds for conferring primacy upon any one of three competing visions of community – the nation-state, the society of states or a community of humankind. These questions have addressed the reasons for preferring the state, for example, as opposed to the society of states, or the community of humankind rather than the narrower communities with which human beings have generally identified. A few examples can explain their character. Does the state exhaust our political obligations or are there wider and more fundamental obligations that survive, so to speak, the fragmentation of the human race into sovereign states? If there are surviving obligations, are they the obligations that states owe one another as members of a society of states? Do individuals have duties to the whole of humanity and can they reasonably claim certain rights against the human species and its political representatives? To what extent are there universal obligations not just to uphold the rights of human beings as far as possible within the 'Westphalian' system but to construct new global institutions and practices capable of promoting higher levels of human solidarity? If each of these societies – actual or potential – has claims upon human loyalty, how is their relative importance to be decided? More specifically, in the event that these communities come into conflict with each other, how are priorities to be defined? These are some of the philosophical questions that have arisen because the issue of who should be included and excluded from political associations has become more and more deeply contested in modern times.

A number of practical foreign policy questions have arisen in conjunction with these questions of morality and obligation. Should states simply be concerned with advancing 'national interests'? To what extent should states forego minor national advantages because of the need to maintain and strengthen the wider society of states? Does the principle of maximizing international consensus oblige states to place serious limits on national ambitions? More profoundly, should foreign policy aim to institutionalize a higher cosmopolitan ethic by ensuring the international protection of human rights or by promoting global social and economic justice? If states do have obligations to promote a community of humankind, how can they be encouraged to create conditions that will effectively erode their power and sovereignty? Put differently, is the purpose of foreign policy to advance the interests of the exclusive nation-state, to strengthen a more inclusive society of states or to promote a logic of moral inclusion by establishing a community of humankind? If there is a place for all three objectives, at least in the current context, then how are they to be arranged within the foreign policy-making agenda of any particular sovereign community?

The third series of questions has dealt with whether or not the state's capacity to attract human loyalty and structure political identity seems likely to change significantly. Although this question was posed prior to the emergence of European sociology, the particular issue of whether modern societies were evolving from exclusive to inclusive social relations (and from particularistic to universalistic moral worldviews) became especially central to social and political thought from the middle of the nineteenth century. The key question of whether industrialization would erode the power and authority of the state and generate consensual forms of world politics continues to set the terms of the debate. Again, a few examples of the central sociological questions may suffice to clarify the points at stake. To what extent do the process of industrialization and the rise of global interdependence create unprecedented prospects for the extension of the moral and political boundaries of community? To what extent are the possibilities that liberals and socialists ascribed to the process of industrialization constrained by its uneven diffusion? How far, therefore, does the uneven development of capitalist and noncapitalist patterns of industrialization trigger ethnic renewal and consolidate the power and appeal of the sovereign state? Is the realist argument that the dominant logic in world politics is the reproduction of the international states-system reinforced by the continuing revolution in military technology fuelled by industrialization? Yet again, are there multiple and competing logics in the world economic and military system, some consolidating state power, particularistic communities and exclusionary practices, others undercutting that power and creating new possibilities for the extension of solidarity and sympathy?

These are, of course, interdependent areas of inquiry, and the answer given in one domain has implications for the position taken on each of the others. The position struck at the sociological level of inquiry has frequently held the key to other levels of discussion. For example, the argument that the dominant logic of international relations precludes any serious expansion of community carries the implication that normative analyses of alternative world orders are redundant and inquiries into the character of 'reformist' foreign policy are otiose. The competing claim that patterns of social and economic change are widening the sense of obligation and community implies that studies of the principles of foreign policy that could advance these trends warrant deeper consideration. In this context, the analysis of the normative purpose of foreign policy, and reflections on alternative global economic and political structures, acquire greater significance.

No single perspective provides conclusive answers to all of these questions but – implicitly if not explicitly – most schools of international relations and many strands of social and political theory provide some of the answers. The question of whether perspectives ought to be judged by the level of their contribution to all three domains is debatable. In any event, one way of restoring coherence to the study of international relations is to draw powerful strands of argument within different disciplinary approaches into a more systematic and comprehensive whole. The development of a critical theory of international relations can promote this objective by connecting normative, sociological and practical analyses of systems of inclusion and exclusion in a more synoptic approach to the field.

Kant and Marx

There are, as one would expect, earlier models of such a standpoint. Indeed, the theoretical standpoint that is outlined here amounts to an argument for the recovery of a project that was developed in different ways by Kant and Marx. The three-layered project discussed above draws on Kant's approach to international relations, which contained a universal ethic (the defence of the categorical imperative), a sociology of logics of development (the analysis of the transformative effects of the rise of republicanism and the evolution of international commercial relations) and the prolegomenon to a new international political practice (the conceptualization of the maxims of an ethical foreign policy that would extend moral and political community). The research programme outlined earlier mirrors the project of historical materialism with its normative vision of a universal society of free and equal producers, its explanatory framework, which maintained that the internationalization of capitalist social relations of production and exchange would destroy the constraints upon the emergence of a cosmopolitan community, and its belief that, at the level of praxis, proletarian internationalism (assisted by progressive national movements) would realize the higher emancipatory possibilities immanent within capitalist civilization.

Yet neither Kant nor Marx provides much more than illustration or inspiration in the present context. Kantian ethics are vulnerable to the charge of ahistoricism. Kant's rudimentary sociology of logics of development in world society reflects the concerns of another era, as does his discussion of the prerequisites of an ethical foreign policy. As for Marx and Marxism, the contention that historical materialism provides the starting point for an emancipatory politics – nothing more and nothing less – pinpoints some of the problems that have yet to be solved by a critical theory of international relations. The most important of these is how to construct a post-Marxist critical theory that takes into account the unyielding qualities of the international system of states (Giddens 1985; Linklater 1990a). The argument for universal ethics and for regarding the progress of world community as a fundamental political goal has to be recovered, as Habermas has observed, and not least because of the current challenge of antifoundationalism (Linklater 1990b: postscript). The sociology of the various logics that may promote or obstruct the expansion of community has to be reworked to consider not only what Habermas (1979a) calls the 'moral–practical' sphere but also the totality of concerns that have preoccupied the principal theories of international relations. Finally, the whole issue of how states can construct foreign policies that can give direction to trends that run counter to existing structures has yet to be theorized with real sophistication. It is improbable, to say the least, that the character of such a project will be shaped to any significant degree by Marxist theories of revolutionary praxis. What appears, therefore, in the following pages is not a defence of either a Kantian or a Marxian theory of international relations but an outline of a contemporary critical theory of international relations that seeks to recover an integrated approach to the normative, sociological and practical problems of community that is inspired by their writings.

The normative dimension

The tension between particularism and universalism is a recurrent theme in the history of Western moral and political thought. Ethical universalism has met with resistance on the grounds that 'it renders our social and moral ties too open to dissolution by rational criticism' (MacIntyre 1984). Yet moral favouritism has been problematical as well. As Miller maintains, the 'duties we owe to our compatriots may be more extensive than the duties we owe to strangers', but their privileged role must be justified nonetheless. The need for justification exists for the simple reason that 'there is a powerful thrust in the ethical theories that are most prominent in our culture toward . . . universalism' (Miller 1988: 647).

  This conflict between particularistic and universalistic codes is exemplified by the specific tension between the obligations of citizenship and the obligations of humanity in the history of international thought. Notwithstanding various attempts to demonstrate the priority of either position, none of the philosophical attempts to realize this objective (or to combine these approaches in a higher synthesis) has commanded any lasting consensus. The main issue for the present argument is whether a critical international theory modelled on the Kantian and Marxian emancipatory projects can overcome the principal arguments against universalism.

  These criticisms take several forms. One objection is that all universalistic codes inevitably reflect the preferences of specific cultures or civilizations, which assume that their moral practices are valid for the entire human race. This criticism is invariably linked with the contention that there is no immutable and universal human reason, no transcendent observation point or Archimedean perspective, that grounds universal moral truths and justifies the inclusion of all persons in one ethical community. Morality is social; moral codes are incommensurable. Community cannot be extended by appealing to universalizable norms because there is, in short, no common ethic to extend.

Yet another line of argument, which was crucial to contractarian perspectives in the seventeenth and eighteenth centuries, did not dispute the existence of moral universals. As the writings of Pufendorf and Vattel indicate, the emphasis of this approach was placed on the 'imperfect' and indeterminate nature of moral universals. The state created the realm of perfect obligation, and, although moral universals survived in relations between separate states, they did so imperfectly. They could neither be demanded nor could they be enforced outside the concrete bonds that tied citizens to the state. Hegel's critique of Kantian universalism sharpened the issues at stake. For Hegel, the notion of universal rights inherent in human personality was one of the great political achievements of the modern age. Nonetheless, Hegel's political thought rejected the cosmopolitan critique of the only social and political association that had proved itself capable of institutionalizing and concretizing ethical universals: the modern territorial state. Universalistic ethical concepts abstracted from specific forms of life went against the historical grain. As numerous thinkers, including Durkheim and Bosanquet, went on to suggest, the ideal of humanity was therefore best served within the confines of particular states and realised through their communal practices (Linklater 1990b).

Various objections have been raised against each of these versions of the 'concentric-circle image of duty' (Shue 1988: 692–3). The presumed incommensurability of rival cultures has been accused of positing the existence of self-contained moral–cultural wholes. In fact, it is argued, cultural boundaries are highly porous, and each culture is deeply shaped by interaction with others. In the modern age, especially, it is evident that a 'diplomatic culture' and an 'international political culture' shaped by the 'cosmopolitan culture' of modernity have been grafted on to most cultural systems (Bull 1977: 315–17).

Furthermore, although the case against universality is often concerned with safeguarding tolerance and diversity, it is invariably implicated in defending one moral universal: the right to cultural difference (Dews 1987: 217–18). In most cases, however, the defence of universalism is not an argument for the destruction of cultural diversity. Its advocates suggest that international political differences are best settled by employing the more critical and universalistic ethical principles and procedures that exist within the more advanced moralities. What is more, the emphasis on group as opposed to universal morality should not ignore the fact that universalistic morality (*moralitat*) is frequently encountered 'within the most enclosed' social groups with their customary moralities *(sittlichkeiten)* (O'Neill 1988: 722). The issue for the universalist is not to replace customary moral differences with a single, universalized moral code but rather to find the right balance between the universal and the particular (Bernstein 1988: 590; Linklater 1990b). The aim is to defend moral inclusion and equality without positing a single human identity and to value difference without subscribing to doctrines of innate superiority and inferiority and correlative forms of moral exclusion (Todorov 1984: 249).

Two observations may help to develop this point further. In support of universalism, it is useful to recall Habermas's claim that social learning in the moral sphere involves the extension of the circle of persons who enjoy equal rights (Habermas 1979a). The rationalization of the moral sphere leads to a deeper understanding of the 'doors to otherness' (Taylor 1985: 383), which have previously been closed, and, concomitantly, to political action to undermine pernicious systems of exclusion based on nationality, gender, race and class. Indeed, the widening of the sense of who counts as a moral person or a moral equal, and the willingness to be bound by universalizable norms, are, arguably, the two main features of the more advanced moral codes. As a result, in the modern age there are powerful reasons for contending that 'any adequate conception of the good life and the virtues is one that cannot and should not exclude in principle any member of the human species' (Bernstein 1986: 137). Without pre-empting some later themes in the argument, it is evident that a commitment to this principle requires a politics of moral inclusion to create a community that is coextensive with the whole human race.

A second observation simply notes one implication for the ethics of decision making. In *Patriarcha,* Sir Robert Filmer argued that if the social contract theorists were right that 'by nature all mankind in the world makes but one people', then 'without a joint consent of the whole people of the world . . . there cannot be any one man chosen King' (Filmer 1949: 285). Filmer's aim was to point to a philosophical weakness at the heart of social contract theory rather than to defend its universalism. In fact, Kant was the first theorist to defend the principle that the organization of political life ought to be guided by the fiction of a universal social contract. In modern social and political thought, the Kantian claim that 'the judging person . . . can only woo the consent of everyone else in hope of coming to an agreement with him eventually' finds its most vigorous defence in the writings of Habermas (cited in Bernstein 1986: 229). What this defence of universalism underlines is the importance of answerability to others; what it highlights is the need for the destruction of all systematic forms of exclusion and the pre-eminence of the obligation to develop global arrangements informed by the ethical ideal of securing the consent of each and every member of the human race. Universalism of this kind does not entail the demise of inner circles of obligations (circles that are not coextensive with the whole human race), but it does imply that the inner sanctum must be open to the scrutiny of outsiders if it affects their prima facie equal right to promote their own ends. This notion of global consent is the essence of ethical universalism (Beitz 1979).

On these foundations, a critical theory of international relations can argue that the state does not exhaust our moral and political obligations. The duties that survive the political fragmentation of the human race are not simply the obligations that states acquire as equal members of a society of states. Universal duties that exist alongside the obligations that individuals possess as members of particular communities require their political representatives to promote higher levels of human solidarity and community. The point, in short, is not to dissolve the obligations at the core of the concentric circles of human obligation but to modify them in response to the rights of those who are located in the penumbra.

The sociological dimension

The philosophical defence of universalism outlined in the previous section is based on the premise that systematic exclusion has become problematical in modern societies. But clearly this has not always been the case. It is therefore important to develop a sociological analysis of the phenomenon of moral inclusion and exclusion in the history of international relations.

This section analyses some perspectives and themes that are relevant to this task. It begins by arguing that realist and English School approaches to international relations analyse two forms of social learning that are central to any sociology of moral inclusion and exclusion in intersocietal systems. These are, first, learning how to control others under conditions of conflict and, second, understanding how to construct order between different states and civilizations. Both perspectives reject 'progressivist' interpretations of international relations, which assume an irreversible ascent toward greater global cooperation and harmony. Nevertheless, the 'Grotian' perspective (to which English School theory belongs) has always stressed the importance of moral and cultural factors in international relations. What is more, the existence of a third form of social learning in modern international relations became a pronounced feature of Hedley Bull's later writings on the Third World's protest against legal, political, racial, economic and cultural systems of exclusion (Bull 1984a). This is moral learning in the form of subjecting political claims to a public test that considers their significance for all human beings who might be affected by them.[1] Bull also maintained that the need to manage the ecological effects of a fourth form of learning (learning how to acquire mastery of nature) has become increasingly important in the modern system of states. In Bull's view, the need for global ecological management created the possibility that states with a much greater commitment to protecting the 'world common good' might yet appear. The more general point is that an analysis of the dominant understanding of moral community in international relations should focus upon the interaction between the four principal forms of social learning.

Realism argues that the dominant logic of competition and conflict between states reveals that any significant extension of community is highly improbable. Its early advocates took issue with nineteenth century liberal and socialist claims that the power of the nation-state would be undermined by the diffusion of capitalist market relations and processes of industrialization. They rejected the liberal supposition that free trade would 'act on the moral world as the principle of gravitation in the universe – drawing men together, thrusting aside the antagonism of race, and creed, and language, and uniting us in the bonds of eternal peace' (Cobden, cited in Bullock and Shock 1956: 53). With equal vigour, they criticized the socialist view that the diffusion of industrial society would lead to new forms of international organization. They dismissed the proposition advocated by Saint-

Simon that 'the continual extension of the principle of association [is] the most salient fact observable in history', and they rejected the prediction that the 'next term must be a still vaster association comprehending the whole human race' (cited in Bury 1955: 287). Needless to say, none of the positions that predicted the inevitability of progress towards higher levels of international cooperation survived the realist challenge. Although the progressivist legacy of nineteenth century social theory has been apparent in more recent analyses of functional and neo-functional integration, and in liberal theories of global interdependence, its themes survive in a significantly reconstituted form.

To consider these points with regard to social learning in international relations, what realism disputed was the supposition, common to liberalism and socialism alike, that developments in the sphere of technical rationality (and associated especially with the quest to control nature) provided the impetus for progress in the domain of morality and politics. Realism stresses the continuing primacy of strategic interaction and the need for states to advance their understanding of how to outmanoeuvre and control adversaries under conditions of actual or impending conflict. Its principal exponents maintained that technical–instrumental rationalization had consolidated national power. This process had not generated the kind of movement towards greater international cooperation that liberals and socialists had expected. Realists have underscored the point that state building and war are the two primary determinants of the boundaries of moral and political communities in all historical eras.

For its part, the English School also stresses the importance of strategic rivalry in the world of exclusionary nation-states. However, the distinction between a 'system' and a 'society' of states is crucial for its argument that it is essential to distinguish learning how to control competitors from learning how to coexist with others in an orderly environment. The fact that states learn how to construct principles of international order that can command widespread consent is therefore crucial for English School theory. In Habermas's terms, international order demonstrates the existence of a realm of practical learning that is interdependent with, but far from reducible to, technical–instrumental rationalization and strategic rivalry.

Approached differently, the English School argues that a process of universalizing norms has been central to the history of the European states-system. Without such a process (and without general agreement about the importance of not universalizing 'essentially contested' national conceptions of justice) international order would have been more difficult to maintain. For the most part, order has been prior to justice in the European states-system. Yet, as Bull argued in his analysis of the rise of the first universal states-system, 'the revolt against the West' is significant precisely because Western powers have been challenged to universalize principles that meet demands for justice as well as order. If we consider this point in conjunction with the themes discussed in the previous section, it seems relevant to claim that recent formulations of the Grotian perspective capture the process of moral learning that has contested international systems of exclusion. The Third World's challenge to legal, racial, political, economic and cultural exclusion reinforces the English School claim that moral and cultural considerations have far greater significance for the international system than most realist approaches are prepared to concede. Moreover, English School advocacy of greater global responsibility for the satisfaction of basic human needs and the protection of essential human rights reveals that these ethical considerations are worthy of pursuit not only for the sake of increased order but because of the intrinsic worth of the universal prerequisites of a decent life (Bull 1984a; Vincent 1986).

The existence of a 'cosmopolitan culture of modernity', which has accompanied the global diffusion of industrialization, may serve to reinforce this general trend (Bull and Watson 1984: 434–5). At the same time, the problems that have arisen as a result of the technical mastery of nature have created the need for new diplomatic procedures and practices. As Bull's later writings noted, there is a pressing need for movement beyond states that are jealous of their sovereign rights to forms of political community that acknowledge an obligation to act as 'local agents of a world common good' (Bull 1984a: 14). The interaction between strategic rivalry, the need for international order and technical–instrumental rationalization, and the reaction against forms of moral exclusion, provides no guarantee that diplomatic interaction will be shaped by increasingly universalistic ethical principles. Even so, if English School analysis is correct then it is foolish to underestimate the prospects for the development of ethical international relations and for the evolution of a stronger sense of cosmopolitan identification with an emergent world community.

There is no doubt that nineteenth century sociology and political economy were wrong to assume that there was an inevitable link between industrialization and internationalism. However, certain themes in nineteenth century social theory remain centrally important to the argument being developed here. The supposition that new social and political relations had begun to appear within the industrial heartland of Europe was a constitutive feature of classical social theory. The foundational sociologists (Marx, Weber and Durkheim) sought to understand the 'great transformation' in which the individual became free from customary and traditional constraints. They focused upon the emergence of the modern ethical subject with a critical and reflective orientation towards the social world and a marked preference for social relations that are based on achievement rather than ascription. The belief that a reflective and universalistic ethic would prevail over inherited, customary and exclusive moralities was present in liberal and socialist interpretations of the modern world alike.

The preoccupation with the rise of the individual and the emergence of new social bonds, which expressed the desire for universality and autonomy, underpinned the renowned dichotomies in nineteenth century social theory – between status and contract, *gemeinschaft* and *gesellschaft,* traditional and legal–rational authority, and mechanical and organic solidarity. In parallel fashion, the analysis of the emergence of individuation, autonomy and universalistic moral codes in different intersocietal systems, and the study of the forces that have given rise to closed and exclusive rules of conduct, can form the subject matter of a critical sociology of international relations.

As with so much contemporary social theory, the project outlined here places culture, community and communication at the heart of the empirical enterprise. Yet it is different from both classical sociology and modern social thought in one important respect. Here, the accent falls not upon the internal ordering of communities, or on change within an increasingly transnational society, but upon the moral conceptions that arise in the relations between different societies, states and civilizations. By way of example, the social construction of the 'other' in different cultures, and the significance of culturally defined differences between insiders and outsiders for the conduct of external relations, are central to the whole exercise. A range of more specific concerns can then be identified. The reasons for excluding the 'other' from moral consideration and the rules that lead to the imposition of inferior moral status are important fields of investigation. (Relations between the 'civilized' West and the 'preliterate', 'historyless' and 'uncivilized' societies outside Europe provide a wealth of examples, as do inter-civilizational encounters between the West and Islam and the West and China.) The move beyond inegalitarian conceptions of the other in the more abstract and universal worldviews is also a matter of special significance. (The rise of universalism in the moralities of the 'axial' age is a case in point. However, logics of moral universalization can be analysed in each of the international states-systems.) Whether the inquiry focuses upon logics of moral inclusion, which permit the expansion of community, or upon logics of moral exclusion, which perpetuate or revive cultural closure, the following principle applies. The purpose of the analysis is to understand how the interaction between different forms of social learning shaped the moral boundaries of interdependent bounded communities; it is also to comprehend systemic potentials for organizing external relations in accordance with universalistic ethical principles as opposed to excessively particularistic and exclusionary norms.

As this sociological project assumes that moral development entails the rise of individuation, autonomy and universality, some observers may protest that it is tainted with Eurocentrism. Yet, the need to define the relationship between the universal and the particular has occurred in a number of civilizations and states-systems, and not only in the modern societies of the West. The universalistic ethic of Mohism in ancient China and the broadly Grotian philosophical perspectives that began to appear in the medieval Islamic world are reminders that the West is not altogether unique (although the considerable importance that universalistic themes have come to possess in the West points to long-term developmental processes that initially set it apart from other civilizations). State building and war led to moral closure in Confucian China, and the dominant political and religious forces in the Islamic world barred alternative paths of moral development that might have been travelled if the gate of *ijtihad* (independent judgement) had not been closed. In the West, a different configuration of forces, including the rise of capitalist development and industrialization against the background of strategic rivalries within a multistate system, generated moral and cultural patterns of development that were resisted elsewhere. Analysing the interaction between the main forms of social learning may enable us to understand the way in which different societies, states and civilizations have defined the relationship between the inner and outer realms of obligation and determined principles for governing their inescapable interconnectedness.

This mode of inquiry can be applied to a range of types of international relations. It can form the basis for a sociology of intercivilizational relations; it can provide a framework of analysis for a study of relations between 'core' states or 'higher' civilizations and the 'backward' peoples of the periphery; and it can be utilized in the context of what Martin Wight (1977: 33) once called the 'sociology of states-systems'. It seems that most states-systems have had a complex relationship with moral development, fostering it to some extent but simultaneously standing in its way. All states-systems – with the possible exception of the Sumerian – have been arenas within which at least the partial universalization of moral beliefs has taken place. Prior to the rise of the modern European states-system, this process occurred during the period of the Warring States in China, in the Greek city-states and in the world of the Hellenistic states. Why was it so? It is certainly the case that each of these states-systems emerged in an area that had previously enjoyed cultural unity (Wight 1977: ch. 1). In addition, to return to an earlier theme, states recognized that their own rights and interests were best promoted within the context of a wider society of states capable of regulating their interaction. However, recurrent opposition to the cosmopolitan critique of the states-system has revealed that states have had a highly ambivalent relationship with the process of moral universalization. Before they had to come to terms with the existence of a multistate system, the state in ancient China and in the medieval Islamic world created closed moral codes that were anchored in custom and tradition and hostile or inhospitable to ethical universalization. A similar concern for moral closure has frequently been displayed by modern states, although it has been held in check by the universalistic themes intrinsic to the West and reflected in the organization of the modern society of states.

In the contemporary international system, moreover, the universalistic morality that developed alongside industrialization has placed further constraints on state-driven forms of moral exclusion and closure. As Gellner (1983) has observed, all forms of social and political exclusion, including cultural and racial exclusion in international relations, have become problematical in the industrial age. But the fact that nationalism has been the main form of resistance to exclusion in the international system reveals that industrialization has also had a dual relationship with moral development. The nationalistic backlash against domination and inequality has often run counter to the universalistic idiom of modern civilization. Notwithstanding this fact, the cultural consequences of industrialization are generally hostile to closed moralities and particularistic ethical orientations, although the prevalent forms of liberal individualism reflect and also fuel exclusionary dispositions. Nevertheless, the prospects for the development of international society through the further eradication of unjust exclusion are kept alive by the dominant systems of ethical legitimation.

The nature of moral argument and the configuration of moral codes possess a degree of autonomy, as writers from Hobhouse to Habermas have suggested. Without any doubt, the realization that the grounds for excluding the other, whether others were slaves, women or 'savages', are morally problematical has been instrumental in generating social and political change in the modern world. The critique of unnecessary social constraints anchored in distorted forms of culture and communication remains an essential part of the critical theory of society. It is also true that the configuration of moral codes has rarely been determined by the force of the better argument alone. The exigencies of production, state-building, war and the search for international political order have left a more profound mark, as the study of multiple learning processes must attempt to reveal. Yet the supposition that the force of the better argument may ultimately play a greater role in world affairs provides the rationale for considering the principles of an ethical foreign policy.

The practical dimension

As we turn to the issue of the conduct of foreign policy, it may be useful to recall some themes that have arisen in the literature on state-formation. Norbert Elias argued that the emergence of the modern state was linked with the development of two interconnected monopolies: the monopoly of the right to own and employ the instruments of violence and the monopoly of the power of taxation. The process of state-building also entailed the creation of new social bonds and the development of new patterns of identity formation (Elias 2000). In short, the rise of the modern state entailed what Wight called 'a revolution in loyalties' in which an 'inner circle of loyalty expanded' and 'an outer circle of loyalty shrank'. New loyalties to the state replaced the inner web of customary loyalties to an 'immediate feudal superior' and the outer web of 'customary religious obedience to the Church under the Pope' (Wight 1978: 25).

From the outset, states have sought to limit the scope of both subnational and transnational solidarities and identities. In the main, they have succeeded in containing the gravitational attraction of inner circles of loyalty. Fearful of 'the invisible connections that ideological movements can establish across their official channels and boundaries', they have often reacted to universalizing ideologies by attempting to attach conceptions of a wider 'community to themselves' (Mann 1986: 368, 522). States have sought a monopoly over the right to define political identity in addition to the two monopoly rights mentioned above. Survival and success in war have depended on it.

Although modern states appeal to national political loyalties to justify their foreign policy behaviour, few have couched their claims to legitimacy in these terms alone. The need to defend international order is reflected in the language of foreign policy, and attendant obligations are concretized in numerous international practices and institutions. On some occasions, the welfare of the entire species is invoked as a principle of foreign policy. These references to a wider moral community – coextensive with humankind – raise the important question of whether the principles of foreign policy might move further along the spectrum from moral exclusion to moral inclusion. Significantly, thinkers as diverse as Kant, Carr and Foucault have answered this question by arguing for extending the boundaries of moral and political community, and for enlarging sympathy and solidarity.

In 'Perpetual peace', Kant argued that states were constrained by the absence of the systematic provision of security in international relations. He did not assume that states would quickly rally around the call for the realization of a cosmopolitan ethic. Nevertheless, in Kant's view, states had become more cognizant of the need to collaborate to preserve international order. New expectations had developed that states would proceed to recognize the importance of complying with the international ethical obligations associated with the age of Enlightenment. In other words, Kant argued that the purpose of foreign policy was to replace force with order and, subsequently, to move beyond order to justice, and to do so incrementally, mindful of the existence of stubborn constraints (Kant 1970b).

The strength of the Kantian position resides in its attempt to specify the maxims of an ethical foreign policy without succumbing to the utopian neglect of international systemic constraints. It is also worth recalling that, in the attempt to avoid a purely sterile realism, Carr (2001: 10, 219) called for a 'broadening of . . . national policy' in which the British government would begin to 'take into account the welfare of Lille or Dusseldorf or Lodz as well as the welfare of Oldham or Jarrow'. A similar sentiment can be found in the writings associated with the World Order Models Project (Johansen 1980: 406).

Furthermore, in some comments on the plight of the Vietnamese boat people, Foucault referred to an 'international citizenry', which must 'raise itself up against every abuse of power, no matter who the author or the victims'. The 'will of individuals', Foucault proceeded to argue, 'must inscribe itself in a reality over which governments have wanted to reserve a monopoly for themselves – a monopoly that we must uproot little by little every day' (Keenan 1987: 20–4). For Foucault, breaking up state monopoly power did not mean incorporating the nation-state within a world community that would come under the dominion of centralized political institutions. Although the precise details of Foucault's position are unclear, his remarks recall the anarchist vision of a world in which the powers of the state are dispatched to local communities and international associations to maximize both universality and difference. For anarchism in general, the construction of a 'post-sovereign' world has involved the enlargement of the sense of community and the recovery of local powers and attachments. In a similar vein, the approach taken by advocates of the 'postmodern' turn in international theory maintains that undercutting the state's role in defining the relationship between the inner and the outer circles of obligation is the real meaning of the challenge to the monopoly powers of exclusionary states. Only in this way can new local and transnational solidarities begin to emerge (Walker 1988).

Assuming this to be so, the issue is whether there are moral universals that have made some inroads into the state's foreign policy and have begun to be institutionalized in new political arrangements and social attachments. The following three developments illustrate some of the trends that are subversive of the idea that state sovereignty is the dominant principle in international relations. A marked increase in the ideal of the international protection of human rights is one such trend. A second is the recognition of the need for collective action to improve the social and economic conditions of the poorer members of the world society. A third trend, encapsulated in the concept of the 'common heritage of mankind' and in the notion of 'world heritage', stresses the need for a global ethic of responsibility for nature (Bull 1984a). The first two trends provide evidence of a logic of moral universalization in which the rights of non-nationals have slowly come to acquire greater significance in discussions about the nature of an ethical foreign policy. The importance of these trends is that they do not concede that foreign policy should be concerned exclusively with national security or with order and coexistence. The third trend indicates how the effects of technical–instrumental rationality may reinforce the importance of strengthening a world community. All three take issue with states that are closed in upon themselves, and all three reveal how the dominant patterns of moral inclusion and exclusion in the modern world might yet be reconstituted, although no one doubts that economic and political interests and responses to 'strategic necessity' will continue to stand in the way. How cosmopolitan principles can give rise to new forms of politics and identity is a central matter for a critical–theoretical approach to foreign policy.

Conclusion

This chapter has identified a range of philosophical, sociological and practical questions about the problem of community in the modern states-system. Its main purpose has been to suggest some new directions for a critical theory of international relations. The argument has been concerned, first, with identifying one method of achieving greater coherence within the field of International Relations and, second, with outlining some means of strengthening the linkages between political philosophy, social theory, historical sociology and the theory of international relations.

   The approach to the critical theory of international relations outlined here calls for three interconnected spheres of inquiry. First, it argues for new models of political theory that consider the obligation between the individual and humanity alongside traditional philosophical reflections upon the obligations that bind citizens to the state. Second, it calls for a form of sociological inquiry that analyses the relationships between state power, culture and moral development, not at the level of society but at the level of intersocietal systems in order to comprehend processes affecting humanity as a whole. Finally, it argues for developing models of the theory–practice relationship that assume that widening the circle of community to include those who are currently excluded by separate states is no less important than striving to improve social and political relations within the boundaries of existing societies. The observation that 'the architectonic role Aristotle attributed to the science of politics might well belong today to international politics' captures the salient point that the study of global politics has become a crucial site for the development of emancipatory social theory (Hoffmann 1960).

3   The achievements of critical theory

Over the past ten years Marxian-inspired critical social theory has exercised significant influence on international theory and has emerged as a serious alternative to orthodox approaches to the field. Critical theory has enlarged the parameters of the discipline by showing how efforts to reconstruct historical materialism offer direction to International Relations in the post-positivist phase. The position covered in this chapter, Marxian-inspired critical theory, should be distinguished from postmodern critical theory, which displays considerable scepticism towards the emancipatory project associated with Marxism. The relationship between these perspectives is a matter to come back to later. The main aim of this chapter is to consider the achievements of the Marxian branch of critical theory, to discuss some of the criticisms that have been levelled against it and to identify further areas for research.

As a strand of social theory and as an approach to international relations, critical theory has four main achievements. First, critical theory takes issue with positivism by arguing that knowledge does not arise from the subject's neutral engagement with an objective reality but reflects pre-existing social purposes and interests. Critical theory invites analysts to consider how claims about neutrality can conceal the role that knowledge plays in reproducing unsatisfactory social arrangements. In International Relations, these themes have been crucial elements in the critique of neo-realism and in the gradual recovery of a project of enlightenment and emancipation reworked to escape the familiar pitfalls of early twentieth century idealism.

Second, critical theory stands opposed to empirical claims about the social world which assume that existing structures are immutable. The central objection to these claims is that notions of immutability support structured inequalities of power and wealth which are in principle alterable. Critical theory investigates the prospects for new forms of political community in which individuals and groups can achieve higher levels of freedom and equality. Its orientation towards existing constraints is shaped by the Marxian assumption that all that is solid eventually melts into air and by the belief that human beings can make more of their history under conditions of their own choosing. It rejects the utopian assumption that there is an unchanging universal ethical yardstick for judging social arrangements and recognizes the constraints upon radical change stressed by perspectives such as neo-realism but avoids the latter's resignation to international political fate. Having overcome the flawed dichotomy between realism and idealism that has lent a peculiar structure to so much debate within the field, critical theory examines the prospects for greater freedom and equality that are immanent within existing social relations.

Third, critical theory learns from and overcomes the weaknesses inherent in Marxism. The project of reconstructing historical materialism associated with the writings of Habermas is especially significant in this regard. This project denies that class power is the fundamental form of social exclusion or that production is the key determinant of society and history. Post-Marxist critical theory extends conventional Marxist analysis by considering axes of exclusion other than class, and by analysing the variety of forces, including production, that have shaped the contours of human history. Particular emphasis is placed on the different forms of social learning. Recent analysis stresses how human beings learn to include some within, and exclude others from, their bounded communities and also how they can develop the capacity to engage others in open and potentially universal discourse. The analysis of boundedness opens up new possibilities for constructing a historical sociology with an emancipatory purpose (see Chapter 11).

Fourth, critical theory judges social arrangements by their capacity to embrace open dialogue with all others and envisages new forms of political community that break with unjustified exclusion. Realist and neo-realist arguments that communities must deal with one another in the currency of military power are rejected by critical theory, which envisages the use of unconstrained discourse to determine the moral significance of national boundaries and to examine the possibility of post-sovereign forms of political life. The theme of dialogue is one area in which different strands of post-positivist theory can converge in charting future possibilities for the study of international relations and in envisaging forms of community that overcome the moral deficits of bounded sovereign states.

The remainder of this chapter is in three parts. Parts one and two consider the first two achievements in more detail. As these achievements are now firmly embedded in the literature this chapter pays more attention to the reconstruction of historical materialism and to the relationship between discourse ethics and international politics. These themes are considered in part three.

Subject and object

In an oft-quoted article Cox (1981) made the important observation that knowledge is always for someone and some purpose. Problem-solving knowledge is always geared to making the international system function more smoothly on the understanding that fundamental change is either impossible or improbable. Critical–theoretical knowledge searches for evidence of change on the assumption that present structures are unlikely to be reproduced indefinitely. If change is not imminent it might seem wise to ensure that existing arrangements operate as smoothly as possible, but critical theory rejects this conclusion because those who belong to the same political order are not treated equally or fairly by it. If international order works to the advantage of the most privileged groups then the well-meaning aim of managing an existing order has the unpalatable political effect of neglecting marginal groups and harming subordinate interests. Observers who analyse the prospects for the smoother functioning of the existing system may claim value-neutrality for their inquiry but they fail to understand that intellectual projects have important moral implications for the national and international distribution of wealth and power. The assumption that critical theory starts from normative and inevitably subjective preferences, whereas problem-solving theory avoids moral commitments in order to grapple with intractable realities, is therefore untenable.

Critical theory collapses the subject–object distinction and emphasizes the human needs and purposes that determine what counts as valuable knowledge. As already noted, Cox identified two interests. Following the publication of Ashley (1981), it is widely known that Habermas (1972) identified three: the technical interest in understanding how to extend control over nature and society; the practical interest in understanding how to create and maintain orderly communities; and the emancipatory interest in identifying and eradicating unnecessary social confinements and constraints. From the critical–theoretical perspective these three interests constitute knowledge, frame the subject's mode of analysis and reveal that serious difficulties attend the claim that knowledge is value-free. Critical theory argues that knowledge about society is incomplete if it lacks an emancipatory purpose.

Claims that the social world is immutable illustrate these points. Critical theorists are inevitably troubled by the immutability thesis, given the assumption that human beings make their own history and can in principle make it differently. According to that thesis, social structures or forms of human action are natural and unchangeable rather than contingent and renegotiable. Critical theory aims to subvert immutability claims and to identify and channel the countervailing tendencies that are immanent within existing forms of life.

Three examples may suffice to explain how critical theory endeavours to undermine perspectives that naturalize what is essentially social and historical. The first is Marx's critique of bourgeois political economy, which supposed that the institution of private property was natural. The second is Hegel's critique of the Indian caste system, which contended that nature decrees that human beings are arranged into unchanging social hierarchies. The third is the feminist critique of the patriarchal claim that the nature of womanhood precludes full involvement in the political realm. For Marx, private property is not a natural institution but a historical product that can be overcome in communist society. For Hegel, caste distinctions are not given in nature but arise within a particular ensemble of social relations in which spirit has yet to be released from the natural world. For feminism, nothing in the nature of womanhood precludes full involvement in a public realm that can be reconstituted in the post-patriarchal state. In each case, the critical–theoretical response is to oppose claims that structures cannot be transformed because they are securely grounded in human nature or in a condition (such as anarchy) that human beings are deemed to be powerless to alter. Critical theory therefore takes issue with accounts of reality that underestimate the human capacity to problematize and transform inherited, and apparently natural, social conventions. It rejects systems-determinism and affirms the capacity of human agents to act collectively to free themselves from structural constraints.

Critical theory is sharply opposed to neo-realism and its variant of the immutability thesis. The immutability thesis here is that political communities cannot escape the logic of power inherent in the condition of anarchy. The thesis fails to provide an adequate account of the relationship between agency and structure (Wendt 1987; Hollis and Smith 1990). For example, Waltz (1979) recognizes that units have the capacity to influence the operation of the international system but argues that, in the main, causality flows in the opposite direction with the result that units are forced into similar responses to the constraints that are inherent in the anarchic system. However, Waltz's observation that the study of international relations is primarily concerned with relations between the great powers recognizes that, although they are forced to act in the context of anarchy (and may be powerless to transform it), they enjoy a capacity to determine the functioning of the system which lesser powers simply do not possess. To adapt Wendt (1992), anarchy is largely what the great powers make it. The incidence of, and the prospects for, peace depend not on the anarchic nature of the international system but on the ambitions of the great powers, the principles of foreign policy to which they are committed and the effectiveness of international norms as constraints on national behaviour (Linklater 1994). The logic of conflict and competition cannot be regarded as unalterable.

Not that it can be easily swept aside either, and one of the virtues of the neo-realist stress on long-standing international constraints is that it counterbalances voluntarism in international relations. Even so, the immutability thesis sanctifies historically specific configurations of power that the weak may resent and the strong are not powerless to change. Contingent political arrangements are placed outside the ambit of legitimate efforts to secure fundamental change. Knowledge that is confined to the problem-solving mode performs the ideological function of perpetuating the international status quo. Not only does the language of immutability convert humanly produced circumstances into quasi-natural forces – it also contributes to the production of political subjects who accept that relations between political communities must be as they are. Immutability claims help to construct political subjects who succumb to sharp and stultifying distinctions between utopia and reality (Ashley 1984).

For Horkheimer (1978) critical theory was contrasted with traditional theory or positivism that sought to explain social laws and regularities. Critical theory regards the analysis of social regularities as useful for understanding the constraints on political change but it transcends positivism by analysing logics which may bring about the transformation of social systems. To illustrate, whereas neo-realism aims to account for the reproduction of the system of states, critical theory endeavours to identify counter-hegemonic or countervailing tendencies that are invariably present within all social and political relations. The sceptical retort that countervailing forces may be ineffectual, and even short-lived, is not a decisive objection because critical theory aims to identify the sources of potentially far-reaching change so that human subjects can grasp the possibility of alternative paths of historical development that can be realized through collective political action. It need only suppose that what is not at present a principal determinant of society and history could become so in future. In contrast, neo-realism privileges structure over agency, provides legitimation for the status quo and assumes that the threat and use of force are an inescapable part of international anarchy. It obscures the crucial point that the reform of the international system should begin with the transformation of the idea of the state as a moral community and with the alteration of past assumptions about the rights and duties of bounded political communities (Linklater 1990b: 26–32).

The reconstruction of historical materialism: from production to discourse ethics

The first and second achievements of critical theory imported critical tools fashioned by Marx and Marxism into International Relations in order to challenge orthodox approaches such as realism and neo-realism. The third and fourth achievements criticize Marxism in order to develop a more adequate account of social evolution and an improved normative standpoint. The crucial theme here is the transition in critical social theory from the 'paradigm of production' to the 'paradigm of communication' in the writings of Habermas, which has immense significance for the development of post-realist international theory.

The limitations of the paradigm of production are well known. The emphasis of historical materialism fell too heavily on modes of production and class conflict whereas the historical importance of race, nation, gender, state building and war was relatively unexplored. Three criticisms of the paradigm of production stem from these observations. In the first place, Marxism pondered the conceptual issue of what it would mean to be free from capitalist exploitation but failed to define freedom in relation to forms of oppression anchored in state power, patriarchy, nationalism or racism. In the second place, Marxism lacked an adequate historical sociology. Too much emphasis was placed on production and too little importance was attached to state-building, war, morality and culture. In the third place, Marxism produced a clear but limited political vision that defended the abolition of class relations, private property and commodity production but offered no clear vision of the social order that was required to secure freedom and equality outside the sphere of production. Recent critical theory has endeavoured to solve these problems by developing the idea of undistorted communication, creating a more complex historical sociology which is based on the idea of social learning and on envisaging the democratization of politics, domestic and international. These developments rework the Marxian analysis of the long-term development of species capacities in order to construct an account of human emancipation that is concerned with enlarging the meaning and scope of discourse rather than with analysing long-term changes in the relationship between the species and nature (Habermas 1979b).

To begin with social learning, the essence of Habermas's critique of Marx is that he assumed that progress in learning how to control nature would create the context in which freedom and equality could be realized. Marx overlooked the danger that the expansion of technological power would allow new forms of domination to develop. For these reasons, Habermas (1979a) argues that technical–instrumental learning that enables humans to increase their collective control over nature should be distinguished from moral–practical learning in which human beings create more consensual social relations. Habermas introduces a third type of learning, strategic learning, in which human beings learn how to manipulate and control others. These distinctions are designed to support an analysis of freedom and history that overcomes the problems inherent in orthodox Marxist analysis. Social evolution is explained by focusing on diverse learning processes involving species-wide competences and capacities.

Having separated the spheres of technical–instrumental and moral–practical learning, Habermas analyses the species capacities that develop in this second realm. Learning in this domain does not have any particular kind of technical–instrumental learning as its prerequisite; the preconditions of freedom include moral and cultural factors that cannot be reduced to material circumstances and undergo separate logics of change. Moral–practical learning refers to the ways in which human beings learn how to conduct social relations consensually, thereby transcending strategic considerations of power. Habermas (1979b: 73ff.) draws on Kohlberg's analysis of stages of individual cognitive development in defence of the claim that there are homologies between psychological and social development. Three forms of morality are identified. Pre-conventional morality exists when actors obey norms because they fear that non-compliance will be sanctioned by authority; conventional morality exists when norms are observed because actors are loyal to a specific social group; post-conventional morality exists when actors stand back from authority structures and group membership to ask whether they are complying with principles that have universal applicability.

The development of various species-powers is evident within the post-conventional stage, which is for Habermas the highest form of morality. Post-conventionalism demonstrates a capacity for ethical reflectiveness in which agents recognize that moral codes are malleable social products rather than immutable conventions to which they must submit. It reveals a capacity for 'decentredness' in which agents recognize that moral standpoints are diverse and contingent and that none has prima facie validity across time and space. It demonstrates a capacity for universality in which human agents move away from efforts to resolve age-old debates about the universalizable good life and seek to define potentially global procedures for dealing with concrete disputes and differences.

Discourse ethics affirms that the validity of principles must be established through modes of dialogue in which human beings strive to reach an agreement. No person and no moral position can be excluded in advance. True dialogue exists when moral agents accept that there is no a priori certainty about 'who will learn from whom' and when they willingly engage in processes of 'reciprocal critique' (Habermas 1990: 26). Dialogue makes it easier for agents to understand how their moral choices and preferences reflect personal biases and local cultural influences that others do not share. Discourse ethics is therefore regarded as overcoming the weaknesses inherent in monologic reasoning such as that employed by Rawlsian contractors separately choosing political principles behind a veil of ignorance (Habermas 1990: 36). Participants aim to be guided by nothing other than 'the force of the better argument' (Habermas 1990: 66, 89) and agree that norms cannot be valid unless they command the consent of everyone who stands to be affected by them (Habermas 1989: 82ff.). The objective is unconstrained communication, although this is an ideal that may never be realized completely because agents could never be sure that they had reached a stage of social development in which there were no further constraints to discover.

Extending this further, moral–practical learning involves, inter alia, a willingness to question all social and political boundaries and all systems of inclusion and exclusion. Systems of exclusion have been problematized in most parts of the world and the critique of the systematic exclusion of women, minority nations and racial and religious minorities is a fundamental dimension of politics in most societies. What Marx took to be the fundamental form of struggle against exclusion (the struggle between social classes) proved to be an instance of the broader phenomenon of resistance to 'the closure of social relationships and the monopolization of opportunities' (Kalberg 1994: 120ff.) in its multitudinous forms. The contention that the human species constructs complex systems of inclusion and exclusion in the course of its development is a better starting point for critical theory.

In particular, human beings learn how the social bond that unites them in one community simultaneously divides them from outsiders. They learn subtle distinctions between insiders and outsiders, but they can also unlearn them and move to new principles of organization in the light of changing normative commitments. Discourse ethics reflects a particular stage in moral development in which human beings question inherited systems of inclusion and exclusion and ask whether the boundaries between insiders and outsiders can be justified by principles that are agreeable to all. The attempt to move beyond Marxism as critical theory is a response to these themes, specifically to the diverse ways in which boundaries and barriers are contested in modern political life (Linklater 1992).

In the contemporary world, critical theory is inevitably concerned with the ways in which bounded communities include and exclude. The focus is on the state although the significance of other political actors is not overlooked. Two main approaches to the state have appeared within critical–theoretical writing in recent years (George 1994). One approach, developed by Robert Cox (1981, 1983, 1989), emphasizes the revolt of Third World states and related political movements that highlight the negative effects of the globalization of relations of production and the impact of linkages between elites in core and periphery on the distribution of the world's wealth. The main emphasis falls upon counter-hegemonic states and social movements and their ability to pool their political resources to transform the world economy. A second approach, closer to Habermasian critical theory, emphasizes the changes affecting the social bond that unites the members of the sovereign state and sets them apart from the outside world. The main emphasis falls upon the tensions within, and the challenges to, the sovereign state, which are evident not just in peripheral areas but in varying degrees throughout the world. The second approach is explicitly concerned with the nature and future of the state as a bounded moral and political community.

To illustrate what is significant from this point of view, it is useful to recall that the social bond that simultaneously unites and divides has been problematical from the beginning of the modern states-system. Great difficulties have arisen in trying to understand the relationship between duties to fellow citizens and duties to the rest of humankind (Habermas 1979b; Linklater 1990b). These difficulties are evident in many areas of international political life including the theory and practice of the law of war, human rights and social justice. Quite what the bond that unites the members of the state means for the rights of those living outside the state – exactly what its moral significance should be – is a matter of continuing philosophical debate, as is the sociological question of whether the social bond is weakening as new patterns of economic and social interaction (usefully captured by the term globalization) entangle national communities.

Recent literature has focused upon the developments that are weakening the ties between citizens and states and undermining tightly bound communities in many parts of the world (Linklater 1995). They are discussed here not in order to reach any definite conclusion about the future of the sovereign state but to outline some important sociological questions from a critical–theoretical point of view. The obsolescence of force between the major industrial powers is one development with substantial implications for the bond between citizens and the state. Given the role that war has played in the creation of national communities, it is hardly surprising that the pacification of the Western or Western-inclined regions of the world-system has been accompanied by calls for greater political representation and voice from minority nations and migrant groups that feel marginalized by dominant conceptions of the national community. Globalization and pacification are interconnected in important respects as Rosecrance (1986) observes in the analysis of the rise of the trading state. If the conquest of territory is no longer necessary for economic growth but is actually detrimental to it, then the cult of violence is less likely to feature strongly in the self-image and behaviour of the great powers. Centripetal forces are, in consequence, freer to develop.

But, as noted, centrifugal forces are also more able to emerge. Globalization fragments national cultures as some groups embrace what Bull and Watson (1984) described as 'the cosmopolitan culture of modernity' while others rebel against the encroachment of predominantly Western images and symbols. The social bond that simultaneously unites and divides is also weakened by the challenge to a dominant theme in the ideology of state-building, namely national assimilationism. Minority nations and indigenous peoples spearhead the politics of identity in which dominant conceptions of national community are challenged and the public recognition of group rights is demanded. For these reasons, the immanent possibility of new forms of political community has become apparent – a possibility that neo-realism blinkered by the immutability thesis cannot explore. New conceptions of citizenship, community and sovereignty are invited by these changes, and especially in Western Europe new constructions of community have already begun to appear (Kymlicka 1989; Connolly 1992; Held 1993; Walker 1993).

One purpose of this brief analysis of the forces currently affecting nation-states is to raise several questions that can be asked about political bounded communities at any stage in the development of the human race. These questions are not concerned with traditional questions in International Relations about how bounded communities interact with one another but with the neglected and prior issue of how boundedness is constituted in the first place (Devetak 1995). The main questions are these:

1 What unifies insiders as members of a bounded community? What is their shared identity? Who is 'the other' within the community and how does 'otherness' within the community help define common identity (Foucault 1979; Habermas 1989: 400)?

2 What level of social and political homogeneity within the bounded community is demanded of insiders, and what level of diversity is allowed?

3 How do members of the bounded community understand their separateness from other communities? What are the principles of separability (Ruggie 1983) to which they are committed?

4 How closed is the community to outsiders? Does the bounded community allow outsiders to become members? What level of internationalization is possible between bounded communities? Which areas of social and political life are most subject to internationalization (Nelson 1971, 1973)?

5 To what extent is the moral significance of boundaries open to question? How far does the boundary between inside and outside include or exclude the forms of moral–practical learning noted above: namely ethical reflectiveness, the decentring of worldviews and open dialogue with outsiders to decide the moral significance of political boundaries and to determine the principles of global interaction?

Some of these questions about bounded communities have been central to Marxist critical theory (Linklater 1990a). Marx's social theory aimed to show that capitalist social relations were being transformed in ways that would deepen and widen communities: deepen them by enabling subordinate classes to enjoy the material wealth of communities that have been traditionally monopolized by dominant classes; widen them by lowering the barriers between the national community and the species in general. But, as already noted, Marx exaggerated the role of the class struggle in his account of political resistance to systematic exclusion, and he obscured wider patterns of change within the moral–practical domain. Arguably, the logic of Marx's project invited the problematization of all forms of social exclusion, but Marx neither articulated this claim precisely nor argued that principles of inclusion and exclusion required the authority of dialogue. Later Marxist writings on nationalism and imperialism asked how the national bond might be reconstituted and how community might come to be shaped by the principles of socialist internationalism, but the paradigm of production meant that the possibilities inherent in the analysis were not explored. The reconstruction of historical materialism, as it is understood here, takes some of the questions that Marxism raised in connection with modes of production, extends them and applies them to the wider sociopolitical domain.

Coming at this from another angle, one of the main sociological critiques of Marxism over the past ten years points to its simplistic single-logic account of human history. Multilogic analysis has been emphasized in the analysis of the nature of social power (Mann 1986, 1993) and in accounts of the state and violence (Giddens 1985; Tilly 1992) but there has been no similar account of how boundedness arises from the interaction between multiple logics. Boundedness arose as a sociological question in the writings of Mauss and Durkheim (Nelson 1971) and in an important essay by Benjamin Nelson (1973) but hardly ever as a theme in International Relations. Much closer cooperation between Sociology and International Relations is required to develop more sophisticated understandings of the origins, reproduction and transformation of bounded political communities (Scholte 1993; Rosenberg 1994).

Discourse ethics: implications for politics

The preceding section set out the main themes of discourse ethics, explained how it renders boundaries problematical and suggested some issues for historical sociology. This section considers the relationship between discourse ethics and practical politics. It begins with the criticism that the universalistic dimension of critical theory generates its own forms of exclusion, and it proceeds to consider the claim that discourse ethics fails to offer guidance on substantive moral issues. Neither claim, it will be argued, is convincing.

Deep concerns about the exclusionary character of Western universalistic reasoning have been raised by many postmodernist writers. Foucault claimed that 'the search for a form of morality acceptable by everyone in the sense that everyone would have to submit to it, seems catastrophic to me' (Hoy 1986: 119). However, as McCarthy (1990) has argued, Foucault and Habermas agreed that the politics of speech was preferable to the politics of force. The gulf between different strands of critical theory is not as great as it is sometimes taken to be, as recent comments by the postmodernist thinker Lyotard reveal. Lyotard (1993: 140–1) claims that the right to speak, and the right of the different not to be excluded from the speech community, are fundamental entitlements. He argues that it is possible 'to extend interlocution to any human individual whatsoever, regardless of national or natural idiom' (ibid.: 139). Through speech, human beings 'can come to an agreement, after reasoning and debate, and then establish their community by contract' (ibid.: 138). Stressing the universalistic theme, which has long been central to critical social theory, Lyotard (1993: 139) concludes that 'civility may become universal in fact as it promises to do by right.'

Although Habermas (1985: 94–6) defends a 'pluralism of life forms' and adds that a 'fully transparent . . . homogenized and unified society' is not a political ideal, his claim that the purpose of dialogue is to determine which interests are generalizable may seem to imply the search for a universal consensus (Benhabib 1993: 9). Feminist theorists have argued that ethical universalism can be gendered and exclusionary. In her critique of Kohlberg, Gilligan (1993) argues that the public domain, which is largely populated by men, is regulated by general principles that apply to everyone irrespective of personal characteristics. Gilligan argues that the belief that the higher forms of moral reasoning are concerned with creating abstract principles of justice devalues the moral skills present in the ethic of care and responsibility, which is concerned with the particular needs of concrete persons. The belief that the most advanced moral perspectives are specifically concerned with universal principles neglects then the moral skills that have been displayed most typically by women within traditional families.

Young (1991) refers to the need for a communicative ethic that does not permit the search for universalizable principles to overshadow efforts to respond to the specific needs of particular human beings. Some theorists such as Benhabib (1993), Gilligan (1993) and O'Neill (1989) argue that the moral agent needs to balance the two moralities that deal with the generalized and the concrete other. Remarking on Gilligan's critique of Kohlberg, Habermas argues that discourse ethics requires the hermeneutic skills that are evident in the ethic of care and responsibility. Discourse ethics is not a form of 'moral rigorism', which applies universalizable principles in a mechanical fashion regardless of social contexts and personal circumstances. The hermeneutic skill of reflecting on the relationship between moral principle, social context and the concrete needs of particular individuals is therefore central to discourse ethics (Habermas 1990: 176–80).

However, the contention that the moralities of justice and care complement one another has more profound implications for the meaning of true dialogue. True dialogue is not exhausted by the quest for generalizable principles governing similar persons in similar circumstances: it requires genuine engagement with the different and quite possibly alien standpoints taken by the 'other'. In her argument for 'post-conventional contextualism', Benhabib (1993: 151, 163–4) makes the crucial point that knowledge of the concrete other is essential before deciding the extent to which the circumstances of different persons are relevantly similar and rightly subject to generalizable principles. In their defence of the 'critical feminist enterprise', Frazer and Lacey (1993: 203–12) have argued for 'dialogic communitarianism' that recognizes the role of community in the constitution of the self and the value of membership of particular social groups. From this point of view, open dialogue recognizes the significance of 'unassimilated otherness' and renounces any commitment to a 'unified public' or stultifying social consensus (Frazer and Lacey 1993: 204). These feminist approaches are not opposed to universalism in all its forms but take issue with a universalism that opposes or attaches little significance to difference (Young 1991: 105). Their effect is to imagine a strong universalism in which dialogue encounters difference and is open to what White (1991) has called 'responsibility to otherness'.

No doubt the debate will continue over whether or not this construction of discourse ethics retains too much emphasis on a universalistic ethic that undervalues and threatens cultural difference. It should be noted, however, that discourse ethics defends procedural universalism and does not claim that any single conception of the good life should be universalized. The contention that critical theory is committed to modes of thought and action that would subsume difference within one totalizing identity is increasingly widespread in the literature (George 1994: ch. 7) but false. The error is to suppose that the idea of reaching an agreement is the same as the notion of arriving at a total consensus (Benhabib 1993: 9).

To develop this further it is useful to identify four forms of understanding. The first is anthropological understanding, which has the aim of comprehending difference for its own sake. The second is strategic understanding, which has the aim of understanding the other's aspirations, interests and intentions in order to outwit and outmanoeuvre the other conceived as an adversary. The third is Socratic understanding in which actors suspend their truth claims and enter into dialogue with others to seek the truth. The fourth is moral–political understanding, which has two dimensions: to understand the plurality of moral views in order to reach agreement about the principles of inclusion and exclusion, and to comprehend the rules of coexistence, which agents could accept for pragmatic reasons should a consensus elude them.

Three of these forms of understanding are relevant for the emancipatory project. Anthropological understanding is relevant because it requires the empathetic skill of appreciating what is unique or different about the other. Socratic understanding is relevant because actors can only arrive at principles that are true for all if they first embrace Cartesian doubt about their standpoints and accept the need for 'reciprocal critique'. Moral–political understanding is relevant as it maintains that principles of inclusion and exclusion and rules of coexistence can acquire universal validity only through open dialogue embracing all points of view. Strategic understanding alone clashes with the emancipatory project because it is geared towards controlling others (and belongs to the sphere of strategic as opposed to moral–practical learning). The accusation that critical theory is driven towards the cancellation of difference misreads the nature of its commitment to 'the goal of coming to an understanding' (Habermas 1979a: 3). Coming to an understanding may not culminate in a moral consensus. But it is the idea of reaching an understanding that captures the most important respect in which critical theory, postmodernism, feminism and philosophical hermeneutics (Shapcott 1994) are involved in a common political project.

One further criticism accuses discourse ethics of formalism. There is some truth in this charge. Discourse ethics sets out the procedures to be followed so that individuals are equally free to express their moral differences and can proceed to resolve them, where possible, through 'the unforced force of the better argument'. Discourse ethics is not an attempt to predict or pre-empt the likely result of dialogue. It does not provide putative solutions to substantive moral debates, envisage utopian end-points or circulate programmatic blueprints, but it is not wholly lacking in content. The gulf between actual social practices and discourse ethics provides an immediate rationale for political critique. In addition to setting out the formal conditions that have to be satisfied before open dialogue can exist, discourse ethics invites a critique of structures and beliefs that obstruct open dialogue. On this basis, critical theory develops a normative vision that is often missing from, although it is not necessarily inconsistent with, postmodernism. Ashley and Walker (1990: 391, 394–5), for example, take issue with claims 'to stand heroically upon some exclusionary ground', and they challenge obstacles to dialogue across the 'institutional limitations that separate nations, classes, occupational categories, genders and races'. This concern with advancing an 'ethic of freedom' (Ashley and Walker 1990: 391) is the starting point for critical social theory.

Illustrating this theme, Cohen (1990: 71, 100) argues that discourse ethics is critical of societies 'based on domination, violence and systematic inequality', which prevent full participation in the life of the community; it therefore supports the equalization of power. Cohen stresses the achievements of liberal–democratic society in this regard without losing sight of its imperfections and without assuming that Western liberal democracy is the model of government that should apply universally. Discourse ethics can be institutionalized in structures of participation, the precise character of which must vary from place to place.

It is important to take this point further by noting that discourse ethics cannot be completed by a number of separate experiments in democratic participation within independent sovereign states. Discourse ethics clashes with the idea of territorial sovereignty, which restricts the capacity of outsiders to participate in dialogue to consider issues that have adverse consequences for them. The important point that such dialogue needs to be embodied transnationally is captured in recent writings on cosmopolitan democracy (Held 1993). The logic of discourse ethics is that moral agents should problematize all social boundaries, including the effects of bounded political communities on the members of other groups.

Discourse ethics therefore invites the questioning of traditional notions of sovereignty and the reconsideration of citizenship. Rethinking citizenship is crucial because this concept is central to the bond that unites the members of the sovereign state and separates them from other communities. Part of the recent challenge to citizenship concentrates upon the denial or inadequate consideration of the rights of persons in other societies. Notions of cosmopolitan democracy imagine communities in which insiders and outsiders can participate on equal terms. An additional critique of the modern idea of citizenship raises issues about the supposition that citizens must share the same identity or have exactly the same rights. Criticisms of this belief argue that particular groups within the sovereign state (such as indigenous peoples) reject the dominant understandings of community and desire the public recognition of particular cultural rights. This critique argues that traditional ideas of citizenship possess an assimilationist logic that indigenous peoples and minority nations reject (Kymlicka 1989). Not only must one imagine communities in which outsiders have greater representation and voice, one must also envisage communities that recognize the claims of the culturally marginal within their boundaries and promote their representation within international institutions which are charged with implementing the principles of transnational democracy. Discourse ethics therefore questions the social bond between the citizen and the state which perpetuates the sovereign state as a system of unjust exclusion.

Finally, some observations are required about the earlier theme of the relationship between universalism and difference in the light of these comments on sovereignty. An account of the prospects for increasing dialogue across bounded communities might note the following developments. Post-nationalist claims and identities are developing in three ways: through the universalization of moral ideas such as the rights of women, through duties of care for the environment and through regionalism. Each move generates fears. The first raises the fear that universalization will assimilate 'the other' within an essentially Western framework. According to this view, the process of universalization might therefore result in the triumph of a worldview in which there is no strongly felt need for dialogue with others. For its part, regionalism raises the fear that new boundaries might be drawn between the regional community and outsiders. Each of the fears recognizes how the rise of post-nationalist frameworks might pose threats to difference and reinstate pernicious barriers.

A further pronounced development in the modern world – the politics of cultural identity in which groups react against perceived threats to their values – may produce several different responses: first, the idea that successful responses should encourage those in the dominant cultures of the West to question the universal significance of their worldviews in the light of their rejection by groups in other parts of the world; second, that expressions of difference can be as unwelcome as the form of universalization mentioned above – unwelcome because some racist and nationalist expressions threaten the existence of different communities; third, that claims to defend any culture invite basic questions about who claims to speak for the community and who may be excluded from representations of its values and traditions. Discourse ethics is an approach to the dangers mentioned above. Discourse ethics encourages open dialogue between the diversity of moral views and facilitates the expansion of the range of moral and political points of view. Open dialogue is a check against the dangers of domination which are inherent in some claims about cultural difference (such as arguments in defence of racial superiority). It seeks to ensure that only those norms that meet with the approval of all who are affected acquire universality. Discourse ethics therefore encourages efforts to strike the right balance between unprecedented levels of diversity and universality. Achieving the aims of critical theory requires the reconstruction of the state as a bounded community and the introduction of post-nationalist conceptions of citizenship (Linklater 1995). This is the meaning of an earlier claim that the reform of international relations has to begin with the transformation of the state as a bounded moral and political community.

Conclusion

Four main achievements of critical theory have been discussed in this chapter: one, its critique of the supposition that subjects can be engaged in the politically neutral analysis of an external reality and its stress on the role that knowledge can play in the reproduction of problematical social arrangements; two, its critique of the immutability thesis and its argument for the analysis of immanent tendencies towards greater human freedom and equality; three, its critique of Marxism and its argument for a more complex account of social learning centred on discourse ethics; and four, its critique of barriers to open dialogue and its support for post-sovereign communities in which new levels of universality and difference are attained. Critical theory keeps faith with the Enlightenment project and defends its universalism by advancing the ideal of open dialogue not only between fellow citizens but between all members of the human race.

Part II
The problem of citizenship

4 What is a good international citizen?

Citizenship can be conceived as a series of expanding circles which are pushed forward by the momentum of conflict and struggle.

(Turner 1986)

It is 'time to go higher in our search for citizenship, but also lower and wider. Higher to the world, lower to the locality...The citizen has been both too puffed up and too compressed.'

(Wright 1990)

I

Senator Evans's proposal that good international citizenship should be a central premise of Australia's foreign policy forms the background to the present discussion (Evans 1989a, 1989b). When advocating good international citizenship, Senator Evans does not claim that the pursuit of national interests must be renounced forthwith. Instead, the argument is that foreign policy must also be animated by more elevated concerns such as promoting world order, encouraging global reform and honouring duties to humanity. The good international citizen will blend the best in – to use Senator Evans's own terminology – realism and idealism.

Although few will contest the proposition that foreign policy should be informed by more than strictly national concerns, this does not mean that various complexities can be quickly set to one side. The normative defence of good international citizenship is a complex theoretical issue in its own right. Deciding the relative importance of national interests, international order and considerations of humanity for good international citizenship is a second complexity. A third – a test for the diplomatic imagination – is how to formulate a coherent vision of Australian foreign policy that specifies the goals and responsibilities of the good international citizen in the region and elsewhere.

Complexities aside, the notion of good international citizen is an attractive one for at least three reasons. In the first place, it promises to overcome the conflict between citizenship and humanity that has been a recurrent feature of the theory and practice of international relations. Second, it appeals as one of the new concepts and ideals that Hedley Bull (1983: 127–31) called for in his searching comments on the mounting problems of world order in the 1970s and 1980s. Third, its attractiveness is further underlined by the way in which recent patterns of global change have prompted the reconsideration of some past diplomatic conventions and encouraged the development of new international norms. In the more fluid circumstances of the present, the concept of the good international citizen can play an important role in 'synthesising the old that is dying with the new that is emerging' and in seizing what Falk (1983: 272) calls 'the Grotian moment'.

The discussion of good international citizen arises in the wake of the more general revival of citizenship theory in contemporary political thought. This renewed interest in the concept is especially evident on the Left, which, traditionally, has been sceptical of the alleged achievements of citizenship. Its critique of citizenship argued that the legal and political rights of citizens have limited significance in the context of profound class inequalities. More recently, faced with the challenge of neo-conservatism, the Left has sprung to the defence of citizenship. It has argued that citizenship was redefined in the early twentieth century to add welfare rights to the traditional legal and political rights of citizens. To be faithful to citizenship, the Left now argues, is to ensure that these welfare rights are not undermined. In recent radical thought, the commitment to citizenship is believed to require support for collective action to assist the victims of unjustifiable forms of exclusion anchored in class, ethnicity, gender and race (Turner 1986; King 1987; Harris 1987; Barbalet 1988; Miller 1989).

In much political theory, the analysis of citizenship deals with the rights and duties of the citizens of particular states; very little attention is paid to the ways in which ideas of citizenship might be developed in international relations. Even so, several writers have added that the current internationalization of economic and political life requires, and might very well generate, the further transformation of citizenship. Bryan Turner (1986: 140) has observed that 'we have a system of national citizenship in a social context which requires a new theory of internationalism and universalistic citizenship'. In a similar vein, Etienne Balibar (1988: 723–30) has argued that the emergence of 'a cosmopolis of communications and financial transactions' means that the 'struggle for citizenship as a struggle for equality must begin again on new ground and with new objectives'. Although it is disappointing that these themes are not accompanied by any discussion of the relevant literature on international relations, the focus on the critique of unjust exclusion in recent discussions of citizenship can enrich the analysis of the good international citizen, as the following discussion attempts to show.

The argument of this chapter is in five parts. The first section considers the meaning of citizenship and proceeds to ask whether its dialectical development within the modern state requires the creation of analogous concepts of citizenship in international relations. With this question in mind, the second, third and fourth sections consider realist, Grotian or 'rationalist' and cosmopolitan responses to, and conceptions of, good international citizenship. These sections argue that these three perspectives can be combined in a more encompassing framework along the lines that Kant developed in *Perpetual Peace*. The fifth section defends Kant's account of the multiple levels of citizenship and points to ways of revising the central themes in his sociology of world citizenship. The main revision is that the development of good international citizenship depends largely on the proliferation of social–democratic, liberal states.

II

At the most fundamental level, citizenship refers first of all to the primary legal rights that all persons have as members of a particular state.[1] In the second place, citizenship refers to the right of participation in the political life of the community as a whole. In the third place, citizenship refers not only to rights but to fundamental duties as well. Emphasizing this moral dimension of citizenship, Aristotle (1960: book III, xiii, section 12) argued that citizens are 'those who are able and willing to rule and be ruled with a view to attaining a way of life according to goodness'.[2] Recent writings on citizenship argue that it entails a willingness to place constraints on self-interest because of duties to promote a more general good. This is the theme that Senator Evans emphasizes in his defence of good international citizenship.

In the twentieth century, the contention that citizens have duties towards the whole community has been linked with the principle that the advantaged have responsibilities to assist the more vulnerable members of society. The belief that citizens do not simply belong to the same community but have an equal right to enjoy its manifold benefits has been a crucial theme in the development of modern states. The goal of dismantling various modes of exclusion that thwart this right is the key to how the original juridical rights of citizens have been expanded over approximately the last two hundred years. Collective action to generalize the rights of legal security and political representation that had been monopolized by dominant groups heralded the new politics of overcoming the systematic forms of exclusion. Socialist arguments about the inadequacy of these first rights led to the development of novel concepts of citizenship that included social and economic entitlements. Resistance to economic and other forms of social and political exclusion has been the hallmark of radical theory and practice for the best part of two centuries (Marshall 1973: 71–4, 91).

A certain dialectic might be thought to be at work here. This was the conclusion that T.H. Marshall reached in his analysis of the development of citizenship in Britain in the nineteenth and twentieth centuries. Marshall argued that civil, political and social rights comprised the three principal stages in the evolution of modern citizenship. Civil rights, which typified citizenship in the eighteenth century, highlighted 'the rights necessary for individual freedom'. The 'institutions most directly associated with civil rights', Marshall argued, '[were] the courts of justice'. Political rights, which became integral to new definitions of citizenship in the nineteenth century, placed the accent on 'the right to participate in the exercise of political power'. These rights were realized through participation in the parliamentary process. Social rights – the crucial addition of the twentieth century – added 'the right to a modicum of economic welfare and security [and] the right to share to the full in the social heritage'. These new rights required political initiatives to give the most vulnerable members of the community access to the educational system and to adequate social services. The link between citizenship and social justice was forged out of the realization that 'the formal recognition of an equal capacity for rights [is] not enough'. This is the theme that is stressed repeatedly in social–democratic and left–liberal conceptions of citizenship.

Marshall's analysis has been criticized for its unabashed 'evolutionism' (Mann 1987). It is far from clear, however, that Marshall believed that extending the original juridical rights of citizens was an inevitable part of the history of modern states. His argument noted that the case for extending citizenship rights grew out of ethical deliberations about what the possession of these first legal entitlements actually entailed. In this respect, Marshall was right to argue that the idea of citizenship has possessed its own forward momentum. Rights of protection under the law were found wanting without the right to participate in the law-making process. These political rights generated demands for measures to redress inequalities of wealth and power. In each case, the original claim made in defence of citizenship engendered additional demands for change and far-reaching, though not inevitable, patterns of political development. Recent stages in the evolution of citizenship have moved beyond confronting class-based forms of exclusion. The dialectic of citizenship has been carried forward into the realm of ethnic and gender forms of exclusion. According to one approach, this dialectic does not stop there but now encompasses questions about the rights of non-human species (Turner 1986: 127–31).

The point that the willingness to tackle unjustified forms of exclusion is intrinsic to citizenship raises crucial questions in international relations. How far does the development of citizenship within the state create the need for the development of new rights and duties in world politics? Many points have been made for and against this proposition. The case against often begins with the observation that citizenship codifies the special rights and duties of those who belong to the same bounded community and cherish similar practices and traditions. In defence of this proposition, the early modern theories of the state and international relations sharply contrasted the concrete rights and duties of citizens with the indeterminate and unenforceable rights and duties of human beings in an original state of nature (Linklater 1990b). At times, considerable emphasis has been placed on the tragic conflict between citizenship and humanity. This is especially so in the writings of Rousseau. In international relations, he argued, where the struggle for security and survival forces citizens to become 'the enemies of mankind', it is impossible to solve the problem of 'how to be a good citizen of a nation and a good citizen of the world' (Hoffmann 1965: ch. 3). In the twentieth century, various writers, such as E.H. Carr and Franz Borkenau, argued that the inclusion of welfare rights within national citizenship had deleterious consequences for the system of states. The concomitant rise of economic nationalism intensified political competition between exclusionary states (Borkenau 1942; Carr 1945). More recently, Raymond Murphy (1988: 74) has drawn attention to the exclusionary role of citizenship by arguing that citizenship laws in the industrialized societies 'prevent the dilution of the benefits of industrialisation . . . through the exclusion of people born elsewhere'. Restrictions on immigration and controls on the intake of refugees are crucial in this regard.

Nevertheless, the conviction that the state marks the outer limit of our moral and political obligations has never been able to prevail. From Pufendorf to Hegel, theorists of the sovereign state have argued that citizenship simply concretizes the imprecise duties that all human beings have to one another (Linklater 1990b: part II). The principle that these human obligations survive the division of the species into sovereign states was not itself at issue. In most cases, those theorists defended the right of states to decide the extent to which they would honour wider moral responsibilities. For this reason, citizenship has been a problematical concept. At one level it has given content to, and been evaluated by, a more basic human ethic; but at another level, as Rousseau noted, it has often been in conflict with more general duties to humanity. For this reason, citizenship has often figured prominently in discussions about the antinomies of political life – antinomies that theory should strive to resolve and practice should seek to eradicate.

The basic point here was foreshadowed in those sections of *The Politics* in which Aristotle explored the differences between the good man and the good citizen. Without developing the theme in detail, Aristotle understood that 'man' and 'citizen' could well come into conflict with one another. Aware of the potential clash between them, he further noted that considerations of humanity ought to be taken into account by the makers of foreign policy. Aristotle regarded the failure to be 'ashamed of behaving to others in ways which they would refuse to acknowledge as just, or even expedient, among themselves' as evidence of moral deficiency. By claiming that foreign policy should be governed not simply by prudence and expediency, but by regard for what was 'lawful', Aristotle (1960: book VII, ii, sections 12–14) defended the sentiments peculiar to the good international citizen. Similar themes are central to Kant's writings on international relations, which directly addressed the problem of overcoming the moral tensions between the claims of humanity and the duties of citizenship.

Overcoming this tension is a compelling objective because, although citizenship has entailed collective action to dismantle the various barriers that prevent the weak from enjoying the benefits of social cooperation, it has always been one of the principal forms of exclusion in social and political life, as aliens and refugees well know. As a consequence, modern ideas about citizenship have been contradictory and unstable. They are linked with the objective of improving the arrangements of a specific society and with the goal of promoting its member's interests, often to the detriment of other societies. On the other hand, modern ideas about citizenship have a radicalizing potential that can be turned against the sovereign state itself. This second point prompts the further observation that citizenship has been 'both too puffed up and too compressed', too exclusionary towards both subnational and transnational loyalties and identities. If the development of citizenship is regarded as the product of various struggles to release the universalistic potentialities of modernity from particularistic constraints (Turner 1986), then its next stage may well involve going 'higher in our search for citizenship, but also lower and wider. Higher to the world, lower to the locality' (Wright 1990: 91–2). Judged accordingly, the idea of the good international citizen can be a means of weakening the particularism of modern states and of overcoming an ancient tension between the rights of citizens and duties to the rest of humanity.

III

The right of individuals to take their disputes to international courts of law (such as the Court of Justice in the European Community), and the right of participation in, for example, elections to the European Parliament, reveal that new conceptions of citizenship have started to develop in Europe. Yet the contention that it is possible to weave good international citizenship into the foreign policy culture of states has always struck some as likely or even certain to fail. Realists have been quick to point out that all forms of 'idealism' fail to note that the struggle for power and security must remain paramount under conditions of anarchy. This observation is often linked with arguments against the domestic analogy, which holds that the prerequisites for order within the state are so similar to the preconditions of order between states that the same 'institutions which sustain order domestically should be reproduced at the international level' (Suganami 1989: 1). Whatever else it may be, the idea of good international citizenship is certainly an example of such analogous reasoning.

Realists are indeed correct that under conditions of profound insecurity, states do not let ethical and humane considerations over-ride their primary national considerations. There is no doubt too that strategic rivalry reinforces the logic of state-building and prevents the emergence of alternative forms of world political organization. To leave the discussion of realism there, however, is to overlook the extent to which realism possesses its own distinctive range of ideas about good international citizenship.

In his recent book, Hidemi Suganami (1989: 100–5, 108–11) has reminded us that Carr endorsed the principle of 'welfare internationalism'; to this one might add that Hans Morgenthau (Mitrany 1960: introduction) wrote sympathetically about David Mitrany's vision of functional collaboration. Notwithstanding his critique of utopianism, Carr thought that the extension of community was a crucial aim of an enlightened foreign policy. The final paragraph of *The Twenty Years' Crisis* argued that an internationalist approach to British policy would take account of the welfare of the inhabitants of Dusseldorf or Lille as well as Oldham and Jarrow (Carr 2001: 219). In his endorsement of this principle, Carr was especially aware of the international consequences of the rise of the modern welfare state. The extension of citizenship from the legal and political to the social realms had introduced conflictual forms of economic nationalism and created new grievances between 'have' and 'have-not' nations. Carr believed that international planning arrangements were needed to ensure that the extension of citizenship within domestic political arenas could be carried further into the realm of international relations (Suganami 1989).

For his part, Morgenthau's sympathy for Mitrany's scheme of functional collaboration and support for the notion of the world state was qualified by the observation that a sense of international community would have to develop before radical institutional change could occur. To this end, Morgenthau maintained that the progressive development of international society required the prior resolution of interstate conflicts and rivalries. Where conflict prevailed, the art of diplomacy required both sensitivity to the interests and fears of adversaries and a willingness to accommodate their legitimate security concerns as far as possible (Morgenthau 1973). Somewhat similar themes are evident in Kissinger's remarks that adversaries can best promote international order by negotiating equivalent levels of security and insecurity amongst themselves (Kissinger 1979). These dimensions of realist thought emphasize that collective responsibility for the maintenance of international order is the foundation stone upon which more ambitious experiments in good international citizenship might eventually come to rest. This emphasis on the importance of replacing adversarial relations with reciprocity, trust and peaceful change (the principal features of Karl Deutsch's pluralistic security communities) has affinities with Senator Evans's proposition that good international citizenship requires the skilful blend of elements of realism and idealism (Deutsch 1970). There is, at any rate, no reason to deny that these realist themes form a legitimate element of any account of the good international citizen. This is the first dimension of good international citizenship.

IV

Although it is present in realism, the idea of great power responsibility for international order has been a far more prominent feature of the Grotian tradition. The importance of being a good citizen of international society was present in Christian Wolff's conception of the *civitas maxima* and in Vattel's subsequent elaboration of a European *res publica*. Vattel's high regard for Britain's willingness to uphold the continental balance of power remains instructive in this regard. For Vattel, the good international citizen is the state that is prepared to put the welfare of international society ahead of the relentless pursuit of its own national interests. It need not sacrifice its own national independence in the process, nor is it legally obliged to act in ways that will jeopardize its survival or endanger its vital national interests, but it is beholden to other states to place international order before the satisfaction of trivial national advantages (Vattel 1916: 251).

Many of the broader concerns that explain the nature of good international citizenship form the core of Hedley Bull's analysis of international society (Bull 1977). Respecting the equal sovereignty of other states, upholding international law, relying on diplomacy and seeking to extend the level of consensus between states are some important considerations. There are several analogies with national citizenship in this account. The legal rights of the citizen have their counterpart in the juridical concept of national sovereignty. The political rights of citizens are approximated by the state's right of diplomatic representation in international arenas such as the United Nations. The supposition that national citizenship implies regard for the common good has its equivalent in arguments that the major powers possess special obligations for maintaining and enhancing international order. Bull's critical comments about the failure of the great powers to assume central responsibility for progress in arms control negotiations and international economic relations in the late 1970s and in the early 1980s, and his remarks about the West's 'appalling lack of vision' in its dealings with the peoples of the South, illustrate the third analogue of national citizenship (Bull 1983: 127–8). Similarly, Keohane and Nye (1989: 268–82) have advanced a defence of 'multilateralism' and global policy coordination, as opposed to unilateralist foreign policy and international institutional neglect, which reflects the belief that states – and the great powers especially – possess the international equivalent of civic obligations to advance the more general good. The need for a commitment to the society of states is central precisely because states have both more and fewer rights than the ordinary citizen – more because the principle of sovereignty allows them to place self-interest before the world common good, fewer because the sovereign rights of small states can always be sacrificed to preserve equilibrium between the great powers. Preserving the society of states in these unique circumstances is the second dimension of good international citizenship.

Hedley Bull's writings offer implicit support for the proposition that good international citizenship entails sympathy for political efforts to overcome unjustified systems of exclusion. The origins of these efforts can be traced back to the nineteenth century. In *The Expansion of International Society*, Bull and Watson (1984: 125) observed that 'European international society' entered 'a state of progressive development' during that century. In that period, 'the first stirrings of internationally organized action about human rights in relation to the slave trade' occurred alongside advances in thinking about disarmament and practical innovations in diplomacy and international law. International action to end the slave trade and slavery formed the starting point for a more concerted attempt to dismantle the exclusionary properties of a Western-dominated international order. In his later writings Bull (1984a) called this process 'the revolt against the West'.

This challenge consisted of five struggles against Western practices of exclusion: the reaction against the structures of political exclusion that deprived the older non-European states, such as Japan and China, of an equal place in the society of states; the nationalist assault upon legal exclusion in which the colonies demanded exactly the same sovereign rights as their imperial overlords; the critique of racial exclusion and white supremacism; the more recent attack upon economic exclusion exemplified by the demands for compensation for past colonial exploitation, a larger share of the world's wealth and effective rights of participation in global economic institutions; and, finally, the struggle against a hegemonic and exclusionary Western culture, which is part of the politics of re-affirming indigenous values. Collectively, these elements of the revolt against the West reflect the main developments in the evolution of citizenship nationally. In each case, there has been an outward projection of the same social and political ethos that has been central to the evolution of citizenship within modern states.

In these examples, the demand for equal legal and political rights and the case for international action to dismantle unjustifiable forms of exclusion are linked specifically with the issue of the proper rights and duties of nation-states. Yet Bull's last published writings argued that the dialectic might not end there (Bull 1984a). New political structures institutionalizing the proper rights and duties of individuals seemed morally desirable to large sections of the world's population. It also seemed perfectly conceivable to Bull that some progress might be made in creating new global structures and attachments. He maintained that recent attempts to affirm not only the rights of weaker states but also the human rights (economic and political) of the most vulnerable sections of the world's population signified a profound change in the character of international relations. What is more, the growing importance of new issues, such as the need for international ecological management, created the context in which states might forego their absolute sovereignty and embrace new obligations as 'local agents of a world common good'. These observations added further meaning to Bull's claim in *The Anarchical Society* that the time may be 'ripe for the enunciation of new concepts of universal political organization that would show how Wales, the United Kingdom and the European Community could each have some world political status while none laid claim to exclusive sovereignty' (Bull 1977: 267). This formulation encapsulates the idea that states should permit the development of multiple forms of citizenship: subnational, national and transnational in character. The proposition that they should permit the growth of subnational and cosmopolitan loyalties, which have previously been foreclosed, is the third dimension of good international citizenship.

V

It is customary to distinguish between the Grotian analysis and defence of the international society of states and the cosmopolitan vision of a greater global community of humankind. In short, one favours while the other rejects the goal of 'altering the fundament structure of international relations as a system of states' (Suganami 1989: 14). The former displays some affinities with the notion that principles of national citizenship can be accommodated within conceptions of citizenship of the society of states; the latter envisages the eventual demise of the system of sovereign states and the appearance of stronger bonds between the individual and the rest of humanity. The cosmopolitan vision of world citizenship can be understood as a more radical experiment in applying the key principles of modern citizenship to relations between states.

'Grotians' stress the point that cosmopolitan principles or beliefs have played a crucial role in international relations throughout the history of the modern system of states. Certain trends within Grotian thought, however, demonstrate that the sharp distinction between the Grotian tradition and cosmopolitanism has also broken down (see Bull et al. 1990). Even so, the suggestion that it is possible to mount a convincing philosophical defence of cosmopolitanism was one that Bull and many other members of the English School have emphatically rejected. In part, their criticisms overlapped with the realist argument that cosmopolitan visions of alternative world orders are bound to be thwarted by the fundamental struggles for power and security in world politics. On another level, they raised the objection that all cosmopolitan perspectives display culturally specific moral priorities and falter when faced with the charge that all ethical concepts are essentially contested.

Charles Beitz (1979) in international theory and Jurgen Habermas (1979a) in social theory indicate how the case for ethical universalism is more frequently presented in recent thought. Notions of consent, contract and discourse are central to their arguments for ethical universalism. Developing a theme which Brian Barry (1973) raised in his criticism of Rawls, Beitz pointed to Rawls's arbitrary assumption that the members of existing sovereign states should determine the principles of their own political communities behind the veil of ignorance. Before that stage was reached, all human beings should have participated in a global social contract to decide whether the establishment of sovereign states was justified in the first place (see Barry 1973). From the beginning, every individual should be included in an imagined contract that decided the basic principles of world politics. A similar theme is central to Habermas's claim that a commitment to universal discourse is a central feature of advanced, post-conventional moral perspectives. These theorists universalize ideas about consent and dialogue that are intrinsic to citizenship in the domestic domain, enlarge the meaning of citizenship by conferring rights of participation on every member of the species, and maintain that every individual is obliged to widen the sphere of moral responsibility to embrace the entire species.

As already noted, these ethical themes are essentially contested. One of the oldest arguments against social contract theory claimed that the values of a specific time and place are always smuggled within supposedly universally valid perspectives. This argument featured in Vico's critique of Grotius and Vattel and in Rousseau's criticism of European portrayals of a lost state of nature (Linklater 1990b: ch. 7). A parallel theme arises in more recent postmodern critiques of universalism which maintain that this perspective privileges the Western, rational subject. Feminist writings on society and morality have argued that abstract, universalistic perspectives reveal a bias towards the traditional public world of men and neglect the ethics of care and responsibility which have tended to characterize the morality of women within the family. What postmodernism and feminism bring to traditional criticisms of universalism is a heightened awareness that notions of global social contract and discourse might not only lack solid philosophical foundations but also have exactly the same potential for exclusion and domination as the perspectives they reject (Der Derian and Shapiro 1979; Benhabib and Cornell 1987: chs 1–4).

If these claims are right, it is not enough to challenge the exclusive sovereign state and an exclusionary, Western-dominated international society; it is also essential to eradicate similar tendencies within Western moral universalism. From this angle, the ethical foundations of cosmopolitan visions of world citizenship are clearly insecure. The argument is strengthened by considering what is at stake for ethnic groups and nationalist movements in the Third World and elsewhere. Their attempts to achieve cultural liberation indicate that they are hardly inspired by the vision of submerging their identities within some higher, all-encompassing universal community. The very most they would aspire to (and the most that others might hope to achieve) is their participation as citizens of a 'pluralist' society of states (Brown 1988).

It is true that no account of cosmopolitan citizenship is adequate unless it recognizes the crucial point that universalistic moral precepts can be just as exclusionary as the sovereign state and the Western-biased society of states that they are pitched against. Whether this puts an end to ethical universalism and the ideals of contract and discourse is debatable. Important as it is to heed warnings about the exclusionary properties of universalistic discourse, it is possible to take scepticism towards, or disillusionment with, Western moral universals too far. Support for the proposition that cosmopolitan moral imperatives are also essential to good international citizenship can be derived from Henry Shue's compelling argument about national measures to ban hazardous work conditions (Shue 1981: ch. 4).[3] Shue's basic proposition is that national legislation to outlaw such practices does not go far enough unless accompanied by efforts to prohibit the export of 'unsafe jobs to foreign parts'. To fail to bring the moral principle that is at issue within the state to bear upon the conduct of foreign policy is to allow one form of exploitation and unjustified exclusion to survive. In this case, there are no moral grounds for preferring citizens to non-citizens, insiders to outsiders. To develop this further, national citizenship gives the members of particular communities some protection from basic forms of harm; one of the aims of the good international citizen is to ensure that similar forms of protection are available to citizens and non-citizens alike.

It is arguable that the cosmopolitan theme that is exhibited here adds force to the ideals of contract and discourse that stand at the centre of current arguments for ethical universalism. Exporting hazards conflicts with the principle of self-determination that is common to liberalism and Marxism. It fails to give outsiders the opportunity either to express or to withhold their consent, and it refuses to allow them the right (in Marx's words) to make as much of their history as possible under conditions of their own choosing. The right of self-determination, which includes the right to protest against actual or potential forms of harm, is the fourth dimension of good international citizenship.

This defence of universalism does not overlook the importance of community for human beings or deny the merits of cultural diversity. Without any doubt, the appeal to bounded communities against 'rootless cosmopolitanism' will endure. By the same token, the appeal beyond citizenship to notions of humanity will survive while there are doubts that insiders have rights to treat outsiders as they please. The complex issue of how to strike the correct balance between the inclusive and the exclusive, or the universal and the particular, will arise as long as human beings regard national boundaries as neither morally decisive nor morally insignificant. As a result, the argument outlined here does not claim that modes of exclusion can never be justified. Considerations of need and merit mean that no society can let its members have automatic access to the entire range of resources; for the same reason, no society can assume a different stance in its relations with outsiders. What is suggested here is that the legitimacy of practices of exclusion (in domestic politics and in international relations) should be decided in the same way: that is, by measures which seek the consent of the included and excluded alike. This is an essential part of the theoretical task of sketching the broad features of good international citizenship.

It may be argued that this principle asks too much of states in practice, especially as they are constrained by public expectations that national interests will remain the supreme guide to foreign policy. For this reason, the argument might continue, states will attempt to preserve their discretion with regard to issues that affect crucial strategic and economic interests. Higher cosmopolitan aspirations that would make various issues (such as immigration, utilization of resources, etc.) open to international negotiation must yield before such realities. Extending this further, the critic might suggest that the question of who is excluded (or who is the greatest victim of exclusion) rarely has an unambiguous answer. Invariably in debates about the intake of refugees, at least two groups can speak the language of exclusion: refugees themselves and suffering hosts. It may also be suggested that because states have competing definitions of who is unfairly excluded, the attempt to broaden good international citizenship to encompass cosmopolitan aspirations may be more likely to endanger than promote international order.

There is little doubt that no matter how far political actors sympathize with cosmopolitan sentiments, they rarely have free rein to follow these in practice. It is also true that the question of who is wrongly excluded can generate a range of competing responses and that, in a great many cases, there may not be (even in theory) a final answer. Yet there is a great deal more to be said.

This area is best approached by recalling Bull's argument that order has priority over justice (Bull 1977: ch. 4). Bull argued that states recognize the value of order and share certain assumptions about how order is best brought about. For the most part, however, they have competing conceptions of justice that no philosophical system has been able to resolve. For this reason, a consensus that projects of realizing justice are best confined to the domestic sphere has long been regarded as essential for the survival of international order.

Notwithstanding these points, Bull wrote sympathetically about cosmopolitan sentiments and argued that these should be of concern both to individuals and states. The philosophical merits of different conceptions of universal ethics were not a central consideration. His more basic theme was that cosmopolitan visions of world order will only make real headway in international politics if they command the support of a significant number of nation-states. As noted earlier, the Hagey Lectures argued that there was a growing consensus that the idea of human rights and the principle of global distributive justice should figure more prominently in the affairs of states. Given these developments, collective action to promote universal moral ideals would enhance rather than threaten international order (Bull 1984a).

The character of the argument was best displayed in Bull's writings about South Africa. In his essay on this subject, Bull argued that hostility to white supremacism was virtually the sole example of a global moral consensus in the modern world. Given the consensus that exclusion on the basis of race and colour was illegitimate, states had the moral right and duty to apply pressure to South Africa to ensure its compliance with global norms. Bull (1982) criticized the Reagan Administration's foreign policy towards South Africa accordingly.

It will be recalled that Bull believed that the legal and political exclusion of Third World peoples had largely been eradicated and that an end to cultural and economic exclusion would have to take place before the transition from a European to a universal international society could be said to be complete. In this discussion there are echoes of Marshall's consideration of the evolution of national citizenship within the modern British state in that forms of resistance to systems of harmful exclusion are not arbitrary, unrelated events but interconnected elements of a coherent pattern of political development. Within this context, it is possible for the theorist to identify desirable forms of change that should be able to command a general consensus. An important case in point is the argument that it ought to be possible in theory as well as in practice to agree that all human beings have a basic right to be free from starvation and malnutrition (Vincent 1986).

It is tempting to suggest that Bull and Vincent were concerned with what Habermas (1979a) calls moral–practical learning: that is, the development of the understanding that various constraints on the life chances of human beings are indefensible and must be lifted. The extension of citizenship within the nation-state and the creation of analogous conceptions of good international citizenship in world politics can also be cited as examples of moral–practical learning. Phrasing the argument in these terms is not to suggest that a world consensus about moral matters is ever likely to be reached. It does not assume that the tragic circumstances that realists emphasize will come to an end or that complex problems about how to preserve international order will become easier to solve. The fact is that a basic consensus about the need to dismantle the illegitimate forms of exclusion does exist in world politics amid a range of complex and interacting forces. This being so, it is possible to analyse the higher moral possibilities that are latent within existing global structures and in the discourse of legitimacy which is employed to secure their reproduction. The case for this project was central to Kant's theory of international relations which considered the possibility that state power would be tamed by principles of international order and that, in time, the world political order would be modified until it conformed with principles of cosmopolitan justice. Kant's approach points to the conclusion that realism, 'rationalism' and cosmopolitanism can all contribute to attempts to define the qualities of the good international citizen.

VI

To recapitulate, the argument has been that the idea of citizenship includes the following dimensions: rights before the law; rights of participation in major political processes; and the duty to promote the widest social good. This last theme overlaps with the argument that citizenship requires support for collective action to improve the conditions of the unfairly excluded. These dimensions of citizenship exist in the different axes of social and political life: in the relations between individuals and the state, in the bonds that link states together in an international society and in the much looser realm consisting of the ties between individuals and humanity. The idea that there are three axes of citizenship is an important theme in Kant's *Perpetual Peace*, which distinguished between *ius civitatis* ('the civil constitution of men in a nation'), *ius gentium* ('the constitution formed by the international law of states in relation to one another') and *ius cosmopoliticum* ('the constitution formed by the laws of world citizenship [Weltburgerrecht] to the extent that men and states, having external relationships with one another, are re-garded as citizens of a universal state of humanity') (Kant 1970b: 206). In Kant's judgement, each axis supported, and was supported in turn, by the others. Certain rights of citizens within the state (specifically the right of self-determination) had to be conferred on outsiders too. What is more, because of the destructive effects of modern warfare, extending rights beyond the national frontier was essential if citizen rights were to be protected within existing states.

Kant understood that many states – autocratic states, for example – were opposed to the development of these multiple forms of citizenship. The central question that Kant's philosophical history sought to answer was whether the ad-vancement of multiple citizenships – required by reason itself – was likely to take place in practice. Kant doubted whether anything straight could ever be made out of something as crooked as human nature; however, he believed that three developments in the modern world provided grounds for optimism. These were the growth of international commerce, the increasingly destructive role of modern warfare, given economic interdependence, and the advance of moral conscious-ness. As far as this last point was concerned, Kant believed that the emergence of republican regimes and moral concerns about infringements of human rights anywhere in the world held the key to future developments. For Kant, support for the three forms of citizenship – national, international and cosmopolitan – arose out of the character of modern republican states.

No doubt a post-Kantian sociology of citizenship must embrace rather differ-ent concerns that reflect contemporary themes. Such an approach to the likely fate of the different conceptions of citizenship needs to consider state-formation, war and geopolitics, material production and patterns of cultural development at the very least. Moreover, various schools of thought are pertinent to the attempt to rework Kant's project. These perspectives can be mobilized to understand the ways in which states display different levels of moral openness and closure to so-cieties elsewhere. What such an inquiry should highlight are the different societal potentials for extending solidarity and community in international relations.

This is not the occasion to try to anticipate what this inquiry might reveal. Suffice it to note that state building, industrialization and war have often com-bined to destroy citizens' rights within nation-states. They have also interacted to challenge analogous forms of citizenship in the international society of states. Authoritarian and totalitarian regimes in the West and in the Third World provide ample evidence of these trends. However, it is also true that war, state-building and industrialization have served to promote the cause of citizenship both within and between nation-states.[4] The fact is that the interaction between various forces has not altered the condition in which the majority of independent societies work to preserve some of the analogues to national citizenship that lie beyond the state. Kant's clear preference for the proliferation of liberal republican states reflected his belief that the next stage in the political evolution of the species would witness neither the establishment of a world state nor the survival of autarchic societies but the extension of the sense of belonging to a universal moral community. Crucially, in his view, the future of international citizenship depended on the spread of republican states.[5]

Waltz's claim that Kant did not grasp the limitations of 'second image' interpretations of world politics is the best-known realist response to this form of argument (Waltz 1959: ch. 4). According to this criticism, second image theorists assume that the issue of whether the state is liberal or authoritarian, capitalist or socialist, is more important than the observable reality that all states compete for power and security in the context of anarchy. In fact, none of Waltz's images (human nature, the state and international anarchy) captures the deeper theme in Kant's writings. None of them refers to the way in which states and their inhabitants define their moral rights against, and duties to, the rest of the world; none of them takes account of the levels of moral exclusiveness exhibited by different states or of what Ruggie (1983), in his critique of Waltz, describes as the principles that separate states from one another. A fourth image of international politics is necessary for the simple reason that some states are less exclusionary than others and more inclined to believe that their own conceptions of national citizenship commit them to upholding fundamental international obligations.

Kant's belief that the constitution of citizenship in the domestic realm is central to the conduct of foreign policy has been restated more recently by Michael Doyle and Christopher Brewin. Doyle's argument that realism cannot explain the pacific nature of relations between liberal states emphasizes the Kantian theme that the construction of national citizenship evidently affects behaviour towards other states (Doyle 1983: 218–20). Brewin (1988) refers to the duties that liberal states must honour if they are to be 'the states they conceive themselves to be'. More specifically, 'a state cannot be liberal unless it acts on the assumption that men in general and its citizens in particular have the potential for ruling themselves in freedom'. In addition, 'if the capacity in human nature for collective and rational self-rule is the end that liberal states exist to promote, they cannot consistently deny that other men also have this capacity'. If liberal states believe that all human beings have the potential for self-determination, then the obligation to promote autonomy 'for other communities and between nations' is incumbent on them (Brewin 1988).

Doyle rightly contrasts the peaceful nature of interliberal international relations with the violence that liberal states have often used in their dealings with illiberal regimes in the Third World. What this amendment suggests is that liberal–social democratic states have a special responsibility for working out the international implications of the more enlightened concepts of national citizenship. In this case, societies such as Australia are obliged not only to comply with their basic moral and political principles by placing real constraints on self-interest; they are also obliged to promote, where circumstances permit, liberal–social democratic principles in other societies and in the conduct of international relations more generally. The notion that this is an appropriate role for the good international citizen is the main conclusion of this chapter.

It is true, of course, that states can exploit terms such as 'good international citizenship' in their efforts to disguise self-interested motives and to make their promotion more palatable. Such terms can be employed to persuade others of the state's ethical bona fides; they may form part of the diplomatic repertoire that is used to deflect moral condemnation of selfish acts. There is no doubt that encouraging states to promote liberal–social democratic principles in other societies and in international relations introduces the risk of cultural imperialism and excessive interference and intervention. These risks are rather less if the emphasis is placed on acting as long as there is an international consensus to proceed, and if the exponents of good international citizenship are particularly sensitive to issues of unwarranted exclusion. Where these considerations are present, the notion of the good international citizen is worth defending for at least three reasons.

First, as Marshall (1973: 84) noted, as 'a developing institution', the idea of citizenship proclaims egalitarian ideals 'against which achievement can be measured and towards which aspiration can be directed'. By the same measure, advocacy of good international citizenship commits governments to universalistic and egalitarian ideals that can consolidate the society of states and strengthen the belief in the community of humankind. Taken seriously, and invoked frequently over time, the concept sets out basic moral criteria for assessing and criticizing foreign policy conduct. Of itself, this can encourage more sophisticated debate about the ethical content and purpose of foreign policy. Second, the idea of the good international citizen can serve as one of the new concepts and ideas that Bull called for in his remarks on the deterioration of international order. More importantly, in the present era of significant diplomatic change, it can have an important role to play 'in the process of fundamental political reconstruction which the seizing of the Grotian moment implies' (Falk 1983). Finally, turning to future developments in the study of international relations, such concepts can provide a useful bridge between reformist or theoretical approaches to world politics and the more policy-related areas of the subject. At present, when the need for connections between these areas is increasingly important, the idea of the good international citizen should encourage further thought about the means of promoting a just world order and about how foreign policy can be harnessed to the project of the Enlightenment.

5   The good international citizen and the crisis in Kosovo

The principal aim of this chapter is to analyse some of the ethical problems raised by the North Atlantic Treaty Organization's (NATO's) military action against Serbia in 1999. The main purpose is to discuss moral factors that are an inescapable feature of decisions to wage 'humanitarian wars' rather than to debate the specific ethical merits and shortcomings of intervention in the Kosovo case.

The argument begins with the premise that post-national or post-sovereign societies are evolving in Western Europe (Linklater 1998). Of course, this may be the only region in which substantially new forms of political community may be appearing. On its eastern boundary there are various political movements that are attached to totalizing conceptions of community and to absolutist notions of the state. Emerging post-national societies have had to decide how to deal with regimes that remain committed to fusing state and nation. They face the question of whether to respect sovereignty without major reservation or make recognition conditional on adherence to liberal ideas of human rights and on support for constitutional politics. Whether or not they have any entitlement to wage humanitarian war against societies that are guilty of serious human rights violations is an additional consideration. Kosovo has introduced the crucial question of whether Western European states and their US ally can act in this way without the express consent of the United Nations Security Council.

In sum, NATO's air war against Serbia has raised at least two important ethical questions: first, whether member states have the legal or moral right to over-ride the sovereignty of a neighbouring power and, second, whether they can assume this right without explicit UN authorization. The answer to the first question depends on a mixture of principle and prudence, as members of the just war tradition have long argued. We return to this point later. As for the second question, many supporters of the war argued that Serb atrocities in Kosovo, and elsewhere in the former Yugoslavia, were so serious that military force was essential even without UN approval. Critics argued that the supposed cure was worse than the disease. From the latter standpoint, the practice, if not the principle, of violating the sovereignty of a neighbouring state was manifestly unwise, and the powers that initiated 'humanitarian war' lacked the moral credentials to embark on such a project in any case. One voice in the debate regarded military action as an example of good international citizenship – another regards it as the latest manifestation of the great powers' selective regard for international law (Evans and Grant 1991; Linklater 1992; Wheeler and Dunne 1998).

Complex issues are raised by these opening remarks, and a short chapter cannot do justice to all of them. The discussion begins by considering the transformation of political community in Western Europe and then notes the rules of recognition that the region has introduced for organizing relations with societies that display traditional attachments to fusing sovereignty, nationalism and territoriality. Whether the former has the moral right to expect other societies in the region to respect its standards of legitimacy, and whether there is a collective right to use force against neighbours that fail to comply with them, are issues discussed in the next part of this chapter. The final section raises the issue of what it means to be a good international citizen in crises such as Kosovo.

Beyond Westphalia

Europe invented the 'totalizing project': the nationalization of political community and the insistence on sharp and morally decisive distinctions between citizens and aliens (Corrigan and Sayer 1985). This peculiar invention occurred against the background of incessant geopolitical rivalry, which led states to strive to ensure the loyalty of citizens in times of war. The disastrous effects of the totalizing project during the twentieth century encouraged Western European states to develop new forms of political community. Three dimensions to the process of remaking Western Europe deserve brief comment.

First, there is declining confidence in the idea that the only legitimate form of political association is the territorial state that exercises sovereign powers over citizens that share a common national identity. Western European states have surrendered some monopoly powers to supranational bodies. The tenet that citizens must identify with the nation has been weakened by the ethnic revolt and by demands for more pluralistic forms of citizenship in the context of increasing multiculturalism. The principle that individuals are subjects of international law who are entitled to appeal beyond the state to international courts of law has gained ground in this region – so has the supposition that the rights of minority nations should be recognized in national and international law.

Second, one of the constitutive ethical principles of the sovereign state has lost its status as a self-evident truth: this is the belief that the welfare of co-nationals takes precedence over the interests of aliens. Of course, some regard for obligations to outsiders has existed throughout the history of the modern European states-system; and clearly the conviction that states have the sovereign right to determine the nature of their international obligations still commands widespread public support. In the European Union (EU), individuals are national citizens first, then European citizens by virtue of that fact. Although the legal rights of European citizens are thin rather than thick – although they mainly reflect the rise of a transnational marketplace rather than some powerful sense of belonging to a regional political community – significant progress towards the ideal of joint rule has occurred (Linklater 1998: ch. 6). Moral preferentialism that grants priority to co-nationals remains the dominant ideology, but there is more support than in the past for the belief that political decisions should have the consent of all who stand to be affected by them, whether insiders or outsiders.

Third, the impossibility of a progressivist interpretation of international society has been a recurrent theme in the theory and practice of the modern states-system. States in the 'Westphalian era' were convinced that war was unavoidable: the belief that international society could evolve peaceful ways of resolving conflicts was dismissed as utopian. Dissatisfaction with this bleak proposition is one of the most striking features of contemporary world politics. Analyses of the liberal zone of peace and globalization have strongly encouraged the view that war, like slavery and the aristocratic duel, is an acquired social practice rather than an immutable phenomenon (Doyle 1983; Ray 1989). The so-called obsolescence of war in the core regions of the world economy has produced new questions about the moral responsibility of states, and specifically about whether involvement in humanitarian war is one of the 'purposes beyond ourselves' which states can and should accept in the post-bipolar era.[1]

One issue raised by Kosovo is how societies that seem to have abandoned the totalizing project – societies that are creating new forms of political community which are more universalistic and more sensitive to cultural differences than their predecessors were – should deal with neighbouring states that are committed to totalizing politics and which are guilty of ethnic cleansing as they attempt to align the boundaries of state and nation. The public debate over Kosovo has revealed that the question of how these two worlds should be related is one of the most controversial moral issues of the age.

New rules of recognition

The questions raised in the last paragraph invite consideration of the principles that govern the recognition of states in international relations. Two rival visions of the society of states address this problem. According to one conception, which I shall call *statism*, regimes should tread carefully when making judgements about the legitimacy of other systems of government.[2] The argument is that, under conditions of ideological conflict, international order requires respect for national sovereignty and its corollary, the principle of non-intervention. New states or regimes do not have to satisfy a public moral test before becoming equal members of international society – there is no consensus in any event about what this test should be. Acts of political recognition should confirm the emergence of viable sovereign states and the existence of new centres of effective power. The former do not confer rights on other states or regimes that they would otherwise lack. In the language of international law, the act of recognition is 'declaratory' rather than 'constitutive' (Akehurst 1992).

This approach to international society can be criticized for regarding respect for sovereignty as more important than the protection of human rights. Its supporters frequently reply by stressing the dangers of humanitarian intervention. Tempting though it may be to intervene to assist other peoples, the fact is that there is no agreement about how the line should be drawn between grave and less serious violations of human rights, and there is no consensus about where the boundary between humanitarian war and military aggression lies. Consequently, those who intervene in other's internal affairs create dangerous precedents which ease the way for predatory states to extend their power under the guise of promoting humanitarian principles (Roberts 1993). From this standpoint, emerging post-national and post-sovereign states with pretensions to be good international citizens should respect the sovereignty of other powers even when they are committed to totalizing politics. Regard for sovereignty does not preclude diplomatic efforts to persuade societies to behave differently, or economic sanctions and embargos in extreme cases, but it does rule out military force for humanitarian ends. These are the central tenets of statism.

This conception of international society has triumphed in the post-colonial world because new states, anxious to preserve the recent prize of sovereignty, have largely rejected the classic idea that they are accountable to the West for their domestic practices. Even so, the global protection of human rights has made important progress in recent international relations. Efforts in this domain draw on a 'solidarist' conception of international society which argues that individuals are the ultimate members of that society and claims that states are obliged to protect their interests (Bull 1966a). How this second conception of international society is to be reconciled with sovereignty remains in dispute but the global human rights culture has made great advances in recent decades and there is less resistance than there was once to the principle that states are answerable to the world community for the treatment of their citizens.

For some, there is unfinished business in this area unless states take the additional step of over-riding national sovereignty when serious human rights violations occur. Under these conditions, it might be argued, the good international citizen should be willing to use force. As custodians of the global human rights culture they should take action to ensure that war criminals are prosecuted and they should be prepared to reconfigure political systems that violate fundamental moral principles. Establishing international protectorates, partitioning societies and promoting the establishment of federal or confederal arrangements are three policies available to good international citizens.

In practice, Western European states gave voice to solidarism in their pronouncements about the rules of recognition for governing relations with the societies of the former Yugoslavia (Akehurst 1992). In their proclamation of 16 December 1991, members of the European Community professed 'their readiness to recognize, subject to the normal standards of international practice and the political realities in each case, those new states which, following the historic changes in the region, have constituted themselves on a democratic basis, have accepted the appropriate international obligations and have committed themselves in good faith to a peaceful process and to negotiations'. Other requirements included 'guarantees for the rights of ethnic and national groups and minorities in accordance with the commitments subscribed to in the framework of the CSCE

[Commisssion on Security and Cooperation in Europe]'. Until Kosovo, it has often been argued that such proclamations were simply another covenant without the sword because the relevant powers had not been prepared to support these commitments with military force.

The present condition is riddled with ambiguities and contradictions. Western European powers can reasonably claim the right to express their domestic political preferences in the rules of recognition pertaining to relations with the former Yugoslavia. Otherwise they leave themselves open to the charge that in their external relations they are not true to themselves (Brewin 1988). They have every right to be anxious about the implosion of multiethnic societies and about the burdens that may fall on neighbouring societies as a result of the mass exodus of refugees. They have good reason to contest the statist position that the principles of sovereignty and non-intervention must be upheld in relations between societies with competing ideologies and to challenge the conviction that the need for international order should trump the ideal of promoting cosmopolitan justice in such circumstances (Bull 1984b). Statist conventions lose their appeal when governments are in a state of war with sections of their own populations and endanger regional stability.

Returning to the question of ambiguities and contradictions, Western European powers and the United States have yet to develop a philosophy of humanitarian war. National governments are anxious to avoid making far-reaching commitments in this domain, and national populations seem to be unenthusiastic about sacrificing the lives of citizens for the sake of desperate strangers, however uneasy they may be with statism. Some principles of the Westphalian order have lost their grip on Western Europe but many groups were critical of the air war against Serbia and of the refusal to deploy ground troops. Military policy was said to damage the cause of solidarism, which requires 'the international soldier/policeman [to risk] his or her life for humanity' (Kaldor 1999: 131). Critics of NATO's action include those who thought its behaviour was illegal, immoral or unwise, as well as those who believed that member states were too hesitant to take the necessary humanitarian action. No consensus appeared about what followed from the new rules of recognition or about how aspiring good international citizens should uphold related humanitarian commitments.

The good international citizen and 'humanitarian war'

The vexed question is what it means to be a good international citizen when neighbouring societies are consumed by ethnic violence and human rights atrocities, as occurred in the former Yugoslavia. Two broad answers to this question are suggested by the competing views of international society noted earlier. First, statists argue that infringing sovereignty, even for humanitarian ends, is illegal and/or injudicious. The second argument is that states which sponsor ethnic violence forfeit their right to the armoury of sovereignty. Some points of convergence between these standpoints will be considered in a moment, but it is important first to recall that European international institutions are committed to supporting constitutional politics in the post-communist societies of Eastern Europe. Western European states may be criticized for turning their backs on human rights atrocities in other parts of the world and for acting inconsistently,[3] but they can also claim that 'national interests' are at stake in Eastern Europe and that they have special rights and duties to use force against violent regimes there.[4]

The question is what sort of action the good international citizen can reasonably take. Failing to conform with Western European conceptions of legitimate political rule authorizes no particular course of action. As noted earlier, various alternatives exist, including the suspension of commercial and other contacts, the imposition of economic sanctions and the reliance on other forms of non-violent pressure to change the ways of unacceptable regimes. We can call the position that favours pursuing one or more of those options, *modified statism*. Modified statism is attractive to many solidarists because it endorses collective action to promote human rights but rules out military force. This doctrine is attractive to those who are unhappy with recognizing regimes just because they enjoy monopoly powers in their respective territories but do not wish to weaken fragile international conventions that limit the use of force.

One objection to modified statism is that its measures are too slow, and too respectful of the conventions surrounding sovereignty and non-intervention, to help vulnerable populations. Modified statism may therefore have the effect of supporting regime security at the cost of human security. Those who supported NATO's action argued that further violence could be predicted in Kosovo and in the wider region and that various diplomatic pressures would probably be ineffective. The main question, however, is whether humanitarian intervention should be avoided in all cases – or in all but the most extreme cases – because of the danger of weakening barriers to the use of force.

The just war tradition is relevant in this context because it sets out various conditions that should be met before the use of force can be deemed legitimate. Many of these are embedded in international law, but whether they are met in any particular case is invariably a contested matter. In summary, just war theorists argue that force is illegitimate unless there is a just cause and all measures short of force have been exhausted. There must be a reasonable chance of success and respect for civilian life. Although civilian deaths are inevitable in war, they should not be intended or disproportionate to the objectives of the war.[5] Furthermore, just war theorists insist that war must be declared by a properly constituted public authority.

This last principle has been crucial for discussions of Kosovo because NATO acted without explicit UN Security Council authorization. Disregard of the principle of proper authority – in essence, the violation of the UN Charter – has been one of the main complaints made by the opponents of the war. Critics of NATO argued that it did not have the legal authority to use force, no right to usurp the will of the global community and, at the very least, dubious credentials to appoint itself the custodian of global moral principles. These are central elements in what might be called the *legalist* position (on legalism, see Walzer 1980). From this vantage point, it would only be appropriate for NATO to take what the UN Charter calls 'enforcement action' if it had secured 'the authorization of the Security Council' and enjoyed the unanimous support of the great powers.[6] For legalists, regard for the UN Security Council is the least to expect from good international citizens.

Real dilemmas arise at this point. The unavoidable issue is whether human rights violations can be so terrible that military action by organizations such as NATO is better than no intervention at all. As Kofi Annan (1999) has argued in connection with Rwanda, a clear tension exists between Article 2, paragraph 7 of the UN Charter, which maintains that the UN does not have the authority 'to intervene in matters which are essentially within the domestic jurisdiction of any state', and support for human rights, which invites intervention in the case of supreme humanitarian emergencies. Legalism defends sovereignty as a buttress against imperialism, but there is the danger that it may prove to be little more than 'a rationalisation of the existing international order without any interest in its transformation' (Vincent and Wilson 1993: 124).

In addition to Rwanda, one other specific case reminds us of key issues surrounding the ethics of intervention – the Vietnamese intervention in Cambodia. In this instance, Vietnam did not claim any right of humanitarian intervention, and most states condemned Vietnam's actions while conceding that terrible atrocities had been committed by the Pol Pot regime (Akehurst 1992: 97). Many private citizens and non-state organizations accepted Vietnamese action because the scale of the atrocities perpetrated by the Khmer Rouge outweighed their concerns about the Vietnamese regime, including the obvious concern that geopolitical factors rather than good international citizens triggered military intervention.

In such circumstances, those who support humanitarian intervention do so with major qualifications, and it is useful to reflect on the standard reservations. First, authorized is almost always preferable to unauthorized intervention. Second, there is inevitably a danger that the intervening power will abuse its superior power and pursue goals that are at odds with humanitarian objectives when it confronts domestic resistance (Roberts 1993). Third, there is the question of whether the intervening power has a serious commitment to a global human rights culture and acts from a genuine commitment to create a more humane international order. Despite these concerns, some may conclude that unauthorized and unilateral intervention – even by a state with no or few credentials as a good international citizen – may be better than no action at all.

The complex question is deciding when human rights violations are so serious as to warrant over-riding the principle of sovereignty and the presumption of non-intervention. On this last point, many argued that Serbia had consistently violated human rights norms and would continue to do so, while others denied that the threshold that could justify NATO's action had been crossed. Likewise, debates have revolved around the question of whether all peaceful options had been fully explored and whether civilian deaths and casualties were proportionate to professed objectives. These are issues that go beyond the present discussion.

Two other issues are more central to considering the general ethical questions raised by NATO's action. The first concerns NATO's authority, or lack of authority, to use force. The second concerns the moral character and credentials of the intervening powers, specifically whether they commanded the respect of large sections of the international community and whether world public opinion concluded that intervention by these powers – notwithstanding the absence of UN Security Council approval – was preferable to inaction.

On the question of NATO's right to use force, critics of the war argued that the UN has absolute authority and that NATO violated the Charter by using force against Serbia. Others have argued that the use of the great power veto in the UN Security Council would have thwarted military action and that, in consequence, intervention by NATO was necessary. From this vantage point, the 'enlightened states' acted to support *progressivism*; for others, NATO's action was an instance of moralism and disregard for international law (Chomsky 1999a).

All parties would agree that the UN Charter should be respected and that any departure from its provisions should occur only in exceptional circumstances. A crucial issue is whether it is right for good international citizens to argue that the great power veto should not be exercised in the worst humanitarian emergencies. Perhaps one of the qualities of the good international citizen is the willingness to challenge the legitimacy of the veto by irresponsible powers that are prepared to block international action to prevent human rights violations.[7] Perhaps, one of its main roles is to initiate a quest for new forms of decision making in the UN when humanitarian catastrophes occur. If so, good international citizens have to offer an explanation for the failure to comply with existing legal conventions while initiating a diplomatic quest for new global decision-making processes that will enforce international humanitarian law (Wheeler 2000a).

As the great powers are unlikely to surrender their veto rights, and they seem to be unprepared to sanction changes that will allow Western powers to intervene anywhere in the world, one must ask whether Europeans can reasonably lay claim to what might be called regional exceptionalism. European progressives might wish to argue that they belong to a political region that is spearheading the human rights culture, which other societies, protective of their sovereignty, do not, and may never, accept. Conceivably, the good international citizen might argue that Europe can reasonably opt out of the wider system of international law and enjoy an exceptional right to wage humanitarian war at least within the continent – a right which it may not wish to claim with respect to the rest of the world, just as they have no right to expect their commitments to sovereignty and non-intervention to bind societies in the European region.

Several problems exist with this position, not the least being where Europe begins and ends. If Europe were to enjoy the right of humanitarian intervention as part of some idea of regional exceptionalism, how far would its jurisdiction extend and who would decide?[8] Furthermore, in trying to define the relevant jurisdiction is there not a danger that Europe will close itself off and create a division between the European continent where human rights violations will be met by force and the rest of the world where violators can proceed with impunity (Derrida 1992)? The issue is whether a Europe that espouses a doctrine of regional exceptionalism is being true to itself. It might be argued that a Europe which is committed to human rights must raise universal claims that demonstrate the depth of its allegiance to Enlightenment cosmopolitanism.

This raises the question of whether the intervening powers have the moral, as opposed to the legal, authority to initiate humanitarian war. Some point to the lamentable record of the United States in its many wars in the Third World (Chomsky 1999b). They note the irony that war crimes trials have been proposed in response to Serbian atrocities whereas the United States has opposed various provisions in the 1998 Rome Treaty on the International Criminal Court on the grounds that 'unwelcome powers' might stand in judgement of US military actions (Roberts 1993: 116; Chomsky 1999a). From this standpoint, at least one leading power must develop appropriate moral credentials before its involvement in humanitarian war can be generally approved.

One might ask how the EU fares when judged by those criteria. Maybe the broad pattern of political development that is evident in the Union points to the conclusion that its participation in humanitarian war is acceptable in supreme emergencies. Some may have greater confidence in those states that have abandoned the totalizing project and recognize that individuals and minorities should have international legal personality on their own account. They may be reassured by states that have taken steps to prosecute war criminals and reject the classical idea that heads of state who have violated human rights are protected by sovereign immunity. They may think that societies that are evolving in post-national and post-sovereign directions may have, or may develop, the skills that are needed to build tolerant multicultural societies elsewhere, not least through partnerships with non-governmental organizations committed to promoting more humane forms of national and global governance.[9]

A final consideration is that societies that lived until recently in anticipation of major war have made progress in eliminating force from their international relations. They have widened the moral boundaries of their communities so that states are not just concerned with harms caused to their co-nationals but are committed to developing 'cosmopolitan harm conventions', which reveal, in Kant's words, that a violation of rights in any part of the world will cause alarm everywhere (Kant 1970b: 216; see also Chapter 8). Inevitably, the question arises of whether they are also prepared to take action against regimes that wage war against national citizens. Whatever the merits or demerits of NATO's action against Serbia, recent events may mark a turning point in the history of European international society. Beyond the specifics of the Kosovo case there lie complex normative questions about whether future commitments to freeing the continent from harm should include support for what Kaldor (1999) calls 'cosmopolitan law-enforcement'.

Conclusion

The last few sentences may be thought to give European societies the benefit of too many doubts, but the question remains whether conditions can be so desperate that military force is justified even when the powers involved do not inspire universal confidence. Complex questions are raised when one region is developing a human rights culture which makes inroads into sovereignty that other parts of the world do not wish to emulate. What follows then for the idea of good international citizenship?

My concluding comments deal with those parts of Europe that are taking part in a remarkable experiment in constructing political communities that are more universalistic and sensitive to cultural differences than their predecessors. The societies involved cannot adopt statism without contradicting their universalistic commitments. They are obliged to take action against states that remain tied to the totalizing project. The question is what form their action should take. Modified statism offers the answer that states should respond in non-violent ways that apply economic and moral pressure to regimes that violate human rights. Its strongest point is that humanitarian wars cause human misery and suffering, however noble the intentions may be. Its most obvious weakness is that more desperate measures may be required to assist vulnerable peoples. In the greatest emergencies, supporters of the human rights culture must countenance the use of military force.

The difficulty then is how to ensure that those who wish to promote humanitarian war respect the conventions that have been developed to control violence. These include the principles associated with the just war tradition and with existing international law, which defines who has, and who does not have, the authority to wage war. Legalism insists that the final decision about whether or not to initiate humanitarian intervention must lie with the UN Security Council; consequently, NATO did not have the requisite authority to take military action against Serbia. However, as Kofi Annan has suggested, decisions to proceed independently of the UN Security Council may deserve support when emergency conditions exist, as in the case of Rwanda. Herein lies one of the fundamental dilemmas for the good international citizen at the present time.

While it is essential that good international citizens should respect existing international legal principles, it is also right that they should apply pressure to them in the name of cosmopolitan principles whose time may have come. Good international citizens must challenge the status quo while avoiding recklessness, arbitrariness and opportunism, but they must convince others of the merits of their case and of their motives and competence with respect to the challenge of repairing war-torn societies (Bain 2006).[10] Significantly, many who supported NATO's actions – albeit with substantial reservations – did so not only because they believed that a humanitarian catastrophe was possible but also because they thought that Kosovo might be the catalyst for a new era of 'cosmopolitan law-enforcement'. There is no certainty that such change will occur, and NATO has not been short of critics who think it foolish to expect powerful states to support progressivism in the shape of large-scale global reform as opposed to moralism in selected cases. Good international citizens must come to the assistance of the victims of institutionalized cruelty, but the dilemma that arises because of the legalist position on the rights of states can be solved only by persuading the international community to adopt a new legality concerning humanitarian wars. Whether Kosovo will give rise to new legal conventions that remove the moral dilemmas of the good international citizen is unclear, as is the question of what form these conventions might take. But one of the fundamental responsibilities of the good international citizen is to attempt to resolve the tensions between legalism and progressivism in a new constitutional framework that alters the traditional relationship between order and justice, citizenship and humanity, and sovereignty and human rights in world affairs.

6   Citizenship and sovereignty in the post-Westphalian state

The rise of the modern state involved 'a revolution in loyalties' in which an 'inner circle of loyalty expanded' and 'an outer circle of loyalty shrank'. Loyalties to the sovereign state replaced the inner web of loyalties to an 'immediate feudal superior' and the outer web of 'customary religious obedience to the Church under the Pope' (Wight 1978: 25). As the twentieth century drew to a close, the subnational revolt, the internationalization of decision making and emergent transnational loyalties in Western Europe and its environs suggested that the processes that created and sustained sovereign states in this region were being reversed. The implications for social and political theory are becoming clearer. It is well known that the transformation of political community in the sixteenth and seventeenth centuries produced the modern vocabulary of the sovereign state. The conjunction of forces transforming contemporary Europe suggests that the time is ripe to engineer a further revolution in political thought or to complete the Copernican Revolution in political thinking, which was initiated by Kant more than two centuries ago (Gallie 1978). What is needed are appropriate visions of the post-Westphalian state.

The idea that the time might be 'ripe for the enunciation of new concepts of universal political organization which would show how Wales, the United Kingdom and the European Community could each have some world political status while none laid claim to exclusive sovereignty' was suggested by Hedley Bull (1977: 267) thirty years ago. His observations provide the starting point for the present discussion. Bull (1977: 275) maintained that 'one reason for the vitality of the states system is the tyranny of the concepts and normative principles associated with it.' He was right to do so. The absence of images of alternative forms of political community that could not be dismissed as utopian or facile has been a striking feature of modern political life. However, Bull (1977: 275–6) posed the question of whether there is 'a need to liberate thought and action from these confines by proclaiming new concepts and normative principles which would give shape and direction to the trends making against the present system'. This issue has acquired deeper significance as nation-states have become more vulnerable to the internal and external pressures summarized above. It has become essential to question the classical relationship between citizenship, sovereignty, territoriality and nationality.

The social bond that has linked the members of each modern European state together and separated them from other states and from the rest of humankind is being challenged by subnational groups and eroded by the advance of regional organizations and globalization. These pressures combine to challenge the exclusionary nature of sovereignty and traditional ideas about community and citizenship. Decisions to enshrine human rights in international conventions indicate that there has been modest but significant progress in Europe in building on the rights that individuals already have as citizens of sovereign states. Equally important is the shift away from 'difference-blind' citizenship to new figurations that recognize the special identities of various subnational groups (Taylor 1994). This chapter makes the case for a normative vision of the state in Europe in which subnational and transnational citizenship supplement existing forms of national citizenship. It argues that one purpose of the post-Westphalian state is to mediate between the different political loyalties, identities and authorities that have become inescapable in the modern world.

The argument is in four parts. Part one surveys Bull's prescient remarks about the possible transformation of state structures in Western Europe. Part two considers intriguing developments in the European political order in the period since Bull was writing that have improved the prospects for the radical extension of democracy not only within states but also in the broader transnational realm. Whether or not it is hopelessly utopian to envisage forms of cosmopolitan democracy 'in which citizens, wherever they are located in the world, have a voice, input and political representation in international affairs, in parallel with and independently of their governments' (Archibugi and Held 1995: 13) is considered here.[1] Part three considers these empirical developments in the light of Habermas's discourse theory of morality, which provides important resources for strengthening the normative foundations of cosmopolitan democratic theory. Part four shifts the discussion to the contemporary debate about citizenship and argues for new models that weave the ideals of cosmopolitan democracy into the organization of the post-Westphalian state.

Bull on the European State

Bull seemed to find the vision of a post-Westphalian Europe perfectly congenial but seriously qualified his support. There were reasons to be sceptical about the extent to which 'neo-medievalism' would represent real progress beyond existing forms of political community. Violence had been ubiquitous in medieval times and it could well become endemic in any future 'neo-medieval order of overlapping sovereignties and jurisdictions' (Bull 1979: 114).[2] Nevertheless, his more positive remarks about the possibility of post-Westphalian states resonate with current discussions about the prospects for transnational democracy in Europe.

Bull (1977: 254) observed that it 'might . . . seem fanciful to contemplate a return to the medieval world, but it is not fanciful to imagine that there might develop a modern and secular counterpart of it that embodies its central characteristic: a system of overlapping authority and multiple loyalty.' The momentous nature of this shift in political organization and loyalty was elaborated as follows:

> One may imagine for example that a regional integration movement, like that in the countries of the European Community, might seek to undermine the sovereignty of its member states, yet at the same time stop short of transferring this sovereignty to any regional authority. If they were to bring about a situation in which the authorities existed both at the national and at the European level, but no one such authority claimed supremacy over others in terms of superior jurisdiction or its claims on the loyalties of individual persons, the sovereign state would have been transcended. Similarly, one may imagine that if nationalist separatist groups were content to reject the sovereignty of the states to which they are at present subject, but at the same time refrained from advancing any claims to sovereign statehood themselves, some genuine innovation in the structure of the world political system might take place.
>
> (Bull 1979: 114)

The new pattern of political organization would not supersede the state entirely but the latter's role in world politics could be diminished to the extent that 'there was real doubt both in theory and in reality as to whether sovereignty lay with the national governments or with the organs of the community'(Bull 1977: 266). Bull further observed that it would be a short step from 'a situation of protracted uncertainty about the locus of sovereignty' to a condition in which 'the concept of sovereignty is recognized to be irrelevant' (ibid.).[3]

For Bull, the move towards a more universal political order would not erase national and subnational loyalties but grant cultural differences in levels of public recognition which had been missing in the past. New forms of political organization would arise from the diffusion of sovereign powers and the dispersal of loyalties to several centres of authority. What would emerge from demands on states to shift power to various domestic locales and to an emergent regional authority would be a complex web of overlapping political identities and authorities:

> We may envisage a situation in which, say, a Scottish authority in Edinburgh, a British authority in London, and a European authority in Brussels were all actors in world politics and enjoyed representation in world political organizations, together with rights and duties of various kinds in world law, but in which no one of them claimed sovereignty or supremacy over the others, and a person living in Glasgow had no exclusive or overriding loyalty to any one of them. Such an outcome would take us truly 'beyond the sovereign state' and is by no means implausible, but it is striking how little interest has been displayed in it by either the regional integrationists or the subnational 'disintegrationists'.
>
> (Bull 1979:114)

The neglect of this possible future is no longer quite as evident among regional integrationists and subnational disintegrationists as it was when Bull formulated these views (Camilleri and Falk 1992). But it still receives too little attention from political theorists who are, with some exceptions, firmly wedded to reflections on the modern state, and from mainstream students of international relations who, by analysing relations between bounded communities, have often ignored questions about how alternative forms of political community and new principles of world organization might evolve. What has been overlooked as a result of this division of labour is the need to rethink the social bond which unites the members of any society, which shapes their conception of their rights and duties vis-à-vis the rest of the world, and which is shaped in turn by the dominant patterns of international relations.

Bull's remarks on possible state forms have considerable contemporary relevance given institutional developments in Europe that promise to shift power and authority down to local regions and up to transnational structures. Powerful barriers to cosmopolitan democracy exist in Europe, but the cosmopolitan turn in democratic thinking (Held 1995; Archibugi and Held 1995) gives expression to real trends that are eroding the classic union of sovereignty, territoriality, nationality and citizenship. Cosmopolitan democracy is not an ideal which is starkly opposed to a reality that is recalcitrant to change but expresses important, but challenged, trends within Europe that favour the gradual democratization of international political life.

Current developments in Europe

Recent developments suggest that the time may be ripe for easing the sovereign state back from its central role in world politics so that stronger subnational and transnational loyalties and authorities can develop. Past references to a Europe of the Regions and the recent establishment of a Committee of the Regions in the European Union are innovations that indicate one way in which the democratic deficit in European institutions can be overcome. The subnational revolt in the former socialist bloc has raised the question of how new political groups might extricate themselves from nation-states in which they do not feel at home without bidding for full sovereignty. Fears that the acquisition of sovereignty will create profound insecurities for ethnic minorities within these fledgling states have prompted European states to ask whether the recognition of sovereignty should be conditional on constitutional guarantees for minority rights. Developments within the CSCE and OSCE (Organization for Security and Cooperation in Europe), and the decision in 1992 to create a High Commissioner on National Minorities, reflect these concerns, as did the adoption in the same year of the European Charter of Regional or Minority Languages by the Council of Europe (Biro 1994). Despite these developments the international protection of minority rights remains lamentably weak.

Resistance on the part of state structures and sections of their populations to the surrender of sovereignty abound, but the circumstances in which modern European states operate have altered significantly since Bull reflected on the possibility of a post-Westphalian Europe. In particular, the weakening of the old bonds linking citizens to the state creates unprecedented opportunities for new forms of political community attuned to the principles of transnational citizenship and cosmopolitan democracy.

Because of the intellectual division of labour previously mentioned, social and political theory and the theory of international relations have not developed a comprehensive analysis of the particular social bonds that unite the members of any society and simultaneously separate them from the rest of humankind. Bull noted that Deutsch's writings on the formation of security communities were pregnant with implications for a more general theory of international relations (Bull 1966a: 42–3; Deutsch 1970). As Bull (1966b: 365) observed, Deutsch was one of the few thinkers 'to think about the distinguishing features of a community, the different sorts of community that obtain, the elements that make up the cohesion of a community, the determinants of mutual responsiveness between one people and another'. The connections between the 'elements' of cohesion and the degree of 'mutual responsiveness' is a central theme that has been ignored by all but a small number of international theorists such as Deutsch and by sociologists such as Benjamin Nelson, who built on Weber's sociology by asking how far different civilizations promoted 'fraternization' by extending 'the rights of dialogue and citizenship to participants hitherto excluded' (Nelson 1971, 1973).[4]

Attempts to build on such work need to recall that developments in the social sciences since the mid-1980s have argued for synoptic explanations that are alert to the interplay between multiple phenomena and distinct therefore from those approaches that tended to focus on one logic – strategic competition in the case of realism, and production and exchange in the case of classic Marxism (Giddens 1985; Mann 1986; Tilly 1992). The unifying and divisive character of the social bond that is peculiar to the modern state bears the imprint of several forces, including state-building and war, the quest for international order, systems of production and exchange, language, culture and belief. Multilogic explanations that highlight the interplay between this array of forces are evident in the analysis of state-building and social power, but similar approaches have yet to appear that explain how the boundaries of political communities expand and contract, fluctuate in their levels of particularism and vary in the extent of their commitment to open dialogue with those who have previously been excluded.

Over the last few centuries, the interplay between state building, geopolitics, production and exchange, culture and identity resolved itself in a specific combination of five monopoly powers which is unique to the modern state:

- first, the monopoly control of the instruments of violence, which reveals the importance of, inter alia, state building, domestic pacification and war;
- second, the monopoly right of taxation, first claimed in order to finance the creation of state bureaucracies and standing armies and later intertwined with the state's responsibilities for the health, welfare and education of citizens;[5]
- third, the state's role in shaping political identity and prioritizing political obligations in the context of modern war and industrial production (but invariably the source of differences between rival visions of community);
- fourth, the state's monopolistic position in determining how legal disputes between citizens will be resolved in the context of domestic pacification;
- fifth, its exclusive right to belong to international organizations and to bind the whole political community in international law.

The interplay between the multiple forces mentioned earlier explains the triumph of the modern state, the nature of the contemporary challenge to its dominance in social and political life, and the prospects for the emergence of new types of political association.

To develop this further, it is important to recall that the territorial state prevailed in Europe because it was large enough to defend itself from external attack but sufficiently compact to be administered from a central point. The state secured and pacified its territory; it defined the legal principles and procedures that citizens were obliged to respect; later, the state acquired new powers and responsibilities by increasing its involvement in economic and social life with the result that powerful national sentiments became easier to instil. The state won the loyalty of its citizens by being the sole provider of these legal, political and economic goods.

Recent literature has focused on various developments that are loosening the bond between the citizen and the state and eroding tightly bound political communities in many parts of the world. The conditions under which the state exercises a monopoly control of the instruments of violence are being transformed in the post-industrial core regions of the world economy. War has long played a central role in the formation of national communities, but the obsolescence of force (Mueller 1989) in relations between the major industrial powers makes close ties between citizens and the state harder to reproduce. Unsurprisingly, the pacification of core regions has been accompanied by calls for increased political representation from minority nations, the claims of which have long been contained on the grounds that national unity is essential for the conduct of war.

The conditions under which the state has exercised its monopoly power of taxation have been transformed by globalization. Global capital markets and the internationalization of relations of production limit the state's capacity to decide national economic policy on its own. Globalization is closely linked with inter-state pacification, as Rosecrance (1986) has observed in his analysis of the rise of the trading state. The conquest of territory has become a barrier to economic growth, and the cult of violence hardly features in the self-image of core powers, at least in their dealings with one another. Numerous 'evasions of sovereignty' (Falk 1990) have appeared, such as inter-regional cooperation and increasing contacts between Brussels and the domestic regions within the EU that bypass national governments entirely. Because of globalization, ancient divisions between separate states are overlaid with new and potentially more important divisions between those who have the capacity to exercise citizenship and those for whom citizenship has been reduced to little more than formal rights. Because of globalization, all citizens are exposed to the rigours of risk society (Beck 1992).

No less important, the conditions under which the state has regulated the identity of its citizens are being altered radically. Mass migration is transforming most societies into diverse, multiethnic communities. Throughout the world, indigenous peoples and minority nations reject national–assimilationist ideologies and practices as part of the 'politics of recognition' (Taylor 1994). All communities are now locked into global communication and information networks embodying new forms of sociocultural power with highly ambiguous results. In most societies, groups espousing cultural closure compete with groups that favour more openness to the outside world. Globalization confronts states with difficult choices about the appropriate levels of involvement in international organizations. A commanding national consensus about questions of national identity and national purpose is increasingly hard to find.

The environment in which the state exercises its legal powers has also been transformed by globalization. Pressures to relax traditional assumptions about sovereign immunity have increased in the wake of commercial developments between states and private economic organizations. The use of international legislation to harmonize areas of national policy is pronounced, as is the development of the closer international scrutiny of the state's regard for the human rights of its citizens and the evolution of international criminal law. As Parekh (1991) has shown, strong pressures exist in multicultural societies to interpret and apply the law sensitively in the light of cultural differences.

The nature of the bond uniting members of the same society and the extent of their separateness from the rest of humanity is being transformed across the world – most dramatically in many parts of Europe. In most societies, the character of the social bond is keenly contested and few communities are now entirely at one with themselves (Derrida 1992: 9–11). In these fluid conditions, new forms of political community no longer seem utopian. The prospect of a post-Westphalian international society is already immanent within a complex web of social, economic, cultural and political change, and new visions of community and citizenship have started to appear (Kymlicka 1989, 1995; Linklater 1992, 1998; Connolly 1992; Held 1993; Walker 1993). Bull's comments about the future European state have acquired greater relevance in recent years, although it is essential to take his argument further in new normative and sociological analyses of the changing nature of bounded communities. It is also necessary to explore the relationships between critical theory, the discourse theory of morality and cosmopolitan democracy in order to advance the case for new polities that can embody higher levels of universality and diversity than the classical 'Westphalian' state permitted (Linklater 1998).

Critical theory, modes of exclusion and transnational democracy

The argument thus far is that the vision of cosmopolitan democracy does not clash with the existing political order but gives expression to important but contested developments within modern European states. Although there are forces that resist shifting power to local regions and transnational structures, complex processes of social change reveal that the notion of cosmopolitan democracy is no longer fanciful in Europe. To show that this is a normatively desirable political future rather than an intriguing empirical possibility, it is useful to link recent discussions of cosmopolitan democracy with critical social theory and the discourse theory of morality.

There is an important parallel between Bull's remark about defending normative principles that support trends running against the present system and the method of critical social theory which examines the extent to which higher levels of political self-determination are already immanent within existing forms of life. Rather like Bull's approach, critical theory argues for higher levels of universality and difference and suggests that the important political question is how structures can be fashioned that strike the right balance between them (Linklater 1998). Bull's position on the diffusion of sovereign power and the dispersal of loyalties to several centres of political authority can be defended on the grounds that it supports advances in democratic accountability, but the link with democratic governance is not as explicit in his writings as in critical social theory (Habermas 1994).

Discourse ethics, as developed by Apel and Habermas, defends the creation of dialogic relations at all levels of social and political life and therefore stands opposed to the principle of national sovereignty, which severely restricts the capacity of 'outsiders' to participate in making decisions that can affect their vital interests. The discourse approach argues that human beings need to be reflective about the ways in which they include some in, and exclude others from, dialogue. It maintains that they should be willing to problematize bounded communities (indeed social barriers of all kinds), and adds that the legitimacy of practices of exclusion is questionable whenever there is a failure to take account of their impact on the interests of 'outsiders'. The discourse approach therefore provides strong normative support for the vision of 'neo-medievalism' advanced by Bull.

The discourse theory of morality argues that norms cannot be valid unless they can command the consent of everyone whose interests may be affected by them (Habermas 1989: 82ff.). A central claim is that the validity of principles can be established only through forms of dialogue that are open in principle to every human being. Starting with this premise, the discourse approach sets out the procedures that are intrinsic to authentic dialogue. These include the convention that no person and no moral position can be excluded from dialogue in advance. Authentic dialogue depends on a particular moral psychology. True dialogue is not a trial of strength between adversaries hell-bent on intellectual conquest but an encounter in which human beings engage in 'reciprocal critique' realizing that there is no certainty about 'who will learn from whom' (Habermas 1990: 26). Involvement in dialogue requires that agents suspend their truth claims, respect the claims of others and anticipate that their initial points of departure will be modified in the course of dialogue. What guides participants is a commitment to being moved by nothing other than the 'unforced force of the better argument' (Habermas 1990: 66, 89).

An important theme in this argument is that public agreements should not be secured by effacing individual or cultural differences (Habermas 1994: 119–20). Habermas (1985: 94–6) emphasizes that a 'fully transparent . . . homogenized and unified society' is not his ideal, but his thesis that the aim of dialogue is to determine generalizable principles has been interpreted as endorsing the quest for a universal consensus on the ends of life. Critics have asked whether cultural differences are valued sufficiently by supporters of the discourse position (Benhabib 1993: 9).[6] Fearing that differences might be cancelled by a stifling consensus, some feminist writers have argued that care should be taken with respect to the idea that dialogue involves the search for general principles that govern similar persons in like circumstances. Dialogue involves engagement with concrete others to ensure that differences are not ignored in the quest for generalizable principles. Moral universals cannot emerge without dialogue between concrete others, but they may not issue from authentic dialogue at all. Since true discourse requires sympathetic engagement with the radically different standpoints that may be taken by the 'other', the outcome may be no more than an agreement to disagree.

Reflecting these developments, Frazer and Lacey (1993: 203–12) argue for a 'dialogic communitarianism' that rejects the goal of a 'unified public' in the name of 'unassimilated otherness', but this argument does not banish universals from the ethical equation. Some theorists such as Benhabib (1993), Gilligan (1993) and O'Neill (1989) argue that the moral agent needs to balance two moralities that deal with the quest for generalizable principles and concern for the differences of the other. These approaches are not opposed to universalism as such but they reject any form that devalues cultural and gender differences (Young 1991: 105). Their effect is to imagine a stronger universalism in which dialogue entrenches respect for 'otherness'. The upshot of these discussions is that the discourse theory of morality supports the development of communities that are simultaneously far more universalistic and open to difference than most modern states have been during the last five centuries. Critical theory therefore strengthens the vision of the post-Westphalian state outlined earlier and endorses the commitment to modes of cosmopolitan democracy that extend the boundaries of political community without endorsing an ethical universalism that is antagonistic to cultural diversity (Beitz 1994).

The discourse approach to morality sets out procedures that should be followed so that individuals are equally free to express their moral differences and able to resolve them, where possible, by employing the force of the better argument. It does not seek to solve substantive moral debates but it has clear implications for how societies should be organized. Illustrating this theme, Cohen (1990: 71, 100) argues that the perspective is opposed to all forms of life that are 'based on domination, violence and systematic inequality' and hostile to full and open participation. It must also be opposed to visions of society which hold that the discourse principle can be implemented by sovereign experiments in democratic politics conducted within self-regarding, separate states.

The discourse theory of morality therefore challenges traditional notions of sovereignty and citizenship with a view to realizing the prospects for new forms of political community that are immanent in modern societies. Rethinking citizenship is crucial as this concept has been central to the social bond that unites the members of the sovereign state and sets them apart from the rest of the world. Troubled by political structures that fail to take account of the interests of other societies, critical theory supports the development of new social bonds in connection with the extension of moral and political community. But while supporting this development, it does not forget the extent to which most societies have excluded the members of minority groups from full participation in their affairs. Critical theory recognizes that traditional ideas of statehood possessed an assimilationist logic that indigenous peoples, minority nations and racial minorities emphatically reject (Kymlicka 1989, 1995). The 'politics of recognition' denies that the citizens of modern states must share the same cultural identity or possess exactly the same rights. Critical theory imagines new forms of political community in which outsiders have greater representation, but it also defends a new social contract with the members of traditionally marginal groups. More radically still, it favours arrangements that combine these two developments by representing minority groups in democratically constituted international institutions.

In summary, the discourse approach to morality contests the social bonds between citizens that perpetuate the sovereign state as a form of dual closure excluding internal and external others. The perspective imagines new dialogic possibilities that require states to dispatch their powers in two directions: upwards in the search for greater universality and downwards in response to claims for the public recognition of valued cultural differences. Such transfers of power and authority to facilitate the realization of transnational democracy have major implications for traditional understandings of citizenship and sovereignty. The next two sections consider them in more detail.

Citizenship

Proponents of cosmopolitan democracy support widening the boundaries of community so that insiders and outsiders can be associated as equals in radical experiments in political participation. Progress in this direction involves the reconceptualization of citizenship and the commencement of a new stage in the development of citizenship rights.

T.H. Marshall's influential account of the development of citizenship in Britain shapes the following discussion. Marshall (1973) maintained that the possibility of enlarging the rights of members was immanent within societies in which the idea of citizenship helped constitute the social bond. Citizenship is clearly linked with deep cultural assumptions about who does and who does not belong to the community, but it involves societies in peculiar tensions and contradictions which arise less starkly, if they arise at all, in social systems that lack the concept. From these tensions, new social bonds have arisen and may develop in future because while citizenship can enforce social exclusion it also has a radicalizing potential that can be turned against the state itself.

Citizenship is intriguing from the vantage point of critical social theory because it has been central to the forms of social inclusion and exclusion that are peculiar to modern states. It has been a means of depriving sections of the population of legal, political, social or cultural rights, but the tensions between the egalitarian claims that are intrinsic to modern ideas of citizenship and actual social inequalities have repeatedly generated resistance on the part of subordinate groups. Limited access to citizenship and restricted definitions of its meaning have frequently triggered political efforts to extend citizenship rights to the previously excluded. The creation of new citizenship rights has been an unsurprising, but far from inevitable, response to deep social contradictions within modern states but, as E.H. Carr (1945) argued, it enveloped these societies in several tensions and conflicts internationally in the 1920s and 1930s. Overcoming these tensions has meant transcending conventional notions of citizenship and reworking traditional ideas about the relationship between the state and humanity. Cosmopolitan democracy is a means of ensuring that the process of extending citizenship rights within states is carried forward into the international sphere in order to create forms of political community that are better adapted to rising levels of human interconnectedness.

Returning to Marshall, as his thesis about the development of citizenship has been discussed elsewhere, only the following points need be noted (see Chapter 4). Marshall traced a dialectic in which the establishment of the legal rights of the citizen in the eighteenth century led to political struggles in the following century to redefine citizenship to include the essential rights of representation or participation in the law-making process. In turn, possession of these rights engendered demands for new citizenship rights that stressed the need for economic security, greater access to education and increased opportunities to enjoy the cultural heritage. Without these economic and social rights, the argument was, legal and political rights would have little significance for large sections of the population (Marshall 1973: 71ff.). There is no reason to suppose that the development of citizenship was ushered along by some historical teleology, but there are good reasons for concluding that initial steps to create legal rights generated the experience of second-class citizenship and led to pressures to promote greater involvement in the life of the political community.

Various ambiguities and antinomies surrounded the evolution of citizenship in the national domain, and attempts to overcome these problems had detrimental consequences for the international realm. As E.H. Carr (1945) argued, states in the first part of the century enlarged the meaning of citizenship to include welfare rights, but 'the socialization of the nation' and the nationalization of economic policy had dire international consequences. As social welfare assumed greater importance in modern states, protectionism and greater international economic and political competition reached new levels. Economic nationalism led to the demise of large-scale immigration, and rivalries between nation-states increased after the momentous decision in 1919 to close national frontiers. National cultures became more inclusive with the introduction of welfare rights but national exclusiveness in foreign policy and tighter national controls over the admission of refugees intensified. Inflamed initially by the drift towards protectionism, nationalism after the First World War encouraged total war, while popular hatred blurred the distinction between military and civilian targets. Coupled with the decline of international law in the 1930s, the deportation of peoples to tidy the frontiers marked the end of the liberal epoch in which nationalism united citizens without creating aggressively particularistic attitudes to other peoples. International order was weakened as political communities in Europe became more tightly bound, more sharply divided from one another and more willing to cause harm.

The extension of citizenship in the first part of the century deepened the tension between obligations to the state and obligations to humanity in Europe. But questions surrounding the morality of war, global social justice and human rights ensured that the normative status of the civic bond that unites and separates has remained controversial. The cosmopolitan strand of thought in the European states-system has ensured that arguments for treating insiders and outsiders as moral equals have retained their importance. Conceptions of national citizenship have invariably been challenged when they have given rise to behaviour that harmed the interests of the members of other societies.

A recent example with clear implications for global citizenship is Shue's consideration of the ethics of exporting hazards. Shue (1981) argues that asbestos-producing plants in the United States were closed and subsequently exported to West Africa in the light of evidence that asbestos production damaged the health of US workers. His principal contention is that there was no moral justification for treating insiders and outsiders differently in this case. This argument lends support to the idea of global citizenship defined as duties to vulnerable non-nationals, to what Beck (1992) calls 'the proletariat in global risk society'. It is important, however, to extend the idea of global citizenship understood merely as moral 'duties beyond borders'. The logic of moral equality, it will be argued, requires transnational democratic processes that bring insiders and outsiders together as transnational citizens with equal rights of representation and participation and with an equal expectation of living without the fear of violent or non-violent harm.

Most recent accounts of global citizenship do not stretch this far: most stop at moral obligations to the rest of humanity. Derek Heater (1990: 163–4) argues that citizenship need not be confined exclusively to the rights and duties that individuals have as members of particular sovereign states. Citizenship as a system of moral duties rather than an ensemble of legal rights can be associated with any geographical unit stretching from the city to the whole of humanity. Heater uses the idea of world social citizenship to defend the duties that the rich have to the poor in world society. Similarly, Martin Shaw (1991: 187) argues for 'post-military citizenship' in which the classical duty to defend the state is replaced by obligations to the poor and duties to the environment. In the world of foreign policy, middle powers such as Australia have introduced the concept of 'good international citizenship' to affirm the need for states to develop significant 'purposes beyond themselves' (see Chapter 4). These efforts to reconfigure the idea of citizenship recognize the possibility of its further dialectical development by encouraging its severance from the relatively closed world of the sovereign state and its attachment to transnational structures which are empowered to reduce the level of harm in international relations. As noted earlier, the relationship between the state and humanity has been a matter of dispute in the modern West because of cosmopolitan ideas about the moral equality of all members of humankind. Addressing this problem, the idea of global citizenship supports the development of universal moral duties as a means of reducing the tension between obligations to the state and to humanity (Falk 1994).

Although it is an important step in carrying the principle of equality forward into the global sphere, the idea of world citizenship has many weaknesses. Its emphasis is on the duty of the strong to help others and on the need for compassion from world citizens. But, as Michael Ignatieff (1991: 34) has argued, citizenship is generally thought to be about rights of political participation rather than moral duties to others. Strictly speaking, citizenship is less about compassion than about 'ensuring for everyone the entitlements necessary for the exercise of their freedom' (ibid.). As noted earlier, ideas about global citizenship rarely extend this far because they are limited to the realm of moral duty. By implication, duty holders retain an important level of discretion about whether or not (and how far) they should honour their international moral obligations. In the language of secular natural law theory, these obligations are not perfect (they are not determinate and enforceable) but imperfect (indeterminate and optional).[7] This points to a crucial weakness in notions of global citizenship, which is that moral duties are not obviously accompanied by support for a long-term project of creating equal rights of participation in transnational democratic structures. Nevertheless, the idea of global citizenship is an important intermediate step between circumstances in which the members of a bounded community limit the ethical constituency to themselves and a possible, but clearly remote, condition in which universal political structures can guarantee the perfect legal, political and social rights of every member of humanity.

Developments such as the Nuremberg Charter challenged traditional conceptions of citizenship by defining the rights and duties inherent in an imagined moral community that transcends sovereign states. The Nuremberg Doctrine established that individuals had the right to disobey unlawful superior orders and could be brought before international courts where they might be found guilty of crimes against peace and against humanity. A nascent form of global citizenship was enshrined in the Nuremberg Charter, although the international rights and duties so defined remained imperfect, the victorious powers retaining sovereign discretion over decisions about who to bring before international courts of law.

Realizing the promise of more active forms of citizenship that might be regarded as immanent within cosmopolitan claims about the moral equality of all human beings remains a distant hope. A conception of an intermediate step between the Nuremberg principles and forms of citizenship that typify the post-Westphalian state can be found in E.H. Carr's remarks on the desirable trajectory of European political development after the Second World War. Carr argued in *Nationalism and After* that interstate violence in the first part of the century occurred because the liberal balance between nationalism and internationalism collapsed following the state's increased role in national economic life. Carr imagined a new European polity that would bind 'insiders' and 'outsiders' together in collective efforts to protect basic welfare rights. New transnational structures that were responsible for economic planning to secure these rights were envisaged in post-Second World War Europe. Carr's observations about the limitations of the state and national citizenship are intriguing in the light of recent efforts to construct notions of transnational citizenship for the peoples of the EU.

In the new world of 'welfare internationalism', Carr argued, the welfare interests of the inhabitants of different European societies should be treated equally. The transformation of political community was required because national citizenship could no longer secure the benefits that had come to be expected from it. Carr's imagined transnational polity placed all citizens on the same level without disregarding their cultural differences. Rather like Bull's neo-medievalism, Carr's vision (1945: 45) argued that 'the international community if it is to flourish must admit [a] multiplicity of authorities and diversity of loyalties.' In this polity, international citizenship would not revolve around benevolent dispositions that might weaken over time. The principle of moral equality would be incorporated in international political structures responsible for the protection of determinate social rights.

Carr set out a major argument in support of the transition from the Westphalian to the post-Westphalian state over fifty years ago and, if anything, the case has strengthened considerably in recent years. Turner (1986: 140) argues that 'we have a system of national citizenship in a social context which requires a new theory of internationalism and universalistic citizenship', and Balibar maintains (1988: 725) that the 'struggle for citizenship as a struggle for equality must begin again' with the emergence of 'a cosmopolis of communications and financial transactions'. These commitments invite the transcendence of the conflict between the state and humanity, which was intensified in the first part of the twentieth century as national citizenship was extended and its meaning revised, but what distinguishes them from global citizenship is the move beyond the advocacy of duty and compassion to support for new forms of democratic politics in post-Westphalian communities.

Carr argued that new political structures would need to take account of the variety of human loyalties, and his writings raised the issue of how the rights of minority nations could be protected. Because the defence of minority rights had provided the pretext for Nazi Germany's annexation of areas such as the Sudetenland, states were unenthusiastic about introducing measures to protect minorities in the aftermath of the Second World War. But at the end of the twentieth century, no serious account of citizenship could proceed without recognizing that one of the main challenges to its role in preserving exclusionary communities comes from indigenous peoples and minority nations. Democratic polities face pressures to revise conventional understandings of citizenship in the light of the contemporary politics of recognition.

Traditional conceptions of citizenship abstract from the particularity of persons to define the rights that all individuals have as moral equals. The politics of recognition argues that modern notions of citizenship are exclusionary because they neglect the different needs of specific cultural groups. A cogent defence of this point of view is provided by Phillips (1991: 81–3) who argues that there is a short step between arguing that all citizens are equal despite their differences to concluding that differences do not matter at all. Furthermore, the invitation to particular groups to transcend their particularity, and to identify with the wider good, can all too easily become a summons to submit to the dominant social strata. For these reasons assimilationist strategies have been challenged by the doctrine that other cultures should be treated as different and equal (see Todorov 1984). The upshot is that minority nations and indigenous peoples should be incorporated in the state consociationally.[8] It is essential to incorporate these themes within post-sovereign visions of cosmopolitan democracy.

To summarize, for the past two hundred years the struggle against exclusion has been central to political life – at first in Europe and now across the wider world. This is the context in which to place the contemporary reinvention of citizenship. Reconfiguring citizenship rights in the twentieth century was integral to efforts to create new forms of political community that were less exclusionary domestically although they became more exclusionary in their foreign policy behaviour. The effects of that process of reconfiguration, so ably described by Carr, can be corrected by developing new visions of global citizenship and by establishing citizenship rights in post-sovereign polities. Without the accompaniment of group rights at the national and international level, such efforts to universalize the achievements of citizenship will remain radically incomplete. Transcending the Westphalian division between the 'inside' and the 'outside' in new forms of political community that allow higher levels of ethical universality and respect for difference to flourish is the key to achieving cosmopolitan democracy (see Walker 1993).

Post-Westphalian communities

Attempts to universalize citizenship by extending rights in international relations, and efforts to particularize it by recognizing special group rights, comprise two crucial means of eradicating unjustified exclusion. Bull's references to a neo-medieval Europe indicated that a polity combining greater universality and difference could result in uncertainty about the locus of sovereignty. A system of multiple authorities and loyalties might prompt the question of whether the concept of sovereignty had ceased to be relevant. The analysis of citizenship in the previous section points towards a similar conclusion. Universalizing the achievements of national citizenship necessarily involves a significant break with the principle of state sovereignty.

What is at stake is the unitarian conception of sovereignty developed by Bodin and bolstered by much subsequent political theory. Unitarianism argues that what 'makes a man a citizen [is] the mutual obligation between subject and sovereign' in which faith and obedience are exchanged for justice, counsel, assistance, encouragement and protection (Bodin 1967: 21). Four points are worth noting about the classic doctrine of sovereignty: first, no one can be the subject of more than one sovereign; second, only one sovereign power can prevail within any single territory; third, all citizens must possess exactly the same status and rights; and, fourth, the bond between citizen and sovereign necessarily excludes aliens (see James 1986: 48, 226–8 for a contemporary formulation).

The ideals of cosmopolitan democracy and the 'Westphalian' principles of sovereignty and citizenship are inevitably in tension. Greater universality and diversity requires that citizens are free to develop subnational and transnational projects in several political arenas that are not arranged hierarchically. Cosmopolitan democracy involves the dispersal of sovereign powers rather than their aggregation in new sites of political authority. If the social bond is transformed to recognize claims for diversity, then the rights of citizens need to have a flexible and varying content: the idea of an undifferentiated public that is subordinate to one sovereign power becomes untenable. Citizenship can then embrace individual rights of access to international bodies to seek redress against abuses of sovereign power. If the social bond is to be modified so that outsiders enjoy equal rights of access to dialogue, then the supposition that citizenship rights must be protected by one sovereign authority has to be abandoned. The upshot is new modes of citizenship in which multiple political authorities and loyalties break with the unitarian conception of state sovereignty.

To develop these points further it is useful to consider the thin conception of citizenship set out within the European Union Treaty and to reflect on what a thicker conception of citizenship would entail. The relevant section of the European Union Treaty (Article 8), which maintains that 'every person holding the nationality of a Member State shall be a citizen of the Union', stresses the following individual legal rights or entitlements: the right of free movement within Europe and to reside in the territory of another member state, the right to petition the European Parliament or the EU Ombudsman and the right to receive assistance from any member state while overseas. The Treaty creates a set of individual political rights: the right to vote and stand as a candidate in local elections in other countries and the right to vote or stand as a candidate for the European Parliament (Wise and Gibb 1993).

What is established by Article 8 of the Treaty is a thin conception of citizenship that is more relevant to an international civil society than to an emerging transnational political community. A thicker conception of citizenship includes the right of appeal beyond the state to European courts of law and participation in international organizations that institutionalize the right of individuals to engage in 'joint rule' (Brewin 1988). A thicker conception reworks the social bond to transcend the claim that all citizens have to share one dominant national identity or owe allegiance to an exclusive sovereign power. It would grant substate national identities and emergent transnational loyalties an unprecedented political role.

Two further aspects of the thick conception of citizenship warrant consideration. The first is suggested by Marshall's remarks that public recognition of formal rights is not enough to ensure full membership of a political community. Social and economic rights that make it possible for citizens to exercise their legal and political entitlements are vital for the reasons given in his account. A second point is that an additional cluster of citizenship rights is necessary to respond adequately to the politics of recognition. Problems inherent in forms of citizenship that abstract from the particularity of persons were noted earlier. Fears that membership of the EU might have the consequence of eroding the distinctive political traditions and identities of smaller countries have featured strongly in recent debates, not least in Scandinavia. These reservations about, or protests against, the widening of the boundaries of political community require that visions of cosmopolitan democracy address ways of bridging the gulf between the national or subnational loyalties of citizens and transnational political institutions.

At least four ways of overcoming the distance between citizens and cosmopolitan democratic institutions exist:

- devolving political power so that citizenship can be enjoyed through participation in subnational or substate assemblies;
- ensuring that minority nations are adequately represented in transnational institutions;
- making it possible for the members of minority nations (and for racial and other minorities) to appeal to international courts that are authorized to scrutinize claims of unfair discrimination;
- providing subnational regions with access to adequate material resources to withstand the effects of de-industrialization upon vulnerable economies and to ensure the survival of minority languages and cultures.

These strategies can help overcome the problem of distance in wider political associations that transcend the sovereign state. It is important that international institutions do not simply represent individuals qua individuals but the entire range of domestic and international groups and voluntary associations to which they belong (Brewin 1994). The modes of citizenship discussed in the preceding paragraphs do not include global citizenship, understood as duties to assist desperate strangers elsewhere. But this notion is important for reflecting upon the ways in which post-Westphalian societies should behave towards the rest of the world. One of the central features of post-Westphalian Europe should be the commitment to avoid 'closing itself off' (Derrida 1992: 29).

What needs further discussion is the structure of citizenship rights that is essential in the post-Westphalian era. Marshall's writings contained a dialectic of citizenship relevant to the modern state. Legal rights were inadequate without rights of participation, but they had limited value where deep inequalities of power and wealth prevented large numbers of citizens from exercising their legal and political entitlements. Taking the dialectic of citizenship further is essential for the reasons outlined in Carr's defence of 'welfare internationalism'. However, it is possible to go beyond Carr's account not only by widening the boundaries of community through the creation of cosmopolitan democratic structures but also by deepening the sense of community by restoring the rights of minority nations and increasing the role of voluntary associations. This is to anticipate the reconfiguration of citizenship to bind different levels of identity (subnational, national and supranational) in new forms of political community. Reversing the processes that led to the formation of the modern European state is necessary, as noted earlier, because citizenship has simultaneously advanced the cause of human equality and stood defiantly in its way. But citizenship might yet be extended beyond the state as part of the process of creating the social bonds that are required to ensure that human beings exercise greater control over their increasing interconnectedness.

It is possible to imagine citizens of a polity that is wider than the state but which does not monopolize control of the instruments of violence, exercise the sole right of taxation, single out one identity and make it superior to all others, function as the final court of legal appeal or claim the sole right of representation in international organizations and the exclusive power to bind the whole community in international law. Although it is not a state, this wider and deeper political community would necessarily encroach upon traditional state monopoly powers and break with the unitarian conception of sovereignty. According to the latter approach, as noted earlier, no one can be subject to more than one sovereign and only one sovereign can prevail within a given territorial area. Further, all citizens must possess the same status and identity, and the bond that links them together must exclude aliens. Citizens of the post-Westphalian state, by comparison, can come under the jurisdiction of several political authorities; they can have multiple identities and they need not be united by bonds that make them either indifferent to, or enemies of, the rest of the human race. The 'Westphalian' state defends national interests against outsiders and frequently takes little account of the interests of minority groups within its borders; the post-Westphalian state can remove these moral deficits by striking a new balance between substate loyalties, traditional nation-state attachments and the sphere of cosmopolitan identification.

Conclusion

This chapter has brought together areas of discussion that are rarely linked: Bull's comments on a possible European future; current trends in the region that invite further development of his schematic observations; the relevance of critical theory and the discourse theory of morality for cosmopolitan democracy; and recent approaches to citizenship and sovereignty that contest traditional accounts of political community. One central theme runs through all four areas of discussion – the possibility of remaking political communities to achieve levels of universality and diversity that modern states discouraged under conditions of geopolitical rivalry and expectations of major war. In the new international environment it is both possible and desirable to realize higher levels of universality and diversity that break with the surplus social constraints of the 'Westphalian era'.

The argument in favour of reconstructing citizenship in the post-Westphalian state supports the claim that, although citizenship is one of the great achievements of modernity, it remains 'too puffed up and too compressed' (Wright 1990: 32): too puffed up because the needs of those who do not share the dominant national culture have frequently been disregarded; too compressed because the interests of outsiders have usually been ignored. The argument set out here builds on the claim that modern states should 'go higher in [the] search for citizenship, but also lower and wider. Higher to the world, lower to the locality' (Wright 1990: 32). 'Higher' forms of citizenship include rights of participation in supranational structures and the international protection of the individual's legal and welfare rights. 'Lower' forms of citizenship involve increasing the power of local communities and substate groups. 'Higher' *and* 'lower' forms of citizenship can be integrated by granting substate groups the right of appeal to international bodies and parallel forms of representation in international institutions.

Europe gave birth to the ideas of sovereignty, territoriality, nationality and citizenship, which it then exported to the rest of the world. Whether the era in which these principles were central to political life is coming to an end is a matter of dispute. Some dimensions of European politics suggest that a new epoch may be emerging in which the principle of moral equality will underpin active citizenship within post-Westphalian arrangements (Falk 1994: 136–7). The new polity that might come about would mark a momentous step forward for the peoples of Europe and might come to be regarded as a historical watershed in the evolution of world political organization. Faced with this prospect, one of the tasks of normative theory is to envisage global political structures that go well beyond efforts to maintain order between settled bounded communities. Various forces are loosening the grip of the nation-state so that a wider range of political identities and authorities are freer to develop. The political task is to give these developments concrete expression in new forms of community that are committed to realizing the Kantian ideal of a universal kingdom of ends.

7   Cosmopolitan citizenship

The idea of cosmopolitan or world citizenship seems to have appeared in Ancient Greece in the fourth century BC when the polis and associated civic virtues were in decline. The cynic philosopher Diogenes called himself a citizen of the world because he believed that the polis no longer had first claim on the individual's allegiances. For Diogenes, the idea of world citizenship was used to criticize the polis rather than to develop a vision of a universal community of humankind. Enlightenment thinkers such as Kant used the concept in a more positive way to promote a stronger sense of moral obligation between the members of separate sovereign states. Since the Second World War, global social movements have resurrected the notion of cosmopolitan citizenship to defend a strong sense of personal and collective responsibility for the world as a whole and to support the establishment of effective global institutions for tackling global poverty, escalating environmental degradation and human rights violations (Dower 2000: 553). Several analysts of social movements maintain that cosmopolitan citizenship is a key element in the quest for a new language of politics, which challenges the belief that the individual's central political obligations are to the nation-state. Cosmopolitan citizenship is regarded as a key theme in the continuing search for basic universal rights and obligations that can bind all peoples together in a more just world order.

The belief that global problems can be solved by proclaiming cosmopolitan rights and duties does not go unchallenged. Critics have argued that cosmopolitan projects are likely to be the vehicles for particular political interests that wrap themselves in the language of universality. Many point to the danger that new forms of cultural imperialism will result from efforts to lay down rights and duties which apply to human beings everywhere. Others argue that attempts to break the nexus between the citizen and the state are destined to fail because there is no sense of international community which can support the sophisticated forms of citizenship that exist within democratic societies. One concern is that the defence of cosmopolitan citizenship is not only rhetorical but dangerous because it threatens to distract attention from the more urgent business of improving viable nation-states.

This chapter begins by considering criticisms of world citizenship which argue that citizenship, properly so-called, exists only within bounded political communities: nation-states. The next task is to assess three ways in which the concept is used in cosmopolitan political theory and practice: to strengthen cosmopolitan duties to the members of other political communities; to champion the realm of individual human rights as set out in the developing realm of world or cosmopolitan law; and to endorse the political project of creating a worldwide public sphere that extends the democratic project beyond national boundaries. The aim of the discussion is to determine whether or not the idea of cosmopolitan citizenship can be defended from the various criticisms that have been levelled against it.

Critics of cosmopolitan citizenship

The simplest and most eloquent challenge to the idea of cosmopolitan citizenship has been put forward by Michael Walzer (2002) who has maintained that:

> I am not a citizen of the world . . . I am not even aware that there is a world such that one could be a citizen of it. No one has ever offered me citizenship, or described the naturalization process, or enlisted me in the world's institutional structures, or given me an account of its decision procedures . . . or provided me with a list of the benefits and obligations of citizenship, or shown me the world's calendar and the common celebrations and commemorations of its citizens.

Three points are worth making about these striking comments. The first is that Walzer argues that national citizens have a clear sense of belonging to a bounded political community; they enjoy common sentiments born from their shared historical experience; and they regard certain dates that define their unique history as worthy of special commemoration. However much globalization impinges on everyday life, and however much it encourages persons to think of the world as a whole, it has not altered the fact that there are no equivalent historical reference points for all members of the human race. It is therefore essential to distinguish between the domain in which citizenship has real meaning and significance – the democratic nation-state – and the domain in which it has no obvious application at all – the world at large.

A second point is that the common culture that binds national citizens together enables them to agree on precise rights and duties that are constitutive of their membership of a distinctive political community. Because there is no global political culture, it is hardly surprising that human beings have not reached an agreement about the rights and duties that world citizens can expect from each other. It is also unremarkable that the world lacks cosmopolitan political institutions that uphold the rights and obligations of cosmopolitan citizens. The central implication of this argument is that, although the idea of cosmopolitan citizenship may well embody noble moral aspirations as its aim is to persuade individuals to take their global responsibilities more seriously, it distorts the meaning of citizenship.

To be a citizen in the true sense of the word is to possess rights and duties that are defined by law and protected by the institutions of the liberal–democratic state.

A third point, the most important of all, is that citizenship refers to rights of participation and representation in politics. To be a citizen is to be a co-legislator, if not directly through the forms of active political involvement that brought adult male citizens together in the democratic phases of the Greek polis then indirectly through elected representatives who make decisions for the community within a democratic public sphere. Walzer stresses that there is no equivalent form of joint rule within world society, nor is there is a global public sphere that brings cosmopolitan citizens together to legislate for humanity as a whole. What is most obviously missing from the idea of cosmopolitan citizenship then are the participatory practices that are at the heart of the civic ideal.

Walzer's critique of world citizenship is part of a broader, essentially communitarian tradition which claims that each political community must have the right to decide who can become a member and who should be turned away. The right of social closure, he argues, is essential if each political community is to preserve its cultural identity. To argue for bounded communities in this way may seem to embrace moral parochialism, which breeds disinterest in, if not outright hostility to, outsiders, but this is not Walzer's position. A passionate defence of moral obligations to outsiders is evident in his remarks on refugees who lack the security of belonging to a viable political community. He argues that bounded communities have a moral obligation to admit stateless persons if they have the resources to accommodate them and if their number does not threaten the survival of the cultural identity of the host nation. What is more, incomers have every right to expect to become full citizens with exactly the same rights as other members of the community. Anything else, Walzer (1995: ch. 2) insists, would be a form of tyranny which violates the principle that all members of the political community are entitled to have their views represented in politics and the right, should they so wish, to participate in joint rule.

Walzer's case for bounded communities is linked with a powerful defence of duties to other members of the human race, but he rejects any suggestion that the idea of cosmopolitan citizenship is necessary to foster compassion for desperate strangers. All that is required, in the United States for example, is that national citizens should define themselves as 'cosmopolitan Americans'. Nothing would be gained by inviting Americans to think of themselves as world citizens but something would be lost by way of conceptual precision as cosmopolitan citizenship does not denote the specific rights and duties of the kind that tie citizens together within nation-states.

Others go further by suggesting that there is more at stake than terminological exactitude. Miller (1999) argues that invitations to conceive of the self as a citizen of the world are a distraction from the pressing task of preserving and developing civic virtues within existing national communities. His argument is that it is important to recall that political associations whose members enjoy the status of equal citizens are a rare accomplishment in the history of government. The social preconditions of citizenship depend on initiatives to encourage individuals to demonstrate loyalty to their community and to make personal sacrifices for the interests of society as a whole. Democratic civic virtues that are intrinsic to citizenship have had to be nurtured within existing bounded political communities, and it is highly improbable that they will develop elsewhere. Nor is the survival of these virtues guaranteed. It is therefore reasonable to suppose that efforts to promote cosmopolitan ideals in a world that lacks a basic moral consensus will weaken the only form of political associations that can sustain the civic ideal. The point is not to loosen the ties that bind citizens together in nation-states but to reinforce them while ensuring that they are compatible with some basic duties to the rest of humanity.

The upshot of these arguments is that cosmopolitan citizenship would be a meaningful concept if humanity was governed by a world state, if the rights and duties of world citizens were elaborated by international law, if the different peoples of the world had similar cultural beliefs and historical memories, and if they were represented in global political institutions that governed the human race. But the term is vacuous in a world of bounded political communities with different mores, with a familiar reluctance to transfer sovereign powers to global economic and political institutions, and a justifiable scepticism that anything resembling democratic citizenship can develop beyond the nation-state.

Despite these objections, the idea of cosmopolitan citizenship features prominently in contemporary cosmopolitan political theory and in the language of global social movements where it is seldom linked with advocacy of world government (Dower 2000). The principal exponents of cosmopolitan citizenship aim instead to revive the ancient Stoic ideal that individuals should regard themselves as belonging to two communities: their particular cities or states and humanity. They regard the concept as a valuable tool for encouraging national citizens to take greater account of the interests of the world as a whole. They advocate cosmopolitan citizenship because sovereign nation-states that assume that the interests of co-nationals must come first are improbable instruments for tackling growing international economic inequalities, rising levels of intrastate violence and human rights violations, and increasing environmental degradation.

The intriguing question is whether cosmopolitan citizenship is a valuable concept in a world in which sovereign nation-states remain the most powerful forms of political community and where citizenship and democracy remain largely national. The interesting issue is whether the concept has real import in a society of states that are highly unlikely to cede powers to a world government but which have established the instruments of global governance for regulating spheres of human interaction that cut across national boundaries. To try to answer these questions, the rest of this chapter asks whether the three approaches to cosmopolitan citizenship outlined earlier provide a convincing response to the critics' objections.

The sphere of cosmopolitan duty

Classic studies of international society and international law addressed one of the most fundamental questions about bounded communities, namely what is the right relationship between duties to fellow citizens and duties to the human race (Linklater 1990a). Thinkers such as Pufendorf (1934a, 1934b) in the seventeenth century, and Vattel (1916) in the following century, envisaged an original state of nature in which all persons were subject to the natural law and had moral rights and duties in common. But there were no institutions in the natural order that specified precisely what it was each individual could expect from the others. Moral rights and duties were a matter for subjective interpretation in the original condition and, inevitably, individuals clashed over the exact nature of their duties and entitlements.

Confusion ended with the establishment of separate civil societies in which individuals acquired determinate and enforceable legal rights and duties as 'national' citizens. As a result of the social contracts that founded sovereign states, each government was obliged to do the best it could for its fellow citizens while remaining subject to the original natural law. Individual governments were not at liberty to ride roughshod over the interests of other peoples but they were largely free to decide the extent of their obligations to them. Neither Pufendorf nor Vattel, nor any of the major contractarian thinkers of the time, argued that the duties to humanity were the duties of world citizens. Anticipating the arguments of many recent theorists of national citizenship, classic writings on the state and international society insisted that citizenship referred to a particular legal and political status that individuals acquired as members of particular sovereign states.

The essence of Pufendorf and Vattel's positions was that duties to fellow citizens are more fundamental than duties to humankind. The difficulty with this standpoint was highlighted by Rousseau, who argued in the *Abstract of the Abbé de Saint-Pierre's Project for Perpetual Peace* that the transition from the state of nature to civil society did not solve the problem of order as the social contract thinkers had suggested. The reality following the establishment of separate states was that individuals were in a 'civil state' in relations with 'fellow citizens' but 'in the state of nature' with respect to 'the rest of the world'; political solution to 'private wars' had kindled 'national wars a thousand times more terrible' (Rousseau 1970: 132). Rousseau did not proceed to imagine a cosmopolitan solution to the tragic consequences of creating multiple political communities. He argued that those who claim to love humanity invariably end up loving no one at all. His preference was for small autarchic republics in which close civic ties were not permanently endangered by cosmopolitan moralities and transcendent religions (Hoffmann 1965; Miller 1999: 67). But for other moral and political philosophers, the impossibility of autarchy and the undesirability of world government are reasons for defending cosmopolitan citizenship. Its role is to ensure that the sense of moral community is not confined to co-nationals but embraces the species as a whole. It is designed to preserve a sense of universal morality in a world of separate states that repeatedly place their interests ahead of the welfare of humanity.

Kant was the first major political thinker to use the idea of cosmopolitan citizenship to challenge exclusionary sovereign states. In so doing, he drew on the Stoic conception of the equality of all human beings as exemplified by Cicero's claim that as 'we are all subject to a single law of nature ... we are bound not to harm anyone' (quoted in Nussbaum 1997: 31). Exactly the same duty to avoid harm to others had been defended earlier by Pufendorf and other social contract theorists, but Kant protested that they had not taken the harm principle seriously in their reflections on international relations (see Linklater and Suganami 2006: ch. 5). Although Kant was more forceful in defending the harm principle, his idea of world citizenship was limited in scope. All the moral law governing 'citizens of a universal state of humanity' required was the duty of hospitality to travellers and traders visiting strange lands (Kant 1970b: 206). The 'universal state of humanity' in question was not a form of world government, a condition that Kant opposed because it would be insensitive to cultural differences and so remote from everyday life as to be prone to despotism. The sovereign equality of states and the duty of non-intervention formed the bedrock of Kant's philosophy of international relations, but space was left for a limited conception of world citizenship which expressed identification with the universal community of humankind that exists above the states-system.

It is useful to draw on other dimensions of Kant's international relations theory to enlarge his conception of world citizenship. They include his claim that the European powers should respect the independence of non-European peoples in compliance with the basic human obligation not to harm other communities (Williams and Booth 1996: 91). They include his central claim that sovereign states should conduct their external affairs in accordance with the principle of publicity and the related contention that states should be bound by moral maxims that apply equally to all. Arguably, a richer conception of world citizenship is implicit in Kant's claim that all individuals and peoples who can affect or harm one another are morally obliged to create 'a cosmopolitan condition of general political security' (Kant 1970b: 210, 1970c: 49).

Mounting global problems over roughly the last century have encouraged many thinkers to develop this broader conception of world citizenship in line with Kant's belief that the objective is to strengthen the sense of belonging to a universal community of humankind rather than prepare the ground for world government. Indiscriminate violence against civilians during the Second World War intensified the challenge to the idea that states can reasonably cause great suffering to ensure military success and to spare their citizens' lives. Indifference to the plight of the global poor and to the victims of human rights abuses is a second reason for the revival of cosmopolitan citizenship. Faltering responses to environmental degradation provide a third stimulus for reviving and developing this ideal. In response to these developments, political theorists and activists have used the concept to challenge the idea that the state's primary responsibilities are to promote the welfare of co-nationals. The concept has also been used to try to instil stronger personal and collective responsibilities for other societies and for the biosphere. (The notion of global environmental citizenship is important in this regard.) It has also been a central theme in efforts to strengthen the belief in personal responsibility for what Arendt (1973: 66) called the aspects of public life that fall within our reach (see Heater 1990: 163–4, 1996; Falk 1994; Van Steenbergen 1994; Christoff 1996).

Arguably, one aspect of what Miller (1999) calls republican citizenship is evident in the idea of global environmental citizenship. This is the sense of personal responsibility for others and the desire to act for the sake of some wider public good.[1] Miller maintains that such similarities are more apparent than real because the civic virtues that typify republican citizenship are combined with respect for all members of the community and with a commitment to finding a compromise between competing views. There are no warranties, Miller adds, that good environmental citizens will subscribe to this ethic. Indeed, some participants in global social movements have ethical commitments that do not leave much scope for compromise with opponents. Miller's point is that the willingness to make personal sacrifices for the sake of the greater collective good is virtually impossible to nurture in the absence of the ties of common nationality.

Miller raises a central question for exponents of cosmopolitan citizenship who use the term to encourage a stronger sense of responsibility for the wider world. This is how to distinguish political conduct that is authentically cosmopolitan from political action that is a vehicle for parochial interests and for culturally biased worldviews. Some account of cosmopolitan virtues which are the counterpart of civic virtues has to be provided, but this may be difficult to achieve because of disputes about what it means to act in a cosmopolitan manner. Disagreements about the rights and wrongs of humanitarian intervention in world politics illustrate the critical point. As the debate over NATO's action against Serbia revealed, there are major disputes between those who believe there is a cosmopolitan duty to breach national sovereignty to protect human rights and those who believe that 'humanitarian war' is the latest example of the West's inclination to impose its will on others (see Chapter 5). In many Third World societies where humanitarian intervention conjures up images of Western imperialism, cosmopolitan citizenship may be regarded as little more than a vehicle for promoting Western interests (Zolo 1997: xiv). Just as various forms of ethical universalism have been criticized for reflecting particular cultural preferences (inevitably, since there is 'no view from nowhere') so have appeals to cosmopolitan citizenship aroused suspicion that Western preferences and prejudices will be forced on to others.

Critics may also argue that, even if some genuinely universal ethic did exist, the concept of cosmopolitan citizenship would be vulnerable to two further objections. The first is that the non-performance of the moral responsibilities and duties associated with world citizenship may lead to personal shame or guilt, but possible beneficiaries have no court of appeal when others decline to help them. They are dependent on charitable actions that it may be virtuous to perform but which potential beneficiaries cannot claim as their right. The second objection, which is central to Walzer's critique, is that appeals to cosmopolitan citizenship merely stress duties to outsiders; there is no reference to traditional associations that stress rights of representation or participation in politics that distinguish subjects from citizens. On such grounds do the critics build their argument that the advocates of cosmopolitan citizenship corrupt the true meaning of citizenship.

Advocates of world citizenship reject this argument. Some such as Dower (2000) champion the concept in order to challenge the assumption that duties to fellow citizens should take precedence over duties to the rest of the human race. Their most important argument does not simply state that individuals should feel a stronger sense of personal responsibility to other peoples or for the environment. The larger point is that across a growing range of issues there are no compelling reasons for preferring the interests of co-nationals to the interests of foreigners.[2] As noted earlier, world citizenship is employed to defend the Stoic conception of belonging to a bounded political association and to the wider moral community of humankind. It is also used to support practical efforts to create stronger transnational moral solidarities and global political institutions that are authorized to protect human interests. Theorists such as Dower (2000: 559, 564) argue that the main difference between those who defend cosmopolitan citizenship and those who claim that it is a pale imitation of national citizenship is that the former are more strongly committed to a 'robust global ethic'. The charge is that critics of cosmopolitan citizenship such as Miller may defend global moral obligations but they do not take the additional step of challenging the traditional belief that the most important political obligations exist between co-nationals. The accusation is that there is a lack of appreciation of the extent to which mounting global problems require fundamental changes of orientation to the social and political world – revised understandings about personal and collective responsibilities for the world at large which the idea of cosmopolitan citizenship can help to bring about.

Debates about cosmopolitan citizenship reveal a clear tension between those who think that citizenship is linked with strong attachments to an existing political community – and with the desire to make personal sacrifices for its welfare – and those who believe that citizenship includes efforts to transform national political communities until their behaviour is powerfully influenced by the Stoic–Christian belief in the unity of humankind. Given their normative commitments, it is unsurprising that proponents of cosmopolitan citizenship have stressed that the linkages between citizenship and the nation-state developed only recently – in the period since the French Revolution. Heater (1990) argues that citizenship was attached to the city before it came to be coupled with the territorial state; it may yet come to be closely linked with European political institutions and, in time, with the world at large.

Miller has been criticized for defining citizenship narrowly and for devaluing the efforts of international non-governmental organizations and global social movements to build a global political community (Dower 2000). A related point is that the critics of world citizenship beg several important questions about political community: that its identity and purposes are clearly settled; that co-nationals do not face moral difficulties about its place in the wider world; and that citizens are satisfied with the rights that the state claims against other societies as well as with its obligations to other peoples and to the natural world (Bankowski and

Christodoulidis 1999). But defenders of cosmopolitan citizenship are invariably dissatisfied with the nation-state and with the lack of support for a robust global ethic. They argue that the criticism that the nation-state is the only community in which effective citizenship can be enjoyed, and the accusation that cosmopolitan citizenship is a departure from citizenship properly so-called, effectively confers legitimacy on imperfect political arrangements and forecloses the discussion of how new forms of community can institutionalize cosmopolitan ideals (Linklater 1999: 36). Critics of cosmopolitan citizenship may respond by arguing that universalistic ethical commitments that are profoundly anti-statist drive such observations about the value of national citizenship. The counter to this argument is that efforts to define citizenship in national terms are no more neutral but are inherently political because they privilege the nation-state and a broadly communitarian ethic. The complaint then is that an unacknowledged or unsupported conservatism underlies the critique of cosmopolitan citizenship (Dower 2000: 560).

The sphere of cosmopolitan rights

Whereas the first conception of world citizenship stresses the need for compassion for non-nationals, personal responsibility for the environment and action to create more cosmopolitan forms of political association, the second begins with the development of a system of universal human rights. It believes that the 'human race can gradually be brought closer and closer to a constitution establishing world citizenship' through the evolution of cosmopolitan law (Kant, quoted in Williams and Booth 1996: 91). The belief that world citizenship is developing in this way can be regarded as a major advance beyond the idea of cosmopolitan moral duty discussed earlier. Critics will argue that there are few mechanisms for enforcing these rights, and they may stress that the second conception of cosmopolitan citizenship still falls short of national citizenship by being divorced from the core notion of political representation and participation. However, its significance might be said to exist elsewhere, namely in challenging the traditional assumption that states are the sole or main subjects of international law. What the second approach to cosmopolitan citizenship claims is that individuals are members of international society and subjects of international law in their own right.

Key developments in the realm of cosmopolitan rights include the Nuremberg Charter, which gives military personnel the right as well as the duty to disobey superior orders to commit crimes against humanity. Additional contributions to the legal constitution establishing the rights of world citizens include the 1948 Convention on the Prevention and Punishment of the Crime of Genocide and the 1984 Convention Against Torture and other Cruel, Inhuman or Degrading Treatment or Punishment. The 1948 Universal Declaration of Human Rights and the 1966 International Covenant on Social and Political Rights can also be regarded as important advances in establishing the rights of world citizens. International law concerning the rights of women and children, and the rights of indigenous peoples and minority nations, also sets out entitlements that all persons possess

as members of a world society. Critics may object that the dominant conceptions of human rights embody the global aspirations of the liberal–democratic
West. They may insist that the universal moral imperatives that are inherent in
these developments lack sensitivity to the cultural preferences of non-Western
societies in an epoch in which there is a growing demand for 'group differentiated
citizenship' – that is for different rights for groups living in the same political
community (Young 1991). These are points to return to later. As for the claim that
there are few instruments for punishing human rights violations, the growth of
international criminal procedures, and the challenge to the principle of sovereign
immunity whereby heads of states are deemed guilty of human rights violations,
lead some observers to conclude that the modern world may be on the threshold
of a new era of 'cosmopolitan law enforcement' (Kaldor 1999: 10–11). Others see
the emerging outline of a new imperialism (Bain 2006).

Although many think that the sphere of cosmopolitan rights simply extends
the dominion of certain liberal–democratic values, others welcome this phase in
the development of commitments to universalistic beliefs on the part of modern
states. As Honneth (1995: 115–18) has argued, the development of universalism
is evident in the institutionalization of the claim that all citizens are entitled to the
same rights and liberties irrespective of their class, race, religion, ethnic identity
or gender. The growth of universalism in the form of pressure on a foundational
principle of the modern state – the principle of moral favouritism, which maintains that measures to promote the interests of fellow citizens are to be preferred
to efforts to promote the welfare of 'outsiders' – has been much slower to develop.
Nonetheless, the growth of world or cosmopolitan law, which differs from classic
international law by being concerned with protecting the rights of individuals
rather than the rights of states, is a small monument to Kant's conviction that
an assault on human dignity in any region should arouse global concern in an
enlightened age (Kant 1970b: 216).

Critics of cosmopolitan citizenship doubt whether these developments represent a major advance in world citizenship. In an argument that is close to Miller's,
Neff (1999) argues that international lawyers often sympathize with the normative
claims of those that expound the merits of cosmopolitan citizenship but is quick to
add that the concept has contributed nothing to international legal thinking. The
outlook of the lawyers 'substantially accords' with the republican conception of
citizenship defended by Miller (ibid.: 106). Interestingly, Miller (1999: 74) argues
that the idea that 'individual people can invoke international law against their own
state does bring us closer to a recognizable ideal of citizenship' beyond the nation-state. He adds that this 'is at most a thin version of liberal citizenship' as the
'citizen is not a lawmaker' in any real sense. Moreover, in the absence of common
national sentiments in world politics, it is advisable to modify national law so that
it does justice to cosmopolitan obligations rather than to create international law
that over-rides the law of the state (Miller 1999: 74–6).

As noted earlier, an equally important point is that international and cosmopolitan law generally lack the enforcement measures that states use in upholding
domestic law. Individuals have basic human rights according to international law,

but the convention has been that national governments are primarily responsible for upholding them. Vulnerable individuals and groups may go outside the state in search of allies in their struggle to ensure respect for human rights, but only a fragment of humanity enjoys the liberty to protest against injustices in international courts of law.

Reflecting on these themes, Neff (1999: 113) has distinguished between two ways in which international law can be used to promote global reform. The first is the 'dualist' approach in which changes are agreed at the international level and then incorporated in domestic law; the second and less common is the 'monist' approach 'in which international legal rules become directly applicable even without state action'. Most international conventions on human rights belong to the former category, and the nation-state remains the '*proximate* source of the rights that . . . individuals have' (ibid.: 115, italics in original). But monism underpins some recent developments in international criminal law. The Nuremberg trials held that it was irrelevant whether war crimes 'were lawful in Germany at the time they were committed. They were unlawful under *international* law, irrespective of their status in German law' (ibid.: 116, italics in original). Monism is also evident in the principles governing the International Tribunal, which is authorized to prosecute persons responsible for serious violations of humanitarian law in the former Yugoslavia.[3] But as Neff (1999: 117) points out, the Statute does not invoke the ideals of cosmopolitan citizenship that are 'otiose' in international legal conventions of this kind.

The important point is that incorporating international obligations in domestic law is not the only way of protecting human rights; also, the role of monism in world politics seems to be growing in response to crimes against humanity and rights violations. It is still the case, however, that monism is strongest in the EU where the principle of *direct effect* obliges national courts to apply Community provisions even though national legislatures have not incorporated them in domestic law, and where the idea of the *supremacy of Community law* holds that EU law prevails when its provisions clash with national legislation (Preuss 1998: 138). Some progress towards a post-national conception of citizenship that rests on notions of individual personhood rather than on any particular cultural identity has occurred through the creation of various social and legal rights in the EU. In Miller's terms, such developments in European international law represent progress in developing a liberal as opposed to a republican conception of citizenship beyond the state. Support for this view is evident in the fact that the rights of European citizens are thin when compared with those of national citizens.[4] Nothing in the Maastricht Treaty, for example, entitles the citizens of the member states of the EU to come together as transnational citizens to elect members of the European Commission or to expel them from office. But as Preuss (ibid.: 139, 149) argues, the decision to uncouple citizenship from the state so that it is possible to be a 'citizen of a supranational entity' is 'a major innovation in the history of political membership', which shows how the ideal of cosmopolitan citizenship may yet come to be embodied more fully in global political practice.

The universalization of particular liberal and democratic rights is no small achievement in an area of the world that was so frequently engulfed in systemic war, and it suggests that one should not be overly pessimistic about the prospects for post-national citizenship elsewhere. Those who are suspicious of efforts to attach citizenship to associations other than the nation-state would be right to emphasize the democratic deficit in the EU and to stress that the development of transnational democracy may well be improbable in the absence of strong attachments to a nation or 'demos'. Even so, notions of cosmopolitan citizenship that emphasize the rights of human beings in a 'universal state of humanity' perform a dual function. They mark some progress in thinking that states have responsibilities to protect the legal rights of all persons, irrespective of nationality or citizenship, and they make significant inroads into the state's claim to be the sole subject of international law. Approaches to cosmopolitan citizenship that defend the sphere of cosmopolitan rights assert that individuals, considered simply as human beings rather than citizens, must possess international legal personality.

The sphere of cosmopolitan democracy

Critics of the two ideas of cosmopolitan citizenship which have been considered thus far argue that they fall short of national citizenship because they are detached from the participatory ideal. However, those who think that cosmopolitan citizenship is to be found in the development of a robust global ethic and in the development of the universal human rights culture rarely leave the discussion there. Many participate in and support international non-governmental organizations (INGOs) such as Amnesty International and Greenpeace in order to promote respect for cosmopolitan principles in a world of states; and in an increasingly prominent trend, many are actively involved in, or supportive of, efforts to democratize global politics. The participation of INGOs in UN conferences and the parallel conferences on the environment and on women, which took place in Rio de Janeiro and Beijing, are important illustrations of the latter trend. Also important are claims for more democratic and accountable international organizations, which were among the demands advanced in Seattle and Prague to coincide with meetings of the World Trade Organization and the International Monetary Fund. Participants in the development of an international civil society frequently use the idea of cosmopolitan citizenship to describe their political involvement in such fora (Boli and Thomas 1999: 39–41, 73–7; Finnemore 1999: 150; Dower 2000: 567).

These emergent trends in world politics resonate with many of the themes that are central to the cosmopolitan turn in democratic political theory (Held 1995; Archibugi et al. 1998). Three arguments in favour of cosmopolitan democracy have been advanced by the proponents. The first is that '. . . the idea of popular sovereignty is doomed to decay into a mere chimera if it remains locked in the historical form of the self-asserting sovereign nation-state' (Habermas 1994: 165). The importance of national democracy, it is argued, has been diminished by globalization, which places national societies at the mercy of external social and economic forces that citizens are often powerless to control. The democratic ideal must be extended into the sphere of world politics if the principles that have been secured through the achievement of national citizenship (transparency, accountability, representation, participation, and so forth) are to survive.

A second argument in favour of cosmopolitan democracy is that various instruments of global governance have emerged to regulate the expanding networks of transnational social and economic interaction. As already noted, several international organizations that have appeared in response to the most recent phase of global interdependence have a democratic deficit because decisions do not require popular assent. Opposition to the system of global governance will intensify if Falk (1998: 320) is right that global organizations such as the UN will be the site for a major struggle between two sets of political actors: transnational business enterprises and multinational banks committed to a neo-liberal global economic agenda and INGOs which seek to highlight the misery of the global poor and the increasing risks associated with environmental degradation. The question is how to bring global economic and political institutions into line with democratic principles of legitimacy.

A third argument for cosmopolitan democracy takes issue with the doctrine of moral favouritism, which maintains that national institutions should be responsible to citizens and do not have the same duty to be accountable to 'outsiders'. This model of democracy arose because it was assumed that citizens had the right to be represented in national political institutions which made decisions that affected them. Citizens could not expect to be represented in the political institutions of other political communities – nor did they believe that they had a duty to grant outsiders representation in their national institutions even if decisions regarding security or trade had ruinous consequences for them (Held 1995: 18). For most of the last two centuries, the power of nationalist ideology in societies that lived with the expectation of violent war ruled out experiments in cosmopolitan democracy and, in any case, the impact of global interdependence on the populations of modern industrial states was much less than it is today.[5] Arguably, the tension between 'man' and 'citizen' should have been of greater concern to the inhabitants of modern states well before the most recent phase of globalization (Linklater 1990a). However, the awareness of increasing vulnerability to global forces, and the consciousness of how decisions in one country can affect the peoples elsewhere, have intensified the challenge to the doctrine of moral favouritism. Reflecting these trends, the third argument for cosmopolitan democracy is that individuals have a moral right to be consulted about any decisions that may affect or harm them wherever these decisions happen to be made. The argument is that all human beings should have this right irrespective of their citizenship or nationality which, for the purposes of this argument, have no more moral importance than distinctions of class, gender, ethnicity, religion, sexuality and age.[6]

The cosmopolitan turn in democratic political theory can be regarded as a radical extension of Kant's theory of world citizenship, which revolved around the more modest idea of duties of hospitality to strangers. One might regard it as a necessary extension of his claim that the 'touchstone' for deciding whether or not something is true is the possibility of 'testing [upon] the understanding of others whether those grounds of the judgment which are valid for us have the same effect on the reason of others' (quoted in McCarthy 1997: 211). However, as noted, Kant did not believe that questions about whether any political action would meet with the consent of all others should be tested in democratic public spheres (Archibugi 1995). He thought that enlightened philosophers would form a cosmopolitan citizenry that would protest whenever and wherever human rights were violated (Habermas 1997: 124). Kant assumed that world citizens would reach beyond states to mobilize world public opinion against human rights violations, but the states in question would not forego the sovereign entitlement to freedom from external interference. The political theory of cosmopolitan democracy concurs with the view that 'Kant's concept of a permanent federation of nations that respects the sovereignty of each is . . . inconsistent. The rights of the world citizen must be institutionalized in such a way that it actually binds individual governments' (Habermas 1997: 127–8). Developments in international criminal law are evidence of movement in this direction. But critics of cosmopolitan citizenship and defenders of transnational democracy agree that 'the rights of the world citizen' are incomplete unless they include rights of representation or participation in global institutions (see Held 1995; Archibugi et al. 1998).

Those who define themselves as world citizens can always raise matters of global concern within their respective national democratic systems although this is not what the concept of cosmopolitan citizenship is usually thought to involve (Bohman 1997: 191). This status involves the capacity to associate with others in a worldwide public sphere that makes decisions for the globe as a whole; it requires 'political representation for citizens in global affairs, independently . . . of their political representation in domestic affairs' (Archibugi 1998: 211). Proponents of cosmopolitan democracy have advanced various suggestions about how institutional innovations can promote the global extension of the democratic ideal. They include direct elections to the United Nations General Assembly and the vision of a second UN Chamber which represents individuals and INGOs directly, two developments that can complement an International Criminal Court with compulsory jurisdiction over violators of humanitarian law (Habermas 1997: 134–5; Archibugi 1998: 221; Falk 1998: 319).

Such institutional innovations are ways of exploring the ground that lies between national democracies and a democratic world government; they are not a prelude to a universal state in which all human beings may come to have citizenship rights of the kind currently enjoyed in separate states. Instead, these organizational innovations would seek to extend the democratic project beyond national frontiers by democratizing existing instruments of global governance. It might also be argued that cosmopolitan citizenship is to be found in individual and collective efforts to promote the democratization of world politics. The struggle to create a worldwide public sphere can be regarded as a crucial way in which cosmopolitan citizenship can exist without a world state.

There is no reason to dispute the claim that, even if the opportunities existed, the level of participation in global political institutions would fall short of that found within democratic nation-states. It is clearly true that there is no sense of international community to rival the sense of national belonging. But, as Dower (2000: 557) argues, the aspirations of cosmopolitan citizens do not stand or fall on the extent to which all the attributes of national citizenship can be transferred to global institutions. The main task is to extend elements of national citizenship (the sense of responsibility for others and the protection of individual rights, including the right of voice or representation in a public sphere) to the global arena so that monopolies of economic and political power are accountable to those who are affected by them. As noted earlier, attempts by INGOs to build a worldwide public sphere by participating, albeit sporadically, in global events running parallel to recent UN conferences advance the claim that global institutions should comply with principles of democratic legitimacy – and the same principle was advanced by many of the protestors in Seattle and Prague. There is every reason to suppose that pressures to democratize world politics will continue to grow and that the extent to which they succeed will depend on whether democratic states use their influence to create more possibilities for participating in an effective worldwide public sphere. The creation of the relevant political institutions structures will take decades, if not centuries, if it happens at all. Even so, one of the strongest arguments in favour of cosmopolitan citizenship is that it begins to equip human beings, who still think nationally for the most part, with the moral and political resources with which to adapt to the increasing challenge of how to control global processes in ways that respect the economic, cultural and political rights of every member of the human race.

Arguably, the most important question about cosmopolitan democracy is whether any progress in democratizing world politics would significantly alter the global distribution of power and wealth, and not whether anything like national citizenship can be replicated at the international level. Critics of the universal human rights culture have argued that this development simply reflects the West's ability to universalize values that do not command the respect of all non-Western peoples. Some protest that efforts to promote respect for individual legal and political entitlements have not been accompanied by attempts to protect social and economic rights or to safeguard the global environment. Support for these views can be found in references to the 'new constitutionalism', which maintains that many central developments in recent international law are largely concerned with creating new opportunities for the expansion of global capitalism and for promoting the interests of highly mobile transnational elites (Gill 1995). The upshot of these remarks for the advocates of cosmopolitan democracy is that the existing sphere of cosmopolitan rights is heavily loaded in favour of Western interests and that efforts to democratize world politics may simply consolidate Western hegemony. This is a crucial point as only the most affluent members of world society could seize any increased opportunities to be represented or to participate in global politics – and these they might exploit to advance sectional interests.

If there is a counterweight to this danger it is to be found in a cosmopolitan ethic which argues that the instruments of global governance should rest on the consent of all peoples, and particularly on the consent of the weakest and most vulnerable members of world society. According to this ideal, global governance is to be judged by the extent to which the vulnerable have the opportunity to protest against the harm that others do to them, to register their views when others benefit unfairly from their weakness and to seek external assistance in reducing avoidable suffering. It is also to be assessed by the extent to which global institutions – whether democratic or not – respond sympathetically to demands for the public recognition of cultural differences. The fact that the vulnerable do not have access to global political institutions where they can make these claims is the main reason why advocates of cosmopolitan citizenship attach so much importance to the sphere of cosmopolitan duty. As previously noted, the development of more democratic forms of world politics would not reduce the importance of this sphere. However remote its institutionalization may be, the fact that reflections on this cosmopolitan ethic have come to the centre of analyses of global politics is a minor revolution in thinking about world affairs (Apel 1979, 1980; Goodin 1985; O'Neill 1991: 301–2; Habermas 1996: 514).

Conclusion

This chapter has discussed two broad approaches to cosmopolitan citizenship. The first maintains that citizenship properly understood exists only within nation-states. This is the only form of political association in which the core ideas of citizenship – the willingness to make personal sacrifices for the sake of the wider societal good and to participate in political life – have been realized. There is no emerging counterpart in world politics. Appeals to world citizenship that urge individuals to take global moral responsibilities seriously may be persuasive but they empty citizenship of its essential meaning. The argument is that citizenship refers to moral dispositions and political practices that exist only within actual national communities.

Advocates of cosmopolitan citizenship maintain that citizenship can also refer to dispositions and practices that can be harnessed to transform political communities and the global order so that they conform with universalistic moral commitments. One of its main roles is to persuade national citizens that they have fundamental moral responsibilities to outsiders that must not be sacrificed in the pursuit of national interests. The universal human rights culture is deemed to reveal the emerging law of world citizens; cosmopolitan citizenship is thought to be exemplified by the increasing global role of INGOs and by efforts to promote the democratization of world politics.

The tension between these views indicates that cosmopolitan citizenship is as 'essentially contested' as all other concepts. Critics insist that cosmopolitan citizenship is impossible in the absence of a world state that grants citizens rights of representation and participation in politics. Supporters maintain that the critics have too restricted a definition of citizenship. Cosmopolitan citizenship is necessary to institutionalize serious moral commitments to outsiders, and it is desirable given the rise of instruments of global governance that do not rest on popular consent.

There is no neutral way of resolving disputes between these competing perspectives; however, shifts in the nature of world politics, including growing expectations that global economic and political institutions should comply with democratic principles of legitimacy, offer some support to those who make the case for cosmopolitan citizenship. The critics of cosmopolitan citizenship are unlikely to be persuaded that they are wrong to support a restricted conception of citizenship that is only realizable within viable democratic nation-states. But as the ties between the citizen and the state loosen, it would be unwise to assume that efforts to extend the achievements of national citizenship into the global political arena are forever bound to be frustrated. It would also be foolish to discount the possibility that humanity in future may use the idea of cosmopolitan citizenship to design international institutions that are responsible for ensuring that global processes do not spiral out of control but answer to shared demands for higher levels of autonomy and accountability.

Part III

The problem of harm

8 Citizenship, humanity and cosmopolitan harm conventions

Social contract theorists in the seventeenth and eighteenth centuries maintained that the establishment of sovereign communities abolished the dangers inherent in the original state of nature. Rebutting this contention, and anticipating Kant's contention that Grotius, Pufendorf and Vattel were 'miserable comforters', Rousseau argued that higher levels of violence and human misery resulted from the transition to civil society: with the appearance of war between states, more died in a single day's fighting than in whole centuries in the state of nature. By becoming citizens of separate states, individuals became enemies of the rest of humankind (Rousseau 1970: 132).

Having contended that new levels of harm appeared as a consequence of state formation, Rousseau proceeded to ask whether a solution to the problem of harm was possible. His realist conclusion was that there was no obvious remedy (Rousseau 1970: 206). Enlightenment cosmopolitans such as Kant believed that human beings could reduce harm over centuries of progress in which they came to see themselves as dual citizens: as members of their respective states and participants in a wider community of humankind.

Other cosmopolitan approaches have argued that world government is the only solution to the problem of harm. Between the polar extremes of realism and cosmopolitanism are the neo-liberal and neo-Grotian positions which observe that most states respect international moral and legal conventions that constrain the use of force. The debate between these approaches is in large part an argument about how far cosmopolitan harm conventions (CHCs) can be developed in the world of states. It is a dispute about whether citizens of separate states are bound to be indifferent to one another's interests, if not enemies of one another, and about whether and how far they can progress together in establishing robust cosmopolitan conventions that protect individuals everywhere from cross-border or transnational harm.

Realists and their critics reach different conclusions about the prospects for such conventions in world politics, but they also understand harm in different ways and disagree about the forms that deserve most attention. For present purposes, harm is defined as in the 1978 *Oxford English Dictionary*: harm is 'evil (physical or otherwise) as done to or suffered by some person or thing: hurt, injury, damage, mischief'. Its effects include 'grief, sorrow, pain, trouble, distress, affliction'. The main forms of harm discussed in this chapter are those that affect individuals and also non-sovereign political associations such as minority nations and indigenous peoples.

Many moral philosophers have argued that the duty not to harm others is the bedrock of ethics on which relations of beneficence can in time be built (Ross 1930: 22). Some have maintained that the duty to avoid harm – otherwise known as the harm principle – is too undemanding of moral subjects. Their contention is that it is 'desirable that [human beings] should not merely abstain from doing harm to their neighbours, but should render active service' to them. However, the author of this remark, Lord Macaulay (1880: 255–6), immediately added that 'in general, the penal law must content itself with keeping men from doing positive harm, and they must leave to public opinion, and to the teachers of morals and religion the office of furnishing men with motives for doing good.' Even so, appeals to the ethic of the Good Samaritan, an ethic that goes well beyond the narrower ethic of avoiding harm, frequently arise in world politics, especially in connection with humanitarian emergencies. On this argument, states should act positively to promote the welfare of human beings elsewhere, and citizen soldiers should be prepared to die for desperate strangers who are victims of genocide and ethnic cleansing (Kaldor 1999). The implication is that states can cause harm by acts of omission as well as acts of commission (for further discussion, see Linklater 2006a).

In response, critics of humanitarian war have argued that intervention may cause more harm than good, especially when the intervening states are major powers with an established history of selective intervention to punish non-compliant regimes. In his critique of NATO's action against Serbia, Chomsky (1999a) defended the Hippocratic injunction *primum non nocere* – above all, do no harm – and there is a long tradition of political theory about intervention which maintains that in the long term more harm than good will come from violating national sovereignty (Wheeler 1997). Perhaps the principle 'above all, do no harm' should be regarded as the most fundamental and least demanding way in which the citizens of one state can respect duties to humanity in the face of clashing conceptions of the good (Barry 1998: 233). Perhaps it should be regarded as a realizable moral aspiration in a world in which the dominant political obligations bind citizens to the state, in which war has been a recurrent phenomenon, but in which there is a growing body of opinion that societies should take responsibility for the injuries they cause each other. The nagging question remains of whether the failure to respond to human suffering elsewhere constitutes harm in its own right and whether 'the prevention of harm', like efforts to promote the welfare of human beings elsewhere, 'is a sink that can drain virtually all of our resources' (Arneson 1998: 85).

There is no easy way of resolving these normative disputes, which also raise interesting questions for the sociology of international relations. Relations between separate communities are one sphere in which 'the production of social distance' means that moral agents have been less concerned with limiting harm to outsiders than with protecting 'proximate' co-nationals from unnecessary suffering (Bauman 1989: 192ff.). A sociology of CHCs can begin with that premise, noting how separate political communities that lack a strong commitment to act altruistically have nevertheless created CHCs that restrict the harms they do to their respective populations. Such a sociology can analyse the development of harm conventions in the modern society of states as well as in earlier forms of world political organization; it can examine the ethical questions about harm that have arisen in these different international systems; and it might also question whether the modern society of states has progressed beyond earlier systems (or seems capable of advancing beyond them) by creating CHCs that seek to prevent injury and suffering to all peoples.

The central aim of this chapter is to develop some of the foundations for a long-term project on the sociology of CHCs. After commenting further on the idea of CHCs, it considers the relevance of the English School of International Relations – or 'international society approach' – for this project. The main argument of this second section is that it is helpful to develop the sociology of harm conventions that is implicit in the writings of the English School and especially important to build on its apparent belief that the modern society of states may be witnessing some progress in making transnational harm an ethical problem for the world political system as a whole. Next, this chapter argues that one function of a sociology of CHCs is to analyse the nature and potentiality of modernity organized as a system of states. A central task is to identify different types of harm in world politics and to consider whether the dominant forms are undergoing radical change in modern politics because of the most recent phase of globalization. These are crucial matters for an inquiry into whether the modern international system is not only different from, but has also progressed beyond, earlier forms of world political organization in developing global conventions that have the function of reducing or eradicating cross-border harm.

Cosmopolitan harm conventions

All societies have harm conventions that define what is permissible in relations with other human beings, what is obligatory and what is officially proscribed; all societies have conventions that define harm and identify the most serious forms of injury that can befall members of the community. Harm conventions are an essential part of the social regulation of human behaviour within bounded communities, and they are no less necessary for regulating relations between them. In addition, all societies have developed harm conventions that stipulate what human beings can and cannot do to non-human species and how they should behave towards the physical world.

All societies have harm conventions but they do not all have CHCs or support them to the same degree. The dominant harm conventions in Nazi Germany legitimated terrible acts of violence to 'insiders' and 'outsiders' alike. Over several centuries, European colonial powers claimed the right to deprive indigenous peoples of their land. Bearing these examples in mind, it is not hard to imagine an international system in which there are no CHCs whatsoever and in which the citizens of each state are literally enemies of the rest of the human race, but this has not been the historical norm. Most forms of world political organization have developed at least some CHCs, and few (if any) societies have endorsed the principle that their members can do exactly what they like in relations with the rest of the world. There are many reasons for this condition including a mutual interest in regulating force and the fear that long-term damage to internal order may occur if members are allowed to treat the enemy just as they please in war.

What makes a harm convention cosmopolitan is the fact that it does not privilege the interests of insiders over outsiders. Its spirit is captured in a statement made in 1919 by Eglantyne Jebb, the founder of Save the Children, that there is no such thing as an enemy child (Chabbot 1999: 231). A related sentiment is evident in the moral conviction that non-combatants should be spared unnecessary injury in war because they themselves do no harm, that prisoners of war are entitled to lead as decent a life as possible during their confinement, and that the captured have obligations too as they must not treat their captors as enemies even though they cannot embrace them as friends (Walzer 1970). In these cases, cosmopolitanism does not mean the absence of national attachments or suggest that loyalty to the whole of humankind should come before duties to particular communities. All it requires is friendship towards the rest of the human race, support for the Kantian idea of respect for persons or some equivalent notion of the equality of all human beings, and the conviction that harm conventions should exist which are, in the words of the *Oxford English Dictionary*, cosmopolitan in the sense of not being 'restricted to any one country or its inhabitants'.

CHCs are anchored in the belief then that the differences between insiders and outsiders are not always relevant reasons for treating them in a different manner. To be bound by these conventions is to accept that insiders are not morally entitled to promote their security and welfare by imposing insecurity on, and instilling fear in, others; it is to recognize that the former do not have the right to act in ways that are widely regarded as reprehensible within their own group. The existence of CHCs means that group members believe that the boundaries of their moral community are not identical with, but extend well beyond, the frontiers of their political associations. Inevitably, obligations to these different constituencies clash periodically, and all societies with a commitment to CHCs have to make decisions about the relative importance of different obligations. How they have dealt with such moral conflicts in different international systems is an additional subject for the sociology of CHCs.

A related issue is that societies display different levels of ethical reflectiveness about the ultimate foundations of duties to insiders and outsiders. What L.T. Hobhouse (1906) called 'the rationalization of the moral code' has been pronounced in Western societies in which professional philosophers have debated the foundations of ethics, considered the reasons for and against regarding obligations to co-nationals as special, and reflected on the matter of how to resolve conflicts between duties to the state and obligations to other peoples. This is not the place to consider the ways in which they have dealt with these questions. Suffice it to note that many international systems have developed cosmopolitan perspectives which state that separate communities are governed by moral principles that should over-ride the obligations that bind citizens together. By agreeing to the humanitarian law of war, for example, modern political communities agree that there are times when cosmopolitan duties are superior to duties to co-nationals and can trump superior military orders.

Important debates have arisen between 'communitarians' who believe that society is the source of moral sentiments and understandings, and 'cosmopolitans' who believe that human reason can understand ethical principles that should apply everywhere. One argument against cosmopolitans is that they claim to enjoy an Archimedean perspective whereas the reality is that no universalistic morality can conceal its cultural origins and resultant biases (Meinecke 1970). A frequent contention is that cosmopolitan principles can be used to oppress culturally different peoples in the name of allegedly universal truths. In short, cosmopolitanism may be a source of, rather than a cure for, transnational harm.

Philosophical disputes of this kind provide interesting material for the sociologist of CHCs; however, debates about whether or not there is an Archimedean perspective, or 'a view from nowhere' (Nagel 1986), should not obscure the simple sociological fact that for many societies a shared capacity for pain and suffering, and a general recognition of common human frailty, is as important as the cultural and other differences between them (Rorty 1989; Turner 1993). The desire not to be cruel, the sense of obligation to those who are vulnerable to our actions (whether or not they stand in any special relationship with us as family, friends or co-nationals) and compassion for the victims of suffering, however caused, have long provided the main impetus for developing CHCs (Goodin 1985).

A desire to avoid cruelty to others is fundamental, but no less important is whether societies are prepared to enter into dialogue with past or potential victims, whether they are willing to compensate them for injuries that have been committed, and whether they are prepared to consult them about decisions that may cause future suffering. Of course, societies do not always need to engage in dialogue with outsiders to discover whether or not they have harmed them. The torturer, who specializes in causing harm, need not consult the victim to discover if certain actions are painful. But it is not always so easy to understand how our actions harm others.

Relations between colonial and aboriginal Australia illustrate the point. Government departments and missionary groups often moved indigenous peoples from their land from good intentions. Missionaries thought they were saving endangered souls, protecting the 'natives' from encroaching settlers with murderous intent and ensuring adequate food supplies in times of severe hardship and drought. They did not *always* know that removal from the land that was thought to have been created by ancestral beings, and for which there was a sacred duty of care, would have disastrous consequences for the peoples involved (Stevens 1994; Rowse 1998). In this particular case, the pain and suffering that resulted from their actions could not have been foreseen without forms of dialogue that could have yielded crucial insights into the world of the other (Shapcott 1994).

CHCs are necessary when societies come into contact with each other and cannot always predict how their behaviour will cause harm (Hanke 1955). Relations between colonial and aboriginal Australia are a reminder that globalization or the greater interconnectedness of the human species creates new opportunities for transnational harm, but this has rarely led to the establishment of legal and political frameworks that give the vulnerable the right to protest against the harms inflicted on them. The lengthening chains of cause and effect that result from globalization have at times produced changes in the moral imagination which meant that the strong became troubled by how their actions could injure others (Tronto 1993). But mere sympathy for other human beings is insufficient: it is necessary to create what has been called 'speech communities' or 'universal communication communities' in which the members of other communities can exercise the right to protest against harm (Habermas 1990; O'Neill 1991: 301–2; Lyotard 1993). Recent studies of cosmopolitan democracy that defend the creation of transnational democratic institutions in the context of globalization address this important theme, as does the analysis of 'cosmopolitan conversations', which regards justice between radically different peoples as a major ethical ideal (Shapcott 1994; Held 1995).

A sociologist of CHCs may seek to analyse harm conventions in international history without passing moral judgement on them, but some earlier comments may be thought to reveal a commitment to a project with an emancipatory interest. Two moral claims underpin the sociological project outlined here. The first is that societies troubled by the harm they do to others are preferable to societies that insist there are morally relevant distinctions between the self and the other that entitle insiders to do what they want. The second is that societies that support communication communities designed to make the powerful more aware of the harms they cause, and that give vulnerable populations the possibility of resistance to injury, are preferable to societies that merely feel pity for others and a duty to behave charitably towards them. In the former case, citizens can be described as cosmopolitan citizens who believe that CHCs should be agreed upon in democratic frameworks of accountability and responsibility or who are politically committed to making progress in this direction (see Chapter 7). Critics may argue that those moral claims already privilege one of the standpoints of modernity and assume some test of moral progress that most non-Western societies are predetermined to fail. Perhaps a sociology of CHCs should abandon this remnant of the nineteenth century philosophy of history; but perhaps the legacy of that approach, freed from its commitment to historical teleology and Western self-congratulation, should be fundamental to the project outlined here. These are matters for future investigation (see, however, Linklater 1998 and Chapter 11).

The English School: civility in international relations

Members of the English School have analysed what they regard as the unusually high level of order and civility that exists in the anarchic system of states. They have highlighted the existence of international legal and moral conventions that limit harm between states and reveal that separate political communities belong to a peculiar 'anarchical society' (Bull 1977). All societies of states possess harm conventions that regulate the use of force, defend the principle of territorial sovereignty and insist that agreements should be kept (Bull 1977). For this reason, members of the English School maintain that international societies, whether ancient or modern, reveal that there is more progress in international relations than the realist suggests but less than the cosmopolitan desires. Wight (1991) positioned 'rationalism' between realism and revolutionism or cosmopolitanism on the grounds that it alone recognized that separate societies are neither in a permanent state of war nor embarked on an irreversible journey towards perpetual peace. Bull made a related point when he noted that states have been able to reach agreements about how to maintain order among themselves but that there have been major disagreements about which principles of justice should apply across the international system as a whole. As a variant on this theme, it might be argued that members of the English School maintain that states find it easier to agree on the harms that should be avoided than on some universalizable conception of the good life that they should cooperate to realize. Many of the practices of international society that the English School have analysed – the idea of sovereignty and the principle of non-intervention, the contrived balance of power, permanent ambassadors and international law – can be seen in this light. These are the means by which states regulate levels of harm in their relations and build elementary forms of cooperation, as opposed to collaborating to realize some universalizable conception of the ends of life.

States belong to a universal communication community of sorts from which other political actors have been excluded, most obviously in the eighteenth and nineteenth centuries when states claimed they were the sole subjects of international law, but this has changed as INGOs have multiplied and grown in strength (Vincent 1990). As international society evolved in the twentieth century, states became more willing to monitor the progress of human rights within what had previously been regarded as the inviolable sovereign domain. Measures to prohibit apartheid, genocide and torture are key examples of collaborative efforts to reduce harm to individuals and non-sovereign communities in the modern society of states. These developments are worthy of support if, as Bull (1977) suggested, international order should be judged by its capacity to promote a world order that protects the basic goals of individuals.

Important contributions to the English School in the 1970s and 1980s observed that some progress had taken place in the area of human rights and that further advances – to prevent starvation, for example – were perfectly feasible (Bull and Watson 1984; Vincent 1986). Many members of the English School doubted that the modern society of states could make more radical progress in reducing levels of harm in international relations. Of course, Wight, Bull and Vincent did not live to witness the collapse of the bipolar era, and we can only speculate about what they would have made of some recent developments that give encouragement to those with more cosmopolitan inclinations. (Their renowned scepticism makes their probable response to the conduct of the 'war against terror' – on which more below – rather more predictable.) The main developments include the pacification of relations between core industrial or post-industrial states because of the dissemination of liberal–democratic values and the new phase of economic globalization; the greater prominence of NGOs in international decision-making and more vociferous demands for the democratization of international institutions; gains for minority nations and indigenous populations which raise hopes that international society may once again become a society of states and peoples; increasing pressure on the principle of sovereignty and the doctrine of sovereign immunity; and the establishment of new international criminal procedures that promise justice for the victims of human rights abuse.

Bull also suggested that important questions must be asked about who supports cosmopolitanism in international relations and whose interests stand to benefit most. One of Bull's remarks about the transition from a European to a universal society of states encapsulates this basic point. Having argued that an international order encompassing new states and their former imperial overlords has been partly constructed, he stressed that the emergent 'nascent cosmopolitan culture' supports 'the dominant cultures of the West' (Bull 1977: 317). It remains the case that many of the global developments mentioned in the previous paragraph have occurred in an era of unusual Western economic and political dominance, and that many in the West and elsewhere believe they reflect its particular material interests and moral values. From that vantage point, there is reason to doubt that a new age of genuinely cosmopolitan as opposed to merely global harm conventions that satisfy dominant interests is appearing.[1] This is to suggest that global harm conventions are being established by the core power or powers, that these conventions frequently disregard the moral preferences of non-Western cultures, and that they place few restrictions on the West's liberty to pursue economic goals and interests that are harmful to large numbers of the world's population as well as to the physical environment.

The general mode of inquiry favoured by the English School focuses on the realm of culture, community and communication in international relations. It provides an alternative to the dominant and more 'structuralist' versions of historical sociology that have been concerned with how the interaction between state building, industrialization, geopolitics and war has shaped human societies (Skocpol 1979; Giddens 1985; Mann 1986; Tilly 1992).

But like Mann in particular, some exponents of the approach consider the role of moral and cultural factors in different international systems, and not only in the one that currently dominates. On the subject of international relations in the Ancient World, for example, Wight (1977: 104) commented on one of the earliest unequal treaties in which a society claimed the right of humanitarian intervention, namely the alleged peace treaty prohibiting human sacrifice that the Greeks imposed on Carthage in 480 BC. While this may be evidence of an early cosmopolitan harm convention – albeit one that was established unilaterally – Rome's later destruction of Carthage demonstrated the total absence of inhibitions against injuring others in at least some phases of classical antiquity (Wight 1977: 105).

For the reasons already given, Wight's sociology of states-systems was princi-pally concerned with order between states. Bull's claim that international orders are to be judged by the extent to which they contribute to world order can be the starting point for a rather different sociological focus, one that analyses the ways in which moral and political communities have been constructed in different international systems and the extent to which political actors have been prepared to protect all human beings from avoidable harm. For this method of analysis, the important questions to ask about past international systems are whether the prevalent assumptions about political community and universal obligations meant that systematic harm to outsiders was an established way of life, whether there were agreements that at least negative duties to minimize distress and suffering to outsiders existed, or whether independent political communities agreed that, separately and collectively, they had positive duties to end transnational harm. By building on English School theory in this way, it is possible to answer one of the criticisms that have been directed against the exponents of critical approaches to international relations, namely the exaggerated contention that they have focused on epistemological and ontological concerns at the expense of concrete sociologi-cal inquiry (Price and Reus-Smit 1998).

Modernity: its nature and potential

Sociological analyses of modernity usually concentrate on the nature of an epoch or condition that is constantly undergoing change because of the impact of science and technology, capitalist industrialization and the prevalence of technical–instru-mental rationality. What the study of international relations adds to this inquiry is a particular focus on modernity as one of the few eras in world history that has been organized as an international system of states. Drawing on the previous sec-tion, the approach invites comparisons between the modern form of world politi-cal organization and preceding global arrangements. One task is to highlight the respects in which modernity differs from past epochs; another is to raise the ques-tion of whether, or how far, it is valid to suggest that the international relations of modernity have progressed beyond earlier states-systems.

Members of the English School argue that one of the main revolutions in recent decades is the expansion of international society from Europe to the rest of the world. Assumptions about Europe's right to conquer and colonize other peoples have been delegitimized; the territorial state has been exported to all regions in compliance with the democratic principle that all peoples have the right to govern themselves rather than suffer alien rule; and progress has occurred in dismantling belief systems that defended harm to the racially or culturally different (in the form of slavery and the slave trade, ethnocide and apartheid). The sociology of CHCs needs to consider whether modernity has made important progress in challenging one of the most prevalent rationales for harm in human history: namely that the differences between insiders and outsiders are so compelling (whether because of the threat the latter pose, because of their perceived inferiority, or whatever) that violent actions that are usually outlawed in relations between members of the same group are judged permissible and even highly prized in dealings with outsiders.

As already noted, the expansion of international society indicates that some progress has occurred in dealing with what I shall call concrete harm: the harm that particular human agents intentionally inflict on specific others who are placed outside the formers' moral community because of religious, racial or other supposedly morally decisive characteristics. Natural hierarchies of the kind endorsed by religious and quasi-scientific accounts of white supremacy have been discredited, as have – but to a lesser extent – teleological or developmental histories that draw sharp distinctions between the 'primitive' world and the 'enlightened' West. Several international legal conventions have outlawed harm anchored in hierarchical representations of human differences. Article II of the 1973 International Convention on the Suppression and Punishment of the Crime of Apartheid prohibits efforts to maintain racial domination by inflicting 'on the members of a racial group or groups . . . serious bodily or mental harm by the infringement of their freedom or dignity, or by subjecting them to torture or to cruel, inhuman or degrading treatment or punishment' (Evans 1994: 218). Other articles that prohibit 'serious bodily or mental harm' to 'national, ethnical, racial or religious groups' can be found in the 1948 Convention on the Prevention and Punishment of the Crime of Genocide and in the 1993 Statute that established the tribunal authorized to prosecute persons responsible for violating international humanitarian law in the former Yugoslavia (Evans 1994: 37, 393).[2] These conventions are evidence of important progress in weaving CHCs into the fabric of international law.

Whether these examples of progress in addressing concrete harm support the proposition that modernity has advanced beyond previous forms of world political organization is a moot point. It has been argued that the Ancient World attached less importance to racial differences than modern Europe has since the Renaissance (Snowden 1983). It may be that progress in tackling harm that has been justified in terms of morally relevant racial differences does not support sweeping judgements about the progressive nature of modernity. All it may reveal is some progress *within* the modern states-system – some movement beyond an earlier phase that tolerated cruelties which are unacceptable today. Broader historical comparisons are complex, and some would advise that they should be avoided entirely. But it is hard to ignore them when, for example, Finer (1997) argues that modern peoples would be appalled by the forms of cruelty prevalent in the Roman empire, and when historians of Ancient Greece, such as Blundell (1989: 52), maintain that few writers in the Ancient World 'ever denied (and no Greek would have done so) that in warfare one has an obligation to inflict maximum damage on the enemy while producing maximum advantage for one's own side'.

Perhaps the claim that modernity has made significant advances in institutionalizing robust CHCs should be taken seriously; perhaps several developments in the post-bipolar age (the obsolescence of force in the core areas of the world-system as post-national elites have become increasingly wedded to the project of economic globalization; the strengthening of international civil society and the proliferation of social movements committed to transnational democracy; the growing realization that the legitimate claims of minority nations and indigenous populations ought to be respected; and measures to enforce international humanitarian law) suggest that modern international society may have an unusual capacity to promote cosmopolitan initiatives to eradicate concrete harm. Arguably, encouragement for this view can be derived from the growing prominence of decentred worldviews that encourage each person to 'think from the standpoint of everyone else' (Bohman 1997), and from a range of ethical perspectives that argue for universalizing communication communities and for the radical democratization of modern political life. Arguably, there has been some growth of cosmopolitan moral consciousness in the form of ethical doctrines which insist that, ideally, global arrangements should have the consent of everyone who may be affected, or who is in danger of being harmed, by them (Linklater 1998). An intriguing question for the sociologist of harm conventions is whether the modern international system has the potential to accomplish more than all previous international systems in this particular domain.

Viewed from a different angle, the achievements of modernity are much less impressive than those comments suggest. Concrete harm between particular 'constitutionally secure liberal democracies' may have declined dramatically (see Doyle 1983, who adds that checks on the liberals' use of force against illiberal regimes are weak by comparison), but violence between ethnic groups within states – or violence directed at oppositional movements – has increased massively over recent decades, first in the form of totalitarian rule and, second, as a result of the collapse of multiethnic states in Africa and Asia and, more recently, in Europe itself. Some argue that it is vital to make a distinction between the 'modern' and 'pre-modern' regions of the international system, adding that many societies that belong to the second category are still mired in tribalism while much of the rest of the world has made advances in eradicating national or ethnic hatred and distrust (see Goldgeier and McFaul 1992; Sadowski 1998). Of course, the notion that modernity has overcome the forces that cause systematic violence cannot be sustained, given the twentieth century experience of totalitarianism (Bauman 1989). But even if it were plausible to think of modernity in this way, immense problems immediately follow. Western societies have been content to avert their eyes as genocide occurred elsewhere, as in Rwanda. Cicero's comment that no one should harm another (quoted in Nussbaum 1997: 31) is a reminder that the harm principle has a long history in Western political thought but that its application remains highly selective in world affairs. Rousseau's complaint about the tension between 'the boundless humanity of our maxims and the boundless cruelty of our deeds', and his question about how 'to reconcile these glaring contradictions', are worth recalling at this point (Rousseau 1970: 135–6). Significantly, as noted earlier, progress in reducing concrete harm has occurred in an era in which industrial societies are considerably freer to pursue economic objectives that harm vulnerable peoples and cause serious damage to the physical environment. But even this progress, the realist might add, is crucially dependent on the absence of actual or perceived security threats, which frequently lead states to ignore the conventions that seek to constrain violence.

In this context, it is essential to consider Foucault's contention that history is not an upward journey towards universal freedom and reciprocity but a cyclical process in which societies move from one form of domination to another (Rabinow 1986). His point was that public spectacles of human cruelty have disappeared from 'more advanced' societies but modern forms of power operate in more sinister ways – through the institutions of the prison, the clinic and the asylum, through new forms of public surveillance and through self-monitoring processes. Drawing on such themes, one might ask if the modern society of states has made progress in eliminating concrete harm, whether the achievements of Western Europe or the liberal zone of peace will eventually be repeated across the world, and/or whether the more powerful trend is towards more diffuse or abstract forms of harm.

Marx was one of the first thinkers to reflect on how industrial capitalism had begun to transform the dominant forms of harm in human history. War and conquest had been the two main instruments that societies used in the past to expropriate wealth; they were the reason for increased interconnectedness between human beings. The main form of harm in international relations was one in which societies exported harm to each other as capitalism introduced unprecedented levels of human interdependence. Because of the continuing global expansion of capitalism, Marx added, an increasing proportion of human harm is transmitted across frontiers by world market forces rather than exported from one society to another through conquest and war. To put this differently, in the past the major forms of transnational harm were concrete as they were part of a deliberate design to injure others; but in the future, Marx believed, harm would have a more abstract quality by being spread haphazardly across frontiers by the uncontrolled forces of global capitalism.

It is also important to note that Marx believed that capitalism was steadily dissolving traditional national distinctions in the most advanced capitalist societies and that he believed, as his comments on India illustrate, that capitalist globalization would erode social systems based on natural hierarchies of power (Linklater 1990a: ch. 2). In advanced capitalist societies, he maintained, hierarchical conceptions of nation and race were being dissolved by modern notions of individual subjectivity and equality. Under capitalism, increasing numbers of the human race were being constructed as free and equal juridical subjects who enter into the contractual relations that are constitutive of societies geared to commodity production. More recent versions of this theme have argued that 'monetarization' and 'marketization' are breaking down many of the old forms of exclusion anchored in hierarchical conceptions of ethnicity, gender or race that once blocked the expansion of capitalism, but the result has been to expose greater numbers of human beings to the vagaries of the world market and to leave them vulnerable to international financial institutions and transnational corporations (Geras 1999). On this argument, the same sensibilities that are offended by violence against the body regard the harms that are caused by 'vast, impersonal forces' as infinitely more acceptable.

There is no need to dwell on the fact that Marx and Marxism before the First World War did not foresee the resurgence of militarism and the interstate conflicts that lay ahead, and that Marx and the early Marxists had been wrong to think that the global proletariat would seize control of the processes that caused abstract harm. While some may argue that the theory and practice of Marxism is no longer relevant to a world in which it is capitalism rather than socialism that has come to have global dominance, others maintain that Marxism is uniquely placed to analyse modern patterns of capitalist globalization, the state's role in facilitating the expansion of global capitalism, and increasing international inequalities (Gamble 1999). Others have argued that 'monetarization' and 'marketization' are steadily reducing the moral relevance of the differences of gender, race and ethnicity in many parts of the world, only to place, as we have seen, an increasing proportion of the human race at the mercy of global capitalism (Geras 1999). Measures that are designed to reduce abstract harm clearly lag behind efforts to reduce forms of concrete harm that are anchored in pernicious racial and other differences. Differential rates of progress in these two spheres, it might be argued, reflect the preference and priorities of the hegemonic, liberal–capitalist societies.

Modernity in comparative perspective

The preceding section began with the observation that sociological studies of modernity have largely overlooked the importance of its organization as an international system of states; it stressed that the study of international relations, and the English School in particular, has been preoccupied with this level of analysis. A central question, it has been argued, is whether this mode of world political organization can make further progress in developing CHCs that control increasing levels of human interconnectedness in ways that reduce injury and distress to individuals and non-sovereign associations across the world. The argument has been that the English School is a useful resource for those that wish to explore this matter further. Its members believe that states have been able to agree on harm conventions that aim to limit the use of force, and most add that some progress has been made in identifying human rights that should be protected everywhere, although the West's upper hand in defining core rights is resented in many non-Western societies. Reference has been made to developments in international law that prohibit concrete harm based on pernicious racial and other differences. Members of the English School might regard these developments as evidence that the modern society of states, which has been especially concerned with maintaining order between monopolies of physical power, has come to regard the harms suffered by individuals and non-sovereign communities as morally important in their own right.

Any effort to build on the English School's study of international societies has to take account of rising levels of abstract harm in the modern world. Its relative lack of interest in international political economy and neglect of the Marxist tradition help to account for the failure to analyse the more abstract forms of transnational harm. It is clear that many of the problems inherent in Marxism resulted from its failure to analyse modernity as a system of states, but several limitations of English School theory arise from the decision to consider the society of states in isolation from the development of modern capitalism (Halliday 1994; Rosenberg 1994). A comparative sociology of international systems that asks whether modern international society is making unprecedented progress in institutionalizing CHCs can profit from reflecting how each perspective can overcome the other's limitations.

Two questions arise at this point. What are the principal forms of harm in the modern society of states, and how should international society deal with them? A provisional answer to the first question is that three forms of harm require attention. The first is the form of harm that has dominated the long history of relations between independent political communities. This is concrete harm that separate communities have deliberately inflicted on each other and which they have justified in terms of strategic necessity or their superiority over others or moral right to ignore their interests. The second is the increasingly important phenomenon of abstract harm that is transmitted across frontiers by transnational economic processes and institutions. The third is the concrete harm that national or ethnic groups inflict on one another within existing nation-states, for example when governments declare war on sections of their own population. A provisional answer to the second question is that international society should strive to reduce those forms of harm by building CHCs that respect all persons as moral equals. As previously noted, global measures to combat concrete harm are evident in the development of international humanitarian law and in the conventions that prohibit genocide and defend universal human rights. Similar declarations that respond to abstract harm are evident in international conventions on the environment (such as the Rio Convention, which obliges sovereign states not to cause injury to neighbouring populations by polluting their environment), and in support for the precautionary principle that is designed to protect present and future generations from the unforeseeable consequences of technological development. Conventions that deal with the harms that despotic regimes inflict on their own populations remain weak, but the rise of international criminal law is a crucial advance in dealing with concrete harm within sovereign states.

These references to international law may be thought to attach too much importance to the state and to ignore the respects in which individuals and groups within international civil society have taken the initiative in creating CHCs (Cavanagh 1997). States are losing some of their powers, most notably in the economic area but not with respect to control of the instruments of violence. Moreover, it remains the case that states have a virtual monopoly in the sphere of rule-making in international society, an unrivalled capacity to decide whether more cosmopolitan forms of national and international law will become part of the global constitution, and an unmatched ability to regulate the pace of international legal change (Hirst and Thompson 1995). There may come a time when states no longer have these rights and privileges, and when the constitutive principles of world society will be decided by transnational business enterprises and NGOs rather than states. But this is not the current reality, despite the partial recovery of the kind of international society that existed in Grotius's time which has weakened the state's monopolistic claim as the sole subject of international law.

A comparative sociology of CHCs must concentrate on the central role of independent political communities, but it must analyse the role that non-state actors, such as religious movements in different historical eras, have played in creating CHCs and on the relationship between 'public' and 'private' power. In the case of the modern states-system, INGOs and global social movements have become increasingly involved in the diplomatic dialogue, as efforts to create a convention banning anti-personnel land mines have indicated (Thakur and Maley 1999). Such private organizations are also especially active in monitoring the extent to which states comply with international agreements (Boli and Thomas 1999). NGOs and private associations aspire to create a global civil society of CHCs that upholds new standards of legitimacy with respect to socially responsible investment, fair trade, ethical tourism, etc. (see also Thomas 1999: 243). It may be that transnational civil society will be the force that decides whether or not the modern society of states develops CHCs that go beyond anything recorded in the history of international relations. Be that as it may, progress in that direction requires different state structures with new understandings of the relationship between the rights of citizens and aliens that are expressed in firmer commitments to cosmopolitan national and international law.

Conclusion

The concept of harm or its equivalent is present in all moral codes; it is universal without being foundational (the keystone of all moralities) or exhaustive (encompassing the full range of moral duties and responsibilities). It is impossible to imagine an international society without a concept of harm or without harm conventions that stipulate what is permissible and what is prohibited in relations with 'outsiders'. Promoting respect for CHCs will remain one of the fundamental themes in global ethics as long as citizens believe that their strongest political loyalties bind them to sovereign states and as long as altruism in international relations remains weak. Although the harm principle and an ethic of benevolence can develop side by side, it may well be that Ross (1930) was right to suggest that the belief that one's actions should not harm others may be the foundation on which more altruistic sentiments can eventually develop.

Interstate war has been the main impetus behind the development of CHCs over the last two centuries, and it remains the principal threat to their survival. The capacity of the state to project its power into the heartland of other societies created the need for new measures to protect the vulnerable. Following the industrialization of war, the most recent phase of capitalist globalization has created longer chains of interconnectedness that reduce the separateness of human societies. In this context the question arises of whether the universalizing forces of the modern age will lead to greater ethical universalism or barely alter traditions of disinterest in the harms suffered by the members of other societies. We cannot know if modernity will succeed in creating CHCs that are unprecedented in the history of forms of world political organization, but a commitment to new forms of domestic and international political community with this ethical ambition should be one of the central aims of a sociology of CHCs with an emancipatory intent.

9   The problem of harm in world politics

Implications for the sociology of states-systems[1]

In the 1960s Martin Wight and his colleagues on the British Committee on the Theory of International Politics wrote several papers on the great states-systems including the Ancient Greek and Chinese systems, medieval international society and the modern international order. A book on the sociology of states-systems was anticipated – a successor to Butterfield and Wight's *Diplomatic Investigations* – but the project was not completed (see Dunne 1998: 124ff.).[2] It would have been the first volume of its kind in international relations and its impact on the discipline would have been immense in a period in which several major works on historical sociology were published by leading sociologists (Skocpol 1979; Giddens 1985; Mann 1986, 1993; Tilly 1992). In more recent times, students of international relations have called for large-scale historical–sociological accounts of world politics, and several works have demonstrated what the field can contribute to the broader project of historical sociology (Hobden 1998; Buzan and Little 2000; Reus-Smit 1999; Hobden and Hobson 2002). As a result, the 'sociology of states-systems' now occupies a more central place in the study of international relations than ever before.

From that 'first period', Martin Wight's *System of States* stands out as the work that did most to set out a grand vision of the comparative sociological analysis of states-systems. The twenty-fifth anniversary of its publication is a suitable occasion to pay tribute to Wight's remarkable contribution to the study of international politics. This will take the form of reflecting, first, on his inspiring sociological vision and, second, on how his argument can be extended from a cosmopolitan standpoint that draws on key theoretical developments in the discipline since *Systems of States* was published twenty-five years ago.

Having offered a brief explanation of the chapter's subtitle, it is important to turn now to its title, 'The problem of harm in world politics'. Brutality has been the custom in world politics. To paraphrase Tzvetan Todorov, equality and reciprocity have usually been the exception rather than the rule, especially during military conflict. Appropriately, harm, hurt, injury – and unprecedented suffering caused by total war – led to the establishment of the academic study of international relations more than eight decades ago. The question of what is to be done with the state's 'power to hurt' – to use Thomas Schelling's expression (Schelling 1966) – has dominated the study of world politics ever since.

Over the decades, central debates in the field have focused on whether harm in the shape of violence and coercion is an inescapable feature of states-systems, whether it would be eradicated if humanity could only agree on some basic moral principles, or whether all we can hope is that separate states will use diplomacy, international law and institutions to reduce the suffering they cause each other.

The English School has been at the centre of these disputes about how far states have made, and can make, progress in controlling the power to harm. Its members regard the society of states as crucially concerned with restraining violence; they value international order knowing that its collapse will bring widespread suffering to peoples everywhere. But as Hedley Bull (1977: 22, ch. 4) argued, the need for order can easily come into conflict with the goal of justice, and international order may or may not promote world order, the purpose of which is the security of individuals rather than states. So in addition to asking how far states have made progress in maintaining international order, we can inquire into how far they cooperated to protect individuals everywhere from unnecessary harm. The English School has addressed this question in its prominent study of humanitarian intervention and human rights.

Those cosmopolitan orientations are central to the sociological approach to harm in world politics that will be outlined here. What is most interesting from this point of view is how far different international systems thought that harm to individuals is a moral problem for the world as a whole – a problem that all states and peoples, individually and collectively, should labour to solve. What is intriguing is how far different states-systems developed 'cosmopolitan harm conventions'. These are moral conventions that are designed to protect individuals everywhere from unnecessary suffering, irrespective of their citizenship or nationality, class, gender, race and other such characteristics (see Chapter 8).

In world politics, unnecessary suffering or superfluous injury – expressions used in the Hague Conventions – usually result from state-building, conquest and war, from the globalization of economic and social relations and from pernicious racist, nationalist and related ideologies. The function of a sociology of cosmopolitan harm conventions is to investigate how far different states-systems drew on the idea of a universal community of humankind to create agreements that individuals should be protected from the suffering such phenomena cause. It is to ask how far the great states-systems developed moral conventions which reveal that human sympathies need not be confined to co-nationals or fellow citizens but can be expanded to embrace all members of the human race.

It may seem slightly odd to pay tribute to Martin Wight's sociological project in this overtly cosmopolitan way. He argued that cosmopolitan and other radical approaches are an important reminder that states-systems contain deep moral imperfections, but he clearly doubted that cosmopolitan approaches and progressivist tendencies will ever enjoy lasting success. As is well known, Wight had a keen interest in what he called revolutionism, and at times he came close to Kant's position by stressing that we should value order because without it efforts to promote justice are bound to fail.

I now turn to some comments about Martin Wight's pessimism. Second, I will note how his writings on Ancient Greece reflected his broader interest in whether or not the idea of the universal community of humankind has influenced the development of different states-systems. Third, some observations follow on different forms of harm that are important for a cosmopolitan approach to the sociology of states-systems. Fourth and finally, the question is raised of whether the modern states-system can be said to have progressed in making the unnecessary suffering of individuals a moral problem for the species as a whole.

Wight's pessimism

Martin Wight (1977: 149) described states-systems as 'the loosest of all political organizations known to us; hence in part [their] fascination' – the loosest because states have no superior; fascinating because the absence of a higher authority does not necessarily mean anarchy and chaos but is compatible with order and society.[3] He had in mind what he called the primary states-systems of Ancient Greece, China in the Spring and Autumn and Warring States periods, and the modern European, now universal, system of states which has its origins in the Italian Renaissance.

Primary states-systems fascinated Wight because there are so few examples in human history. He focused on the three examples just mentioned, adding that a fourth may have existed in Ancient India (Wight 1977: ch. 1).[4] Barry Buzan and Richard Little (2001: 174) have extended this list in their recent book by adding the city-state systems that appeared in what are now Pakistan, southern Mexico and West Africa. A recent work on medieval frontier societies notes that an embryonic states-system may have existed in Wales for much of the twelfth and thirteenth centuries (Davies 1989). No doubt the list could be extended further.

Wight's fascination with states-systems owed something to their remarkable flair for self-destruction. Earlier states-systems had ended in empire; none survived for more than a few centuries. He therefore asked whether certain laws or patterns have existed in all states-systems, and by way of a preliminary answer suggested that three phases seem to recur. In phase one, the number of independent powers decline as the smaller states are eliminated, the casualties of military expansion and war. In phase two, increasingly violent competition between the surviving great powers dominates the system. In phase three, we witness the end of the states-system, as one of the remaining predators achieves the goal for which it has been striving – preponderant power and the ability to law down the law.

Martin Wight did not advance the comforting thought that the modern states-system will be the first to break the historical mould. His argument was that every states-system ultimately rests on the balance of power, which is inherently unstable and which is eventually destroyed by the struggle for domination (Wight 1977: 44).[5] Conceivably, he believed that the modern states-system, reduced at the time he was writing to two superpowers weighed down with nuclear weapons, was moving inexorably towards its violent end. In all this, we can see Wight at his most fervently realist – the Wight remembered in the textbooks for maintaining that international politics is the realm of recurrence and repetition, the sphere in which progress does not occur. We know from his undergraduate lectures at the London School of Economics that he was not persuaded by the cosmopolitan argument that the human race could or would unite in a universal community free from destructive states and poisonous nationalism.[6]

Wight added that cosmopolitanism 'is theoretically the least important' form of radical thinking about world politics. He went on to state that no major work of international political theory had propounded this doctrine although it has enjoyed some influence in practice (Wight 1991: 45). Cosmopolitans might choose to respond by arguing that this belief-system should be more influential than it has been in the past as it is the obvious remedy for so many of the world's ills, but Wight was quick to stress that cosmopolitan perspectives harbour their own dangers. It is important to remember his claim that the modern states-system has known systemic war and international revolution in almost equal degree. Our system has been unusually susceptible to the horizontal divisions that result from conflicts between transnational ideological or religious movements over universal goals, and from messianic struggles that threaten international order by weakening respect for sovereignty and encouraging intervention.[7] But pessimism is not the same as fatalism, and it is important to repeat his claim that order is not an end in itself but a possible staging post to justice.

Two concepts of cosmopolitanism

Despite 'the long peace', 'the end of geopolitics' and the 'obsolescence of war', events may yet prove that Wight was correct that our states-system will finally be destroyed by violence. We do not know if progress in curbing violent impulses will last indefinitely or if the modern states-system will revert to type as great powers rediscover their enthusiasm for imperial domination and appetite for war. The literature that defends the idea of an enduring peace raises the question of whether the modern system will reinforce existing constraints on the 'power to hurt' and whether the ability to extend compassion across national boundaries will come to have unusual success. One might ask in this context if Wight focused too much on the dangers inherent in cosmopolitan doctrines that hope for the withering away of the state and the dissolution of national sentiments, and too little on cosmopolitan perspectives that complement his own rationalist thought.[8]

Helpfully, the *Oxford English Dictionary* identifies two forms of cosmopolitanism. The first holds that provincial attachments should yield to the allegedly higher ethical conviction that our primary loyalties are to the whole of humanity. The second does not reject national ties, but opposes them when they ignore the legitimate interests of outsiders. The *cosmophil,* which the *Oxford English Dictionary* defines as someone who is 'friendly to the world in general', exemplifies the latter approach. On this view, one should not defend or celebrate national affiliations and cultural differences when they burden outsiders with intolerable costs; on this view, cosmopolitans need to combine loyalties to co-nationals with moral obligations to the members of other societies such as the duty not to harm them unnecessarily. This is the position that was taken by Stoic philosophers such as Cicero (see Rowe and Schofield 2000: ch. 24).

The observation that societies can agree on some basic universal moral rights and duties, however much they are divided on other scores, is one point on which the Kantian and Grotian traditions of thought converge (Wight 1991: 19).[9] Pointing to the harmony between these standpoints, Wight argued that Kant and Grotius shared the belief that independent political communities have moral obligations to three constituencies: to fellow citizens, to the society of states and to the wider community of humankind (Wight 1991: 73–5).[10] Raising one of the most important themes in the first chapter of *Systems of States,* he asked if parallels to these three moral constituencies existed in other states-systems, and if powerful commitments to human equality influenced the behaviour of states. The chapters on the Ancient Greek city-state system, and on relations between Greece and Persia, explored the question of how far different states collaborated to reduce unnecessary harm.

Ancient Greece

In those chapters Wight argued that loyalties to the polis were far stronger than loyalties to Hellas and the world at large. Ideas about the solidarity of the Hellenes and the unity of the human race clearly existed but they were far too 'hesitant' to check egoism in foreign policy (Mann 1986: ch. 7). Some states made noble pledges not to destroy each other, or starve one another's peoples or endanger their precious water supplies in peacetime or in war, but oaths to avoid cruelty to outsiders were rarely effective.[11] There was no counterpart in the Ancient World to the modern conviction that certain violent acts of state so shock 'the conscience of humankind' that they invite humanitarian intervention (Wight 1977: 67ff.), and nothing quite like the modern law of war or the universal culture of human rights. The Greeks' apparent disgust at human sacrifice and their alleged intervention in Carthage to bring an end to child sacrifice were possible exceptions to this more general rule (Wight 1977: 104). Their horror at the Carthaginians' habit of drowning foreign sailors revealed, Wight (1977: 103) thought, that the Greeks had some respect for human life outside the state of war. But there were no ingrained habits of creating cosmopolitan harm conventions to protect Greeks and individuals everywhere from unnecessary suffering.

While Wight was not persuaded by any cosmopolitan ethic or political vision, he was clearly intrigued by the sociological matter of how far visions of the universal community of humankind have shaped the evolution of different states-systems. At no point did he argue that all states-systems can be measured by some common ethical yardstick – and such an exercise may have been anathema to him. Be that as it may, some foundations for a cosmopolitan approach to the sociology of states-systems can be found in his comments about cruelty in Ancient Greece and in various expressions of his professed 'rationalist' preferences (Wight 1991).

The problem of harm in world politics

As noted earlier, it is not surprising that an interest in harm has dominated the study of international relations. Arguably, the will to harm has been the dominant pattern in world politics since the appearance of the Sumerian city-state system and the emergence of the first empires.[12] References to harm and injury are plentiful in the academic literature, but there is no distinguished body of work, no great tradition and no emergent sub-field of inquiry that examines how harm to individuals has been understood, managed and controlled in different international systems. This is something that a new sub-field of the discipline must seek to remedy.

The English School has said more than most approaches about the problem of harm in world politics.[13] Its members are drawn to societies of states because they are made from conventions that place moral and legal constraints on the power to harm and the right to hurt.[14] As noted earlier, the question of whether it is possible to extend cooperation to prevent harm – by strengthening the human rights culture or by creating new principles of humanitarian intervention, for example – has long been central to the English School.

The approach outlined here takes this further by starting with the assumption that the universalization of the harm principle – the global extension of the principle that obliges us to avoid harming others unnecessarily – is central to any cosmopolitan ethic (see Linklater 2006a).[15] The harm principle is only one part of that ethic; other vital ingredients include altruism, benevolence and charity. That said, there are two reasons why the harm principle is a critical dimension of a global ethic and a core element of a sociology of states-systems with a cosmopolitan intent. There is, first, the need to deal with what Geoffrey Warnock (1971) called the 'damaging effects' of 'limited sympathies'.[16] Warnock's point was that loyalties to particular groups often lead their members to act cruelly to outsiders or to adopt a stance of indifference to the ways in which their association damages their interests – whether accidentally or by design. He added that many basic moral conventions in domestic societies aim to protect the vulnerable from the negative consequences of limited sympathies. Of course, this is also true of international society in which loyalties to sovereign states frequently have dangerous effects.

There are parallels here with the notion of the cosmophil because it is the harsh consequences of limited sympathies rather than the existence of bounded loyalties that a global ethic needs to address. The second point connects the question of limited sympathies with the fact that human collectivities are divided over the nature of the good society and good life. A central theme in the English School, and particularly in Bull's writings, is that international societies are possible only because independent political communities recognize – despite their radically different conceptions of the good – the need for 'mutual forbearance', particularly with respect to the use of force.[17]

Rousseau maintained that a state can die without any members being injured. Perhaps, but, especially since the rise of modern nationalism, it has been impossible to distinguish harm to the state from harm to citizens. As E.H. Carr argued, the political struggles to make states correspond with nations often displaced minorities and encouraged total war and made it necessary for the society of states to develop cosmopolitan moral and legal principles to protect individuals in their own right.[18] Because of nationalism, it has become even more important to judge international order by the extent to which it promotes world order in Bull's sense of the term. Bearing this in mind, it is possible to explore the development of cosmopolitan harm conventions in the modern society of states and to ask how our world compares with the states-systems of the past.

Varieties of harm

Analysing the dominant cosmopolitan harm conventions in different states-systems is one way of building on Martin Wight's sociological imagination, one way of further exploring the region in which the Grotian and Kantian traditions intersect, and one way of making the Kantian ethical ideal of 'a cosmopolitan condition of general political security' more central to the English School than it has been in the past (Kant 1970c: 49). To develop these points, it is useful to identify different forms of harm, of causing distress, suffering, apprehension, anxiety or fear, of damaging vital interests. Five types of harm can be identified giving rise to five reasons why international society needs stronger cosmopolitan harm conventions. In what follows, they will be treated as if they were completely separate, but the events of September 11 and the war against the Taliban have demonstrated their close interconnectedness more than any other recent events (Linklater 2002).

Deliberate harm in relations between independent political communities

The first form is deliberate harm in relations between independent political communities, the most obvious example being war. As noted earlier, Wight believed that states-systems have enjoyed some success in limiting the use of force but no states-system had succeeded, or seemed likely to succeed, in eradicating violence. His sociological approach concentrated on institutions such as the balance of power, diplomacy and international law which preserve order in world politics. A cosmopolitan variant on the approach can compare efforts to prevent excessive violence in war, a project that requires the analysis of how far different states-systems developed harm conventions that were designed to prevent 'superfluous injury' to combatants, to protect the rights of the captured and to spare civilians, especially women and children, unnecessary suffering.

Deliberate harm caused by governments to their own citizens

The desire to spare individuals suffering in war has been the main reason for the development of cosmopolitan harm conventions but serious human rights violations in the modern world have led to the conclusion that it is just as important to protect individuals from a second form of harm, the harm that governments do by waging war against sections of their own citizenry. As noted earlier, the English School has long been interested in sovereignty, human rights and intervention. Especially since the implosion of the former Yugoslavia, sharp differences have emerged between those who believe that the current international order should promote an experiment in humanitarian intervention (and is obliged to do so if the universal human rights culture means anything at all) and those who fear that weakening the principle of territorial sovereignty has the dangerous effect of removing one of the central constraints on the ambitions of the great powers. Wherever these debates may lead, the modern states-system seems unusual, and possibly unique, in creating international legal conventions that contract national jurisdiction and also in reflecting on the moral responsibilities of 'bystanders' who witness distant suffering as part of everyday life (Barnett 2000; Linklater 2006b).

Deliberate harm by non-state actors

Deliberate harm by non-state actors, such as pirates and mercenary armies, criminal organizations involved in the traffic of women and children and in the international drugs trade, transnational economic organizations and global terrorist movements, is a third form of harm. Cross-border or transnational harm that is caused by such actors is a third reason for designing harm conventions with universal scope.

Unintended harm

Thus far the emphasis has been on the will to coerce, but not all harm takes this form. Reflecting on capitalist globalization, Engels (1969) observed that new technological breakthroughs in Britain could destroy livelihoods in China within a single year. Those that caused long-distance harm were not always aware of how their actions affected foreigners, and it would have been futile to criticize them for intending to cause harm. Engel's insight was that the growth of the world market exposed an increasing proportion of the human race to unintended, long-distance harm. For Marx and Engels, a double revolution in world history was taking place. The old types of deliberate harm, caused by warring states and expanding empires, were being replaced by the diffuse forms of harm transmitted across frontiers by global capitalist forces. In addition, an extended sense of moral responsibility to the human race was necessary and would emerge, they believed, with the movement to global socialism.

   Whatever one thinks of their predictive skills and their utopian vision, Marx and Engels were right to stress the growing importance of unintended, transnational harm, and correct to defend, although Marx and Engels did more than this, universal conventions to protect the vulnerable from global market forces.[19] In recent times, the increase in what Ulrich Beck (1992) calls the imperceptible harms that are inherent in global risk society has underlined their central point.

Environmental degradation is the best example of how the countless repetition of everyday actions that are seemingly harmless in themselves can, with the passing of the generations, have damaging outcomes that no one desired.[20] Many approaches to global governance and environmental ethics, and many international legal conventions, respond to the problem of 'unintended consequences' by arguing for new global responsibilities for avoiding harm (Mason 2001).[21] This is a fourth reason for supporting the development of more robust cosmopolitan harm conventions.

With some exceptions, the English School has not been concerned with this form of harm.[22] In his study of human rights, John Vincent highlighted the ethical issues which are raised by harm that is transmitted across frontiers by global economic forces. His argument that every human being has an equal right to be free from starvation is worth recalling at this point. Vincent's central contention was that the affluent have a moral duty to assist the starving, but he added that the former's awareness of how they benefited from global structures that disadvantage the vulnerable should strengthen their resolve to end starvation and reduce global inequalities.[23]

Vincent identified an orientation to global moral responsibilities that has grown in importance in recent years as individuals have reflected on what Ted Honderich (1980) has called the 'wrong [we do] in our ordinary lives'. Whether the focus is on child labour, sweatshops in the fashion industry, fair trade, socially responsible investment or ethical tourism, there is some evidence of growing concern with the moral problems that arise from association with harmful institutions and practices. The point is that institutions may cause harm that individuals would not do of their own volition (Kutz 2000). The core moral issue is complicity in the misery of others – complicity by benefiting from the exploitation and suffering of others (Wertheimer 1996). An additional reason for developing cosmopolitan harm conventions is provided by the forms of global connectedness that bind the affluent and the vulnerable together (Pogge 2002). A central ethical question that arises in this context is whether causing harm is always morally worse than profiting from harm and doing nothing about it (Feinberg 1984: ch. 4; see also Kutz 2000 on gradations of responsibility).

Negligence

A fifth form of harm is negligence – the failure to take reasonable precautions to prevent the risk of harm to others.[24] Two examples are 'nuclear colonialism': testing nuclear weapons in the South Pacific with apparent indifference to the health of local populations (Dibblin 1988: 205), and 'environmental apartheid': the practice of exporting hazardous waste to societies where safeguards are weaker than in the West (Shue 1981; Shiva 2000). In each case, the ethical question is indifference rather than cruelty although, interestingly, the *Oxford English Dictionary* does not care for the distinction.[25] The main point, however, is that the negligent knowingly expose others to risks and hazards which they may regard as unacceptable in their own societies (Shue 1981). Here is a further reason for supporting efforts to weave more demanding cosmopolitan harm conventions into the structure of international society.

A cosmopolitan approach to the sociology of states-systems

The main reason for classifying forms of harm is to identify some key questions for a cosmopolitan approach to the sociology of states-systems. One can then proceed to ask if all states-systems developed moral conventions in order to prevent unnecessary suffering in war, if all developed moral conventions on the grounds that the harm that governments do to their citizens should concern the world as a whole, and if all created conventions that offered peoples everywhere protection from private international violence, from the effects of long-distance and unintended harm, from exploitation, complicity and negligence.

Admittedly, it is difficult to compare how different states-systems responded to long-distance harm because earlier systems did not experience the level of global interconnectedness that now exists, but the virtually universal phenomenon of slavery raises questions about how far guilt about profiting from the vulnerable, and moral concerns about complicity in the suffering of others, have been present in all states-systems (see Buzan and Little 2000 on different levels of cross-border interaction in international systems). Having made these points it is possible to build on Wight's discussion of the part that visions of a universal human community have played in the evolution of states-systems. Part of the endeavour is to ask whether the modern states-system has surpassed its predecessors in creating global conventions that protect all persons from avoidable harm.

Modernity and progress

Perhaps the temptation to ask this question should be resisted. What conception of cruelty or unnecessary suffering should inform the analysis, and where is the Archimedean standpoint that allows useful comparisons to be made? Perhaps the more sensible strategy is to ask whether the most recent phase in the development of the modern states-system represents an advance beyond its more violent past.

Interestingly, Wight noted that the idea of progress was a factor in the study of states-systems promoted by members of the British Committee. The assumption that states-systems mark an advance beyond other forms of world political organization 'underlies', he wrote, '[the] choice of states-systems as a subject of study' (Wight 1977: 44). Robert Jackson (2000: 408) goes further by arguing that the modern society of states is the best form of global political system yet devised for promoting peaceful coexistence between separate communities.[26] Important issues arise here that deserve further investigation. A useful place to start is with three perspectives on whether the idea of progress is relevant to the sociology of cosmopolitan harm conventions.

The progressivist interpretation of international relations

The first is the 'progressivist interpretation of international relations', an approach that Wight famously rejected. This is the view that steady progress has occurred in world politics not only in recent decades but, more profoundly, over the whole course of human history. Studies of the unique liberal–democratic peace and the growth of the universal culture of human rights offer the best contemporary academic statement of this approach.

The English School is usually thought to be at odds with progressivism although Bull and Watson defended a progressivism of sorts when discussing advances in the nineteenth century in abolishing the slave trade and slavery, and in developing the humanitarian law of war. In his influential Hagey Lectures, Bull (1984a) referred to progress in human rights and in applying the welfare principle to international relations. Similar themes are present in the writings of Vincent (1986) and Wheeler (2000b).

But such progressivism is surrounded by major reservations including an emphasis on the precarious nature of international order and on the evidence that cosmopolitan harm conventions have usually been controversial in their application and design. Wight's comments on Kant in his London School of Economics lectures, which stress the dangers of thinking that all societies should be committed to the same principles of government, suggest that the idea of the liberal peace should be treated with care.[27] Others have developed the point by arguing that the liberal peace is all too easily grounded in the belief in superiority over the non-liberal world, in disinterest in the suffering of non-liberal peoples and in the belief that the liberal faith in constraints on war is unlikely to be reciprocated by dictatorial regimes (see Doyle 1983; Goldgeier and McFaul 1992; Sadowski 1998 on the American abandonment of the illiberal world to its fate). These themes have considerable contemporary relevance. But that does not mean that evidence of progress is nowhere to be found, for example in the area of human rights.[28]

The anti-progressivist standpoint

The anti-progressivist standpoint denies that there has been progress in history or much more than short-lived diversions from more persistent trends. In his sombre conclusion to *Mankind and Mother Earth*, Toynbee (1978: 590) stated that there has been no progress in human history outside the technological sphere. On this view, there are no grounds for thinking that the modern states-system supersedes earlier states-systems in the desire to end senseless suffering.

Liberals may protest that the Assyrian and Roman empires, and the Mayan, Aztec and other Amerindian civilizations, differed from the modern states-system by specializing in physical cruelty (Kyle 1998: 134ff.). Certainly, Ancient Romans seem to have derived what now seems to have been unusual pleasure from public 'spectacles of death' in which enemies, traitors and exotic animal species were slaughtered in staggering numbers (Finer 1997: 440; Kyle 1998). Norbert

Elias (2000, especially part II, ch. 10) may have been right that the 'civilizing process' that tames aggressive impulses and suppresses the pleasure derived from cruelty sets the modern European world apart from many other historical eras. Others – Michel Foucault (1979) most famously – have argued that modern societies have devised new forms of power that are less manifestly cruel than their predecessors but impossible to reconcile with the idea of progress. Still others – Zygmunt Bauman (1989) for example – maintain that modernity introduced new opportunities for bureaucratized or 'industrial' killing.

The anti-progressivist point can be underscored in other ways. Progress in defending human rights and in promoting the humanitarian law of war has to be viewed against a background of human rights violations and civilian casualties in war that have few parallels in history. Progress in the struggle against racism has also to be placed in the appropriate historical context as Ancient Greeks and Romans do not seem to have subscribed to later European ideas about the profound moral significance of racial differences (Snowden 1983). Progress in curbing violent impulses occurs at the very moment when economic globalization determines the fate of an increasing percentage of the world's population. Certain forms of physical coercion are deemed contrary to international law whereas various forms of economic harm are regarded as just how it is with markets. None of this supports the claim that the modern system has made much progress beyond all other states-systems in tackling unnecessary suffering.

Changing standards of international legitimacy

Elements of the progressivist and anti-progressivist standpoints can be combined in an approach that focuses on standards of legitimacy in world politics and asks whether modern states are judged by higher moral standards than the states of the past.[29] Standards of legitimacy are evident, first, in the rules about how decisions should be made or in understandings about what counts as fair procedures, and, second, in the actual decisions that states reach about what is permissible in statecraft and what should be proscribed (Luard 1976).[30]

The English School has been especially interested in how standards of legitimacy which decide rights of representation in world politics have changed over the centuries. Evan Luard argued that in the Ancient Chinese states-system dynastic rulers made foreign policy for themselves, as did the absolutist states of early modern Europe (Luard 1976). Ian Clark (1989: ch. 6) has argued that new standards of legitimacy at the end of the Napoleonic Wars enlarged the boundaries of the decision-making community: a concert of the great powers institutionalized consultation about matters of common concern. Developing the narrative, one might note how support for the idea of national self-determination gave smaller nations the right to be heard in the global dialogue at the end of the First World War. The anti-colonial revolution, and to a lesser extent the revolt of indigenous peoples, have also transformed past assumptions about who has rights to be represented in global decisions. Many non-governmental associations and social movements that resist globalization strive to take the process further, as do the advocates of cosmopolitan democracy (Held 1995). All these developments are relevant to the question of how the international order has changed – and can be changed more radically – so that vulnerable groups can protest against actual and potential forms of harm.

Those developments and demands would appear to be unique in the history of international relations, and would seem to confirm Buzan and Little's judgement that the idea of human equality had little importance in earlier states-systems. They suggest that no analysis of the modern states-system will be complete if it fails to note how the idea of human equality has influenced its principles of legitimacy – not only its decision-making procedures but also the concrete decisions about what is permissible and what is proscribed in human affairs that emanate from them (Buzan and Little 2000: 340). It is no longer extraordinary in enlightened circles to argue that decisions should have the consent of everyone who may be harmed by them – although realists, expressing the anti-progressivist viewpoint, will be quick to stress the continuing gulf between principle and practice that is largely the result of the exigencies of statecraft. There is no point denying this, but it is important to emphasize that modern standards of legitimacy embedded in international law repeatedly declare that individuals have a right to be spared 'serious mental or bodily harm'. This may be a new phenomenon in the history of world political organization, but the conjecture has yet to be put to the test.

The universalization of the harm principle

The crucial question then is whether the modern states-system has progressed beyond its predecessors not only in the way in which decisions are made but also in universalizing the principle that no individual should cause unnecessary harm to any other member of the human race.

Physical cruelty in relations between states

A preliminary answer to this question might start by noting how physical cruelty came to be regarded as a problem for the world as a whole, especially during the last century. This change is evident in important shifts regarding what is deemed permissible and what is forbidden in war as exemplified by the assault on sovereign immunity introduced by the Nuremberg Charter and restated by the resolutions that established the International Criminal Tribunals for the former Yugoslavia and for Rwanda. Along with the UN Security Council resolutions, which include rape in war in the list of crimes against humanity, such developments have embedded the idea of human equality in international society, so enlarging the dominion of cosmopolitan law. To focus on a matter of great contemporary importance, one should also note increased public concern about civilian suffering in war, but continuing selectivity at the level of great power reponses.

Physical cruelty in relations between governments and citizens

New standards of legitimacy regarding physical cruelty have also addressed the violence that governments inflict on their citizens. Several international legal documents, such as the conventions on the Suppression and Punishment of the Crime of Apartheid, on genocide and torture, as well as the United Nations Declaration on the Elimination of Violence against Women, have outlawed 'serious bodily or mental harm' (see Evans 1994). Significant progress has occurred in contracting the sphere of domestic jurisdiction. The evidence does not suggest that other states-systems went down this particular path.

Changes in the areas just mentioned reveal progress in expanding the geographical 'scope of moral concern' (O'Neill 2000: 188); that is, movement has occurred in expanding the circle of those with rights to be free from senseless violence. But this is only part of the story. Critics of NATO's military action against Serbia highlighted the selective enforcement of international law (Schnabel and Thakur 2000). One might wonder how far the new principles of legitimacy made a difference to the women and children of Iraq in the 1990s, and many doubted that they would alleviate the suffering of innocent civilians in Afghanistan (although humanitarian considerations seem to have had some influence in that war). But it is important that the tension between principle and practice does not escape close scrutiny in world politics, and that contemporary standards of legitimacy equip states, NGOs and other actors with important moral resources with which to conduct struggles against unnecessary suffering. From these tensions and forms of resistance more ambitious experiments in universalizing the harm principle as part of a 'global civilizing process' may yet grow (see also Chapter 10).

Unintended harm and negligence

The advances that have been made in institutionalizing an ethic that puts cruelty first constitute progress along one axis (Shklar 1984: ch. 1). But a second axis exists that is concerned with the depth rather than with the scope of moral concern, with vertical rather than with horizontal dimensions of global morality. The importance of depth has been highlighted by those who criticize Western conceptions of human rights for stressing liberal and political, as opposed to economic, rights. Their claim is that more radical harm conventions are needed to address unspeakable squalor and extreme vulnerability to global market forces. The recurrent theme is that the dominant harm conventions will continue to lack legitimacy in the eyes of large numbers of the world's population until they address questions of depth as well as scope.[31] Much has been heard about this in recent times (Linklater 2002).

The modern states-system seems to be unique in having to respond to the multiple forms of harm described earlier. It does not lack the moral resources with which to increase the depth as well as the scope of moral concern, but whether it will utilize them to reduce harm caused by capitalist forms of production and exchange as well as by state-building and war, and various doctrines of cultural, racial and religious supremacy, is unclear. Recent events are not encouraging, but hardly the final word. Perhaps the main issues regarding the future are how far the dominant economic and political interests will need to respond to calls for institutionalizing cosmopolitan harm conventions in order to ensure the legitimacy of global arrangements. It is hard not to approach these issues without recalling Wight's pessimism but important to connect scepticism about the prospects for reform with support for the requisite cosmopolitan ethic.

Conclusion

This chapter has relied heavily on two of Martin Wight's insights: first, that the sociology of states-systems is a crucial yet neglected area of scholarly inquiry; and, second, that it is important to analyse the extent to which ideas about the universal community of humankind influenced the evolution of different states-systems. The aim of the chapter has been to develop these themes in a sociological project that focuses on the problem of harm in world politics, to reflect on Wight's comments about how the Grotian and Kantian traditions overlap in important respects, and to recall his observation that international order should be valued because justice will not develop without it.

Bringing Kant into the discussion is not to set revolutionism against Wight's realism. Because the struggle for power will never cease, and because the tensions between principle and practice may never disappear, the question is how far the exercise of power can proceed with 'a minimum of domination' (Foucault, quoted in Moss 1998: 20–1), with less cruelty, with lower levels of negligence or indifference; the question is how far it can operate with greater accountability to others, especially the most vulnerable members of world society. These moral matters, which are ultimately concerned with how far the human species can organize its affairs on earth so that unnecessary harm and senseless suffering are reduced as far as possible, enjoy a permanent place in human affairs and a heightened importance at the present time. This is why the problem of harm deserves pride of place in a cosmopolitan approach to the sociology of states-systems.

10 Norbert Elias, the civilizing process and the sociology of international relations[1]

Things that were once permitted are now forbidden.[2]

Efforts to forge connections between historical sociology, world history and the study of long-term processes of change are at the forefront of current scholarship in International Relations (Buzan and Little 2000; Denemark *et al.* 2000; Hobden and Hobson 2002). Norbert Elias's analysis of 'the civilizing process' – the process by which modern European societies have been pacified over approximately the last five centuries, and in which emotional identification between the members of each society has increased – has much to contribute to historical–sociological approaches to international relations. However, Elias's writings have been largely neglected in the Anglo-American discipline,[3] and there has been no detailed examination of the importance of his work for the sociology of long-term patterns of change in world politics.[4]

Amongst sociologists of his generation, Elias was unusual in recognizing the importance of international relations for the wider social sciences, but he did not write extensively on world politics or display an acquaintance with the relevant literature.[5] Many of his comments on relations between states will be familiar to students of world politics. This is especially true of his realist observation that 'elimination contests' will prevail as long as independent political communities are locked in a struggle for power and security in the condition of anarchy. But it is important to look beyond such Hobbesian themes in Elias's thought to his comments about dominant attitudes towards cruelty, violence and suffering in different eras for insights that can enrich historical–sociological approaches to international relations. Elias raised the question of how far the civilizing process had influenced the evolution of the modern international system. This was an underdeveloped area of his research – one that can obviously profit from engaging with, inter alia, English School, constructivist and legal approaches to global norms and principles that echo many of Elias's principal concerns.[6] This chapter considers the significance of Elias's analysis of the civilizing process for the specific project of creating a 'sociology of states-systems' as outlined in Wight's pioneering essays on this topic (Wight 1977). Attention will be paid to the Hobbesian and Grotian elements of Elias's writings and to the particular significance of Kantian themes for efforts to develop the 'Wightian' project.

The discussion begins by drawing attention to the significance of 'civility' and the 'civilizing process' for English School reflections on international society. There are clear parallels between this mode of analysis and Elias's account of the rise of the modern European state, and it is important to integrate their different strengths in a more comprehensive analysis of the development of human society. Elias's theory of the civilizing process will then be discussed prior to providing a short overview of his comments about whether Ancient Greek international relations differed from the modern states-system in their attitudes to suffering and in the extent of their tolerance of cruelty to foreigners. The discussion concludes by outlining ways in which a sociology of states-systems can profit from engaging with Elias's analysis of long-term patterns of change in modern Europe, and specifically from his reflections on changing sociopolitical attitudes to harm (see Chapter 11). A typology of forms of harm is introduced to show how elements from Wight's and Elias's perspectives can be combined to prepare the foundations of a new research programme that compares global civilizing processes in different states-systems. Analysing dominant attitudes towards human cruelty and to various forms of bodily and mental harm is central to the proposed field of investigation, as is considering how far 'cosmopolitan emotions' shaped the long-term development of these distinctive forms of world political organization.

The English School, civility and international order

Evidence that the idea of civility remains important for the investigation of modern social systems can be found in a recent collection of essays that builds on the historical writings of Sir Keith Thomas (Williams 1976: 48–50; Burke *et al.* 2000). Civility refers to social conventions, manners and habits, and related psychological traits and emotional dispositions that bring order to human affairs.[7] Of course, the role of moral and legal conventions and psychological dispositions in preserving international order is the English School's point of departure; however, the literature on the School has largely overlooked the ways in which the concepts of civility and civilizing processes have been used to analyse anarchical societies (see, however, Sharp 2003).[8] Important illustrations of the latter are Butterfield's claim that global political stability needs to be understood in conjunction with 'the whole civilizing process' that underpins international order (Butterfield 1953: ch. 7). Curbs on aggressive impulses and threatening behaviour, and internal and external checks on egotistical behaviour, are core elements of the global civilizing process as Butterfield described it.[9] His definition of civilization is broadly similar to Elias's idea of a civilizing process. Butterfield stated that civilization refers to 'patterns of behaviour which emerge over time through the experience of people who are capable of empathy with others and capable of denying themselves short-term gains for the long-term goal of maintaining ordered relations' (quoted in Sharp 2001: 11; Sharp 2003). His stress on empathy was mainly concerned with affinities between members of the diplomatic community, whereas Elias was interested in long-term patterns of social and political change, including the development of empathy and other emotions, within modern states, but the two approaches can be usefully linked together to ask how far 'cosmopolitan emotions' (see Nussbaum 2002) influenced long-term patterns of change in different states-systems. More specifically, Wight's comments on how far commitments to visions of a universal human community influenced the development of international societies can be significantly extended by engaging with Elias's investigation of changing levels of emotional identification within European societies over approximately the last five centuries.

Several more recent works by members of the English School have used the ideas of civility and civilization to analyse the moral, cultural and emotional foundations of international orders. Watson (1992: 20) describes the 'diplomatic dialogue' as '*a civilized process* based on awareness and respect for other people's point of view; and *a civilizing one* also, because the continuous exchange of ideas, and the attempts to find mutually acceptable solutions to conflicts of interest, increase that awareness and respect' (italics added). Jackson's claim that the modern society of states is the most successful form of world political organization thus devised for promoting 'mutual intelligibility, recognition, communication, and interaction between people of different civilizations' emphasizes the importance of 'civility' for bridging different accounts of civilized conduct (Jackson 2000: 408). He argues that 'civility' is preferable to 'civilization' as it is not associated with the view that societies can be arranged hierarchically in terms of their stage of moral and political development. Civility for Jackson has a vital role to play in understanding the modern 'global covenant'. Like Butterfield, he states that mutual understanding, tolerance and self-constraint are central to how political entities with divergent or discordant worldviews learn to coexist.

A key point to make is that Butterfield, Watson and Jackson have used the idea of civility or civilization in world politics without derogatory connotations to describe shared understandings about the need for constraints on force and for sensitivity to the cultural preferences and political interests of others.[10] (There is a parallel with Elias who claimed that he did not use the idea of a civilizing process pejoratively to denote the superiority of the West.) Of course, members of the English School are well aware that European states in the nineteenth century used 'the standard of civilization' to justify excluding non-Western peoples from the society of states and to describe the changes they had to undergo to acquire equal membership (Gong 1984). Indeed, their interest in the nature of Europe's professed civilizational identity and in the impact it had on other societies can be usefully connected with Elias's analysis of how Europeans understood the civilizing process to include a global civilizing mission. The English School's analysis of how Europe distinguished between civilized, barbaric and savage societies runs parallel to Elias's reflections on how distinctions between the 'established' and the 'outsiders' were constructed and amended during the civilizing process (Elias and Scotson 1994). Great emphasis has been placed on how the idea of civilization shaped the self-understanding of states that were involved in preserving an international society that excluded 'uncivilized' peoples, and on how the development of global civility has allowed diverse European and non-European political communities to coexist as at least notional equals in the first universal society of states (Jackson 2000). Butterfield's remarks on the centrality of empathy for international order is crucial for understanding 'the expansion of international society', a process that was intimately connected with profound changes in Western emotional responses to the plight of subordinated peoples (see n. 43 below).

Various English School references to civility and civilizing processes emphasize that international order cannot be reduced to the constraining role of the balance of military power.[11] They stress that order depends on internalized constraints including a common desire to limit violence, a highly developed capacity to empathize with others' fears and interests and a moral outlook that prefers compromise to egotism, self-righteousness and mutual recrimination. Exactly the same stress on the importance of internalized constraints on violence and self-control was central to Elias's account of the civilizing process.

A key difference between the approaches is that Elias focused on how these internalized constraints developed within territorial states whereas the English School considers global civility or civilizing processes in anarchical societies. Bull and Watson (1984: 9) argued that such phenomena reveal that 'international political life, including its normative or institutional dimension, has its own logic, and is not to be understood simply as the reflection of economic interests or productive processes'. They recognized that civility in international society is connected with civility in its constituent parts but they did not analyse the linkages in order to assess the relative importance of endogenous and exogenous processes.[12] The opposite bias is found in Elias's approach. But just as the English School is aware that global civility is not cut off from domestic civility, so was Elias clear that the long-term patterns of social change that he examined had to be analysed in conjunction with international politics and with large-scale developments affecting humanity as a whole (Elias 1991: 139; see also Elias 1987a: 82).[13] It will be argued below that Elias devoted more attention than members of the English School have done to the inter-relations between these different levels, and specifically to the connections between domestic and global attitudes towards cruelty and suffering. This is one of the main respects in which his perspective can contribute to the 'sociology of states-systems' outlined in Wight's essays.[14]

Civilization and its discontents

Contemporary social and political theories – post-structuralist and post-colonial perspectives in particular – are understandably suspicious of narratives about modernity that make reference to civilization – so often this language has promoted binary oppositions between 'advanced' and 'backward' peoples with violent consequences. Elias's choice of terms was unfortunate if the idea of the civilizing process was not designed to argue for the progressive nature of Western modernity. The first issue to discuss in considering the significance of his writings for international relations is whether his account of the civilizing process shared the progressivism of the major nineteenth-century metanarratives.

Elias and writers influenced by him have been emphatic that modern European societies are not alone in undergoing a civilizing process. A recurrent claim is that there is 'no zero point of civilizing processes, no point at which human beings are uncivilized and begin to be civilized' (Elias 1992: 146). Elias's central point was that all societies have to socialize their members into shared understandings about the importance of observing constraints on violence, and all need to equip them with skills in adapting behaviour to the legitimate needs of others. Elias makes this point most forcefully in a crucial claim for the argument of this chapter, namely that all societies confront:

> the problem of how people can manage to satisfy their elementary animalic needs in their life together, without reciprocally destroying, frustrating, demeaning or in other ways *harming* each other time and time again in their search for this satisfaction – in other words, without fulfilment of the elementary needs of one person or group of people being achieved at the cost of those of another person or group.
>
> (Elias 1996: 31, italics added).[15]

In short, civilizing processes are universal features of human society, and a sociology that endeavours to understand them can embrace all times and places without pejorative connotations (see Mennell 1996a).[16] A central sociological task is to compare 'social patterns of individual self-restraint and the manner in which they are built into the individual person in the form of what one now calls "conscience" or perhaps "reason"' (Elias 1992: 146). An analysis of civilizing processes could therefore compare 'different stages of the same society' or 'different societies' without assuming that the modern phase of European history is superior to all others (Elias 1995: 8–9).[17] To avoid misunderstanding, it is essential to remember his claim that his research had 'not been guided . . . by the idea that our civilized mode of behaviour is the most advanced of all humanly possible modes of behaviour' (Elias 1998b: 44).

Elias's most celebrated contention is that over recent centuries Western societies have developed constraints on aggressive or violent behaviour that surpass functional equivalents in the Middle Ages and possibly in Ancient Greece. This formulation immediately raises the question of how such a claim can be made non-pejoratively – that is, without assuming that the West is more civilized than at least those two historical epochs.[18] Elias maintained that his empirical statements about the greater tolerance of wounding and killing in the Ancient World were not designed to 'cast a slur' on Greek civilization. In Ancient Greece, greater tolerance of physical violence coexisted with very high levels of artistic, philosophical and scientific achievement. Comparative observations about civilizing processes in different eras were not 'ethnocentric value-judgments' bred from the assumption that 'we are good' and 'they are bad' (Elias 1996: 133–4). Sociological analysis could not begin with the observation that other societies 'had been free to choose between *their* standards and *their* norms and ours, and having had this choice, had taken the wrong decision' (Elias 1996: 135).[19] Crucially, such comparisons would reveal that the lower threshold of revulsion against violence in modern Europe is neither irreversible nor free from social and political dangers.

Three points need to be made in this context. The first is that Elias repeatedly observed that the modern civilizing process has had little influence on interstate relations.[20] Constraints on force between members of the same society have long been accompanied by a high tolerance of force in relations with other societies, with the consequence that a major contradiction exists at the heart of modern civilization. Elias did not leave matters there. A more detailed account of how Grotian and Kantian themes moderated his Hobbesian position will be offered later in the discussion.

A second point is that the civilizing process, though usually 'unplanned', has often been advanced by social groups that employed invidious distinctions between the 'established' and the 'outsiders' to achieve their ends (see Mennell 1996b: 126). Indeed, the very idea of civilization is only possible through contrasts with the less civilized, contrasts that have frequently provided the grounds for acts of violence, humiliation and exploitation, as the history of Western colonialism so clearly reveals. Elias's claim that 'civilizing processes go along with decivilizing processes', and the supporting observation that the key 'question is to what extent one of the two directions is dominant', explicitly rules out complacency regarding the achievements of Western modernity (see Fletcher 1997: 83). Modern peoples may regard constraints on physical violence as evidence of their advancement beyond other social systems. However, Elias's analysis of the civilizing process does not validate their collective self-images but rather highlights their hypocritical and violent qualities in relations between members of the same society and in relations between separate states.

Elias's distinction between civilization as a 'condition' and as a 'process' helps to clarify these observations. One point of the distinction was to stress the dangers that were inherent in the temptation to which Europeans succumbed in the nineteenth century, namely the belief that civilization was evidence of 'inborn superiority' rather than the result of complex historical processes that required 'constant effort'. The delusion that Western civilization was a natural condition, a conceit that began in the Napoleonic era, led Europeans to claim a natural right to civilize savage or barbaric peoples (Elias 2000: 43). This collective myth about their naturally civilized state had the disastrous consequence of leaving European societies 'ill-prepared' for the rise of Fascism (Elias 1997: 314). One of the main illusions of the epoch was that genocide occurred only in the 'primitive' phases of human development when states and empires wallowed in cruelty and demonstrated little or no compassion for outsiders (see Fletcher 1997: 158). Many came to believe that excessive violence had been eliminated from modern Europe. A central objective of Elias's study, *The Germans,* was to explain how the Nazis destroyed the faith in the civilized condition by unleashing decivilizing processes that broke with the main course of European social and political development over the previous five centuries. The Nazi era demonstrated that ostensibly civilized states were not immune from the barbarism that was deemed characteristic of earlier stages of human history or typical of the allegedly less advanced regions of the world.[21]

Along with Adorno and Horkheimer (1972) and Bauman (1989), Elias set out to understand what it is about Western civilization that permitted 'barbarities of this kind' and why 'such an outbreak of savagery and barbarism' as occurred in Nazi Germany 'might stem directly from tendencies inherent in the structure of modern industrial societies' (Elias 1996: 303; Fletcher 1997: 158ff., 168ff.). Part of his answer was that the development of modern territorial states created new levels of individual security and enabled high levels of social interdependence to develop. The 'paradoxical effect' of this process was the rise of unusually high levels of personal detachment (Smith 2001: 21). As will be discussed later, Elias thought that the importance of external constraints on individual behaviour declined over approximately five centuries as atomized individuals became increasingly responsible for constraining aggressive inclinations. Public cruelty and violence became less essential for social integration, and what is now widely regarded as disgusting and distasteful (not only punishment but the slaughter of animals and death itself) came to be screened from view. Elias proceeded to argue that these social and political developments were crucial for understanding how genocide was possible in a modern European society. The broad logic of the argument appears to agree with Bauman's claim that greater social distance between individuals made modern forms of bureaucratic violence possible.[22] Large numbers of those who participated in the Holocaust were not active participants in public acts of cruelty, and indeed they did not encounter (or need to encounter) the victims of genocide in their everyday lives. Rather than express aggressive impulses, many were merely required to play what they purported to be trivial roles in the bureaucratic apparatus of industrialized killing (roles that required the very suppression of violent instincts which the civilized process required).[23] Modern structures of bureaucratic power checked the development of personal responsibility and collective guilt with respect to human suffering in the context of the unusually high levels of personal detachment that were required by the civilizing process (see Mennell 1998: 248).[24] Such observations about the violent tendencies that reside in the very structure of modern industrial societies resonate with Arendt's discussion of the 'banality of evil' and also with analyses of 'bystanders' whose conscience is untroubled as long as violence is hidden from view (Arendt 1994; Barnett 2000; Smith 2001: 26).[25] For Elias, as for Foucault, the civilizing process placed constraints on certain forms of public power (public execution for example) but made other forms of domination possible – hence the claim that civilizing processes are invariably attended by decivilizing possibilities and effects.

The modern civilizing process

Having argued that Elias did not defend a nineteenth century 'grand narrative' that defended Western triumphalism, it is important to consider his account of the civilizing process. As noted earlier, Elias used this idea to describe patterns of

Western social and political change stretching back to the fifteenth century. Social controls on violence and constraints on impulsive behaviour were the 'most basic elements' of the civilizing process, but they were not the whole of it. In a parallel with English School comments on global civilizing processes that were noted earlier, Elias (1996: 109) claimed that 'the extent and depth of people's mutual identification with each other and, accordingly, the depth and extent of their ability to empathize and capacity to feel for and sympathize with other people in their relationships with them' were also 'central criteria of a civilizing process'.[26] His main objective was to understand long-term patterns of change in Europe which affected not only the organization of economic and political life but also the emotional lives of individual persons. Analysing the relationship between social and political structures (the sociogenetic) and the emotional lives of individuals, including their perceptions of guilt, shame, and so forth (the psychogenetic) is a strikingly original feature of Elias's standpoint with immense significance for the study of international relations. On those foundations, Elias developed the argument that the inhabitants of modern societies have come to enjoy levels of physical security that are rare when viewed in the broadest historical context.

To account for this development, Elias argued that the rise of stable monopolies of power (in the form of absolutist states) promoted internal pacification and allowed lengthening chains of social interdependence to develop. In this condition, higher levels of self-discipline became necessary, along with greater foresight. Absolutist states had relied initially on external constraints to control the behaviour of knights, but 'the self-restraint apparatus [became] stronger relative to external constraints' and to 'the direct fear of others'. The rise of inner constraints was first evident in the court societies of England and France, but spread in a largely unplanned fashion over subsequent centuries to shape what Elias called the 'habitus' of modern life. Over the five hundred years that Elias investigated, the 'long-term civilizing trend [led] towards more even and more thorough control over the emotions'; in this period individuals came 'to identify more readily with other people as such, regardless of social origins' (Elias 1978: 155). Greater 'self-control in the harmonization of people to each other's activities became something more taken for granted' and was essential for the social integration of persons performing highly specialized tasks (Elias 1996: 34; 2000: 367; 2001a: 136). The analysis of how internal constraints on aggressive impulses became stronger relative to external checks emphasized the development of the modern conscience and profound changes in the dominant 'attitudes with regard to the perpetration of violent acts causing harm to other people, animals or even property in Western societies' (Elias 1996: 335; 2000: 161ff.; Fletcher 1997: 19). Modern societies developed a lower 'threshold of repugnance' to public acts of cruelty which set them apart from the medieval period.

It is seldom realized, Elias (2001b: 48) argued, that 'physical security from violence by other people is not so great in all societies as in our own'. The historical evidence revealed that 'the scope of identification' has become wider in modern Europe than it was in earlier centuries. As a result of the civilizing process, most inhabitants of European societies 'no longer regard it as a Sunday entertainment to see people hanged, quartered, broken on the wheel . . . As compared with antiquity, our identification with other people, our sharing in their suffering and death, has increased' (Elias 2001b: 2–3). In the preface to *The Civilizing Process*, Elias (2000: ix) maintained that:

> [if the] members of present-day Western civilized society were to find themselves suddenly transported into a past epoch of their own society, such as the medieval-feudal period, they would find there much that they esteem 'uncivilized' in other societies today . . . They would, depending on their situation and inclinations, be either attracted by the wilder, more unrestrained and adventurous life of the upper classes in this society, or repulsed by the 'barbaric' customs, the squalor and coarseness . . . encountered there.

They would discover a radically different social world in which public displays of extreme emotional responses were commonplace:

> in warrior society, the individual could use physical violence if he was strong and powerful enough; he could openly indulge his inclinations in many directions that have subsequently been closed by social prohibitions. But he paid for this greater opportunity of direct pleasure with a greater chance of direct fear . . . Both joy and pain were discharged more freely.
>
> (quoted in Smith 2001: 111; see also Elias 1992: 147)

Contrasts between 'great kindness' and 'naked cruelty' were 'sharper' than in modern societies where 'anything distasteful' or repugnant is usually hidden 'behind the scenes' (Elias 2000: 102; 2001b: 15).[27]

We have seen that Elias stressed the coexistence of civilizing and decivilizing processes in his account of how the violence of the Nazi period could possibly have occurred in Western Europe, and this raises the question of how far modern constraints on violence can resist political efforts to weaken them or are easily dissolved. Elias (1996: 196) maintained that, in the case of 'state violence in the Hitler era', 'the long build-up period which preceded the great acts of barbarism' was 'hardly visible' at first, but then 'became more obvious as though they had sprung from nowhere'. As for the relations between states, the two world wars had revealed that 'the sensitivity towards killing, towards dying people and death clearly evaporated quite quickly in the majority of people' when faced with growing insecurity (Elias 2001b: 51). But a strong theme in Elias's writings is that the 'process of brutalization and dehumanization . . . in relatively civilized societies always requires considerable time'. For reasons given earlier, the violence of the Nazi era may well confirm his general thesis about changing emotional responses to public cruelty over five centuries, although rather more empirical research is needed to decide whether Elias's account of European modernity is basically correct (see Garland 1990: ch. 10; Spierenburg 1991: ch. 7).[28] Certainly, as Elias argued, the Nazi persecution of the Jews did not diminish the widespread revulsion against cruelty that is a principal feature of European modernity.[29] At least this aspect of the evolution of modern societies has not been, and cannot be, easily reversed if Elias's analysis is broadly accurate (see Fletcher 1997: 24).[30] In these comments about general responses to the violence of the Nazi era, Elias argued that the civilizing process has not been confined to relations within modern societies but has had some impact on the larger development of human society and on the conduct of international relations. This observation has enormous importance for the sociology of states-systems, but before considering this theme in more detail it is necessary to comment on the relationship between Hobbesian, Grotian and Kantian themes in Elias's occasional reflections on world politics.

A global civilizing process?

The last few comments raise several questions about the relevance of Elias's project for the study of international relations. To what extent has the civilizing process that Elias identified in the relations between states and citizens, men and women, parents and children, and in the treatment of non-human species, influenced relations between political communities?[31] Is there a global civilizing process that weakens the sovereign state's capacity to behave violently towards its own peoples and which demands greater compliance with the humanitarian laws of war?[32] To what extent has the economic and technological integration of the human race contributed to a global civilizing process in which the members of different political communities come to identify more closely with one another? Are emotional responses to human suffering changing so that growing numbers of citizens believe that they have moral and political responsibilities to the world at large? Is the modern era witnessing fundamental changes in the ways in which human beings are bound together and yet set apart in world politics?[33] Is there evidence of collective learning processes which reveal that the human race can control increasing global connections and establish how different societies can live together without domination and force?

The Hobbesian response that Elias often gives to these questions is that international politics have persistently lagged behind developments within modern states with the result that 'a curious split runs through our civilization' (Elias 1996: 177). He drew on Bergson's writings to argue that, throughout human history, most societies have possessed moral codes that condone, and often actively encourage, acts of violence towards other peoples that are usually proscribed within the in-group (see also Elias 1996: 461). Elias used the expression, 'the duality of nation-states' normative codes', to describe this condition in the modern world (see Elias 1996: 154ff., 461). He maintained that the formation of stable monopolies of power was crucial for the pacification of modern societies, but added that the absence of a global monopoly of power has meant that relations between states have largely consisted of 'elimination contests' in which political actors respond to what Elias called the 'double-bind process' – or the security dilemma as it is called in International Relations (1996: 176–7; 1978: 30).[34] 'On this level', Elias (1996: 176) argued, 'we are basically still living exactly as our forefathers did in the period of their so-called "barbarism"' (see also Elias 1987a:

74). He added that the 'vicious circle' of 'mutual distrust between human groups', and 'unbridled use of violence' when leaders 'expected an advantage and were not afraid of retaliation', has been almost 'normal throughout the ages'. Only rarely has this condition of endemic distrust and conflict been 'tempered' by the 'fear of retaliation by superhuman agencies' (Elias 1996: 137–8); and only rarely have societies recognized 'that if they want to live without fear of each other . . . they can only do so by imposing certain common rules of conduct and the corresponding restraints upon themselves' (ibid.).[35] Just as formerly each tribe was a constant danger for the other tribes, so nowadays each state represents a constant danger for other states. Moreover, war is one social practice that remains largely free from human control.[36] All such comments are emphatically realist.[37]

Of course, many approaches to international politics – realism and neo-realism aside – have quarrelled with this interpretation of world affairs. Members of the English School will be struck by Elias's failure to note that societies of states (the Greek, Ancient Chinese and modern) developed legal and moral mechanisms for constraining violence in the relations between separate monopolies of power. Many will add that the modern society of states has made progress in promoting respect for the principle that all persons should be free from human rights violations and spared 'unnecessary suffering' in war; and they may stress how far global civilizing processes can develop in the absence of a single monopoly of power, whether regionally, as in the EU, or across the world as a whole (Linklater 2005). As noted earlier, the English School has stated that international society can be the site for the development of forms of global civility that are not as developed as their national equivalents but which influence the conduct of sovereign power monopolies nonetheless.[38] On this argument, Elias's approach inclines too much to the Hobbesian view that global civilizing processes cannot develop in the absence of a single, worldwide monopoly of violence.

Despite his realism, Elias was often sympathetic to the Grotian interpretation of world politics. He maintained that societies have not constructed dualistic normative codes with their emphasis on the welfare of citizens as against duties to humanity in uniform ways (Elias 1996:154ff.). Many nineteenth century German political thinkers stressed 'the incompatibility of the two codes' of morality (private and public) whereas British counterparts were more inclined to seek a compromise between these ethical positions (Elias 1996: 160ff.). This reference to the British zest for compromise immediately brings to mind the view that the Grotian approach represents the *via media* between the Hobbesian and Kantian approaches to international relations (Wight 1991: 15). Elias (1996: 134ff.) came close to the Grotian view that states can moderate the Hobbesian dynamic when he stressed how aristocratic internationalism in the nineteenth century supported interstate rules of conduct. In an argument that will be familiar to readers of Carr (1945) and Morgenthau (1973), he stated that the aristocratic code of honour and chivalry applied the same moral standards to domestic and international politics.[39] Subsequent changes in the European class structure made their own mark on relations between states. In the struggle against aristocratic rule, the bourgeoisie invoked 'a code of rules in the form of a morality regarded as valid for all people';

its support for egalitarian and universalistic moral principles was designed to advance a global civilizing process. Those comments suggest that Elias transcended the Hobbesian position by recognizing that independent political communities have become involved in a global civilizing process, but his comment that the bourgeoisie succumbed to the conflictual interpretation of international relations that had held sway in earlier eras indicates there were no guarantees that civility would survive (Elias 1996: 143). Indeed, Elias went further by suggesting that multistate systems might seem destined to be destroyed by force and replaced by empire (see Mennell 1990: 364). Here, Elias is at one with Wight (1977: ch. 1) and broadly shared the latter's belief that international politics is 'the realm of recurrence and repetition', the sphere of human interaction that is most resistant to change (Wight 1966a). In Wight's terms, Elias's views about international politics may be best placed at that point on the spectrum where the Hobbesian and Grotian traditions intersect.

Although Elias did not develop these remarks, he was unusual among sociologists of his generation in lamenting sociology's neglect of international relations.[40] He insisted that sociologists should not close their 'eyes to the fact that in our time, in place of the individual states, humanity split up into states is increasingly . . . the framework of reference, as a social unit, of many developmental processes and structural changes' (Elias 2001a: 163). Goudsblom (1990: 174) suggests that the analysis of the civilizing process was not an account of parallel national histories and that Elias was disposed to the view that 'humanity at large should be the unit of investigation'. Mennell (1990: 364) adds that the focus on processes affecting humanity as a whole was basically Hobbesian: the idea of 'the globalization of society as a very long-term social process' was firmly anchored in the belief that 'competition between states [is] a force for globalization'.[41] But perhaps the deeper issue raised by Elias's comments on globalization is whether the widening of emotional identification at the level of the human race may yet prove to be its most enduring effect.

These are matters to consider in the next section. Suffice it to note for now that it would be curious if the civilizing process (understood as the development of changing attitudes to cruelty and suffering and constraints on violence) did not make some impression on international affairs, and indeed Elias provided several examples of its effects. The barbarism of the Nazi years was widely regarded as violating European codes of conduct:

> Up till then . . . European wars had always been relatively limited regressions. Certain minimum rules of civilized conduct were generally still observed even in the treatment of prisoners of war. With a few exceptions, a kernel of self-esteem which prevents the senseless torturing of enemies and allows identification with one's enemy in the last instance as another human being together with compassion for his suffering, did not entirely lapse.
>
> (Elias 1998e: 114).[42]

These comments raise questions about whether the modern states-system is unusual in developing constraints on violence and in witnessing the rise of empathy for the suffering in other societies.

Recent works on international relations that analyse the delegitimation of colonialism in the twentieth century, changing emotional responses towards ethnic homogenization, and public expectations that governments will protect non-combatants from unnecessary suffering in war have contributed to this inquiry (Thomas 2001; Crawford 2002; Rae 2002; Wheeler 2002),[43] but these are unusual works in the field. It is striking that there is no tradition of inquiry that compares levels of cruelty and compassion in different states-systems, no systematic examination of long-term trends with respect to civilizing processes in international societies, and very little discussion of whether cosmopolitan responses to human suffering are stronger in the modern society of states than in earlier times. The works mentioned earlier in this paragraph are excellent examples of how analyses of central themes in Elias's thought can advance the study of long-term processes that affect humanity as a whole. Of special importance is their focus not only on state interests and global norms but also on emotional life, and specifically on attitudes to cruelty, harm and suffering (Scheff 1994). However, to develop these forms of analysis it is valuable to engage with Elias's account of the civilizing process and to note how it can contribute to developing a sociology of states-systems that considers the importance of 'cosmopolitan emotions' for projects of controlling world affairs with a view to minimizing senseless harm. Elias's comments on the 'Kantian' dimensions of international relations are of special importance because they can contribute to the development of Wight's achievement in carving out the sociology of states-systems as a distinctive area of intellectual inquiry.

Cosmopolitan emotions, modernity and the sociology of states-systems

Elias's writings contain intriguing observations about changing attitudes to violence and suffering, and about varying levels of intersocietal identification in the history of the modern states-system. The 'wars of the seventeenth century', it was claimed:

> were cruel in a somewhat different sense to those of today. The army had, as far as possible, to feed itself when on foreign soil. Plunder and rapine were not merely permitted, but were demanded by military technique. To torment the subjugated inhabitants of occupied territories . . . was, as well as a means of satisfying lust, a deliberate means of collecting war contributions and bringing to light concealed treasure. Soldiers were supposed to behave like robbers. It was a banditry exacted and organized by the army commanders.
>
> (Elias 1998f: 22–3; 2000: 162–4)

Similar contrasts separated the modern states-system from even earlier times, as these passages indicate:

The ancient Greeks . . . who are so often held up to us as models of civilized behaviour, considered it quite a matter of course to commit acts of mass destruction, not quite identical to those of the National Socialists but, nevertheless, similar to them in several respects. The Athenian popular assembly decided to wipe out the entire population of Melos, because the city did not want to join the Athenian colonial empire. There were dozens of other examples in antiquity of what we now call genocide.

(Elias 1996: 445)[44]

[Moreover, in that period] the level of 'moral' repugnance against what we now call 'genocide' and, more generally, the level of internalized inhibitions against physical violence, were decidedly lower, the feelings of guilt or shame associated with such inhibitions decidedly weaker, than they are in the relatively developed nation-states of the twentieth century. Perhaps they were entirely lacking.

(Elias 1996: 145)

Elias (ibid.) observed that the 'difference between this and the attempted genocide in the 1930s and 1940s is at first glance not easy to grasp. Nevertheless it is quite clear. In the period of Greek antiquity, this warlike behaviour was considered normal. It conformed to the standard'. Tolerance of unrestrained force in international affairs reflected the greater acceptance of violence in society at large.[45] The relationship between emotional responses to violence in these two spheres was a central theme in the Eliasian sociology of sport (Elias and Dunning 1986). Sport, Elias and Dunning argued, is one sphere of human activity that frequently encapsulates the prevailing attitudes towards violence, not least because of its historical importance as a training ground for developing warrior skills. Elias (1996: 136ff.) claimed the Greek *pancration*, a mode of ground wrestling in which it was legitimate to kill the adversary, indicated that 'the threshold of sensitivity with regard to the infliction of physical injuries and even to killing in a game-contest' was very different from what it is today in domestic and in international politics (Elias 1996: 137). Such remarks were designed to show that modern Europe is separated from Ancient Greece, as it is from the Middle Ages, by its higher level of repugnance towards cruelty and violence.

Was Elias correct that acceptance of violence was greater in the Greek polis and in ancient Greek international relations than it is today? Such questions about the relations between domestic and global civilizing processes have not received much scholarly attention in international relations although, interestingly, Wight drew a similar contrast between the international relations of Ancient Greece and modernity. Commenting on Churchill's reaction to Stalin's suggestion that the entire German General Staff should be liquidated at the end of the Second World War, Wight (1966b: 126) mused that it could be that 'modern Europe has acquired a moral sensitiveness, and an awareness of the complexities, denied to simpler civilizations. The Greeks and Romans gave small thought to political ethics, still less to international ethics'.[46] Perhaps this is correct but, as already noted, a closer analysis of the international relations of that epoch is needed in the light of recent scholarship. More generally, plausible though Elias's account of changing attitudes towards cruelty and violence may be, the core thesis requires 'further empirical corroboration', minor correction and even substantial revision (see Fletcher 1997: 19; van Krieken 1998: 131).[47] An important question for a sociology of states-systems that investigates levels of 'moral sensitiveness' is whether Elias's claim that cruelty in war was greater in the Ancient World than in the present era is broadly right.[48] These are large issues that must be left for another occasion. The main point is that Elias raised questions about the relationship between 'national' and 'international' civilizing processes and about levels of cruelty and emotional identification in international relations, which provide new directions for the sociology of states-systems.

The final task of this chapter is to consider how Elias's approach can contribute to the sociology of states-systems set out in Wight's landmark essays.[49] Wight (1977: ch. 1) was principally interested in the moral, cultural and institutional underpinnings of order between political communities in the Ancient Chinese, Hellenic–Hellenistic and modern systems of states. He was mainly concerned with civility in international relations. His focus was predominantly state-centred, but he also considered the extent to which visions of a community of humankind have had a civilizing role in different systems, and also a decivilizing one when used to dominate or exterminate allegedly inferior peoples (Wight 1991: ch. 4). His comments on ancient Greek attitudes towards cruelty in war addressed the question of different degrees of 'moral sensitiveness' in international systems. There are several parallels between Wight's remarks on these subjects and Elias's comparison of attitudes to violence and levels of emotional identification in antiquity, the Middle Ages and in modern Europe. Wight's references to prevalent attitudes to violence in warfare can be taken further in a sociological project with two primary ambitions: to examine the extent to which different states-systems tried to prevent or minimize the harm that separate political communities and other actors can inflict on one another's populations; and to consider whether or not the modern states-system is unusually committed to the ethical view that its constituent parts should regard unnecessary suffering as a global moral problem that all societies should try to solve.

An appropriate point of departure is how different states-systems have addressed 'the problem of harm in world politics' (see Chapter 9). The question of harm has long been central to the Grotian approach to international society. As Donelan (1990: ch. 4) argued, one of its central ethical tenets is that states have a responsibility to refrain from causing unnecessary injury. Echoing the point, Jackson (2000: 20) defends the importance of prudence in world affairs, the 'political virtue' that requires human beings 'to take care not to harm others'. Bull's claim that all societies have developed means of protecting members from 'violence resulting in death or bodily *harm*' (Bull 1977: 4–5, italics added) recalls Elias's statement that civilizing processes are designed to solve the problem of how human beings can satisfy basic needs without 'destroying, frustrating, demeaning or in other ways *harming* each other' in their attempts to satisfy them (see above

p. 164, italics added). A more complex account of what constitutes harm than either Elias or the English School have provided is necessary to develop this further. Arguably, a sociology of global civilizing processes should consider at least the following seven types of harm:[50]

- deliberate harm to the members of other communities which takes the form of maximizing the suffering of combatants and non-combatants in times of war, intentionally causing economic hardship, or promoting representations of other peoples that degrade and humiliate them;
- deliberate harm whereby a government harms its citizens through unlawful arrest and imprisonment, torture, degrading representations and other abuses of human rights;
- deliberate harm caused by non-state actors whereby, for example, terrorist groups target civilians, transnational corporations take advantage of vulnerable communities, and criminal organizations engage in the traffic of women and children and in the global drugs trade;
- unintended harm whereby, for example, a government or business enterprise unknowingly damages the physical environment of another society or the 'global commons';
- negligence whereby a state or private organization knowingly submits others to the risk of harm (for example by failing to ensure that workers in hazardous industries are protected by adequate health and safety provisions);
- harm through unjust enrichment whereby the members of affluent societies benefit unfairly (but perhaps unintentionally) from the rules of global commerce or the vulnerability of foreign producers;
- harm through acts of omission whereby a community fails to alleviate the suffering of others in circumstances where there is no or little cost to itself.[51]

This typology attempts to capture the complexities of the civilizing process, as Elias defines it. It is advanced in the light of his claim that it involves constraints on the human ability to cause mental and physical injury, as well as the rise of the 'capacity to feel for and sympathize with other people' (see above, p. 167). The upshot is that a sociology of global civilizing processes should focus on the extent to which efforts to prevent cruelty – and forms of emotional identification that embody the willingness to protect all human beings from unintended harm, negligence, unjust enrichment and omissive harm – developed in different states-systems. Such a typology raises two sets of questions about the extent to which cosmopolitan emotions influenced the long-term development of states-systems:

- To what extent did the members of different states-systems collaborate to ensure that military personnel and civilian populations, and especially women and children, were protected from unnecessary suffering in war? To what extent did the sense of a global responsibility to protect individuals from the violence of governments develop in all or most societies of states? To what extent have different states-systems developed universal obligations to protect the vulnerable from violence, domination and exploitation caused by non-state actors (pirates, mercenaries, merchant groups, and so forth)?

- To what extent have the members of different states-systems acted to reduce or eliminate unintended harm and the adverse effects of negligent behaviour? To what extent have they sought to protect all human beings from unjust enrichment or from the negative effects of acts of omission?

Those questions provide the basis for an empirical research programme that has two main purposes: to understand how far global civilizing processes that demonstrated what Hegel called 'anxiety for the well-being of humankind' (quoted in Elias 1996: 262) have developed in all states-systems; and to consider whether or not a global conscience or cosmopolitan moral emotions have greater influence in the modern states-system than in earlier epochs. Such questions, which are partly the result of engaging with Elias's reflections on European modernity, represent an attempt to take the sociology of states-systems in new directions.[52]

It would be wrong to look to Elias's writings for a detailed assessment of how far the modern states-system differs from its predecessors; however, his writings raised important issues that deserve closer attention. One such issue is the contention that the transition from peace to war is more complex for modern citizens than it was for the subjects of medieval principalities, the reason being that the former have internalized constraints on aggressive impulses that did not exist five centuries ago when 'social prohibitions' against violence were weaker (Elias 1996: 210; 1987a: 80–1; see also Verkamp 1993). Superpower competition to 'protect the individual against laws of his own state that they regard as inhumane' was evidence of a global civilizing process that reveals changing attitudes towards physical cruelty (Elias 1991: 140). Perhaps their rivalry represented 'the early stage of a long process in the course of which humankind as the highest level of integration may gain equality' with the state (ibid.). The emergence of regional associations might permit ethical commitments to the welfare of all human beings to escape national constraints (see Smith 2001: 130–1, 141).[53]

Elias posed what may be the key question about the meaning of globalization – whether it will increase emotional identification between the members of the human race. More cosmopolitan emotions might develop, he argued, as lengthening chains of human interconnectedness presented diverse societies with the challenge of finding new ways of living together.[54] But globalization could give rise to a powerful 'decivilizing counter thrust' in which groups react aggressively to alien values and to the insecurities that attend closer interdependence (Elias 1995: 36; 2001a: 222; see also Fletcher 1997: 79–80). Elias also noted that globalization means that more people than ever before are aware 'that an enormously large part of humanity live their entire lives on the verge of starvation' (Elias 1996: 26). Although the 'feeling of responsibility which people have for each other' has probably 'increased', the truth is that 'relatively little is done' to solve the problem (ibid.).[55]

For Elias, concerns about poverty suggested that a global civilizing process affecting the 'conscience' of modern peoples had grown out of the long-term patterns of change within European societies.[56] However, the current era could be placed in perspective by imagining how it might appear to future generations, assuming that 'humanity can survive the violence of our age'. Should 'our descendants' promote a global civilizing process that strengthens constraints on force, extends the protection of individual human rights and reduces starvation, they would be justified in concluding that modern peoples were the 'late barbarians' (Elias 1991: 146–7). In this alluring formulation, Elias summarized the achievements and limitations of the modern civilizing process.

Conclusion

Elias's analysis of the civilizing process described the rise of state monopoly powers, the appearance of internal constraints on violence and the widening of emotional identification between citizens of modern European states. He did not believe the civilizing process had made much impression on international politics although Grotian and Kantian sentiments existed alongside realist themes in his writings. These emphases are evident in his remarks on the revulsion against genocide and on the role of the humanitarian law of war in the modern world. Elias suggested that cosmopolitan emotions had made some advances in recent times, but how far modernity differs from earlier epochs in condemning cruelty is a matter for the undeveloped sociology of systems of states. Some parallels with Wight's interest in different levels of 'moral sensitiveness' in international societies have been noted, but Wight did not develop this area of inquiry. An engagement with Elias's account of European modernity – with his analysis of repugnance towards violence and discussion of the scope of emotional identification within and between societies – can make a significant contribution to the idea of a sociology of states-systems as outlined in Wight's pioneering essays.

Larger matters arise for those who lament the continuing divisions between International Relations and Sociology. The analysis of the civilizing process was not just or even primarily concerned with developments within separate states but also considered long-terms patterns of change affecting humanity as a whole, even though it failed to engage with the academic literature on international relations. An engagement with the relevant literature would have enlarged Elias's analysis of the connections between domestic and global civilizing processes; building on his comments about the relations between the two is one way of constructing new linkages between Sociology and International Relations. The prize is a deeper understanding of the tolerance of violence in different systems of states and the degree of emotional identification, and also a deeper appreciation of the forces that will decide whether cosmopolitan emotions come to play a greater role in controlling global interconnections between human beings than they have done in the previous phases of human history.

11 Towards a sociology of global morals with an 'emancipatory intent'[1]

Numerous thinkers have denied that the idea of shared humanity can provide the philosophical foundations for a cosmopolitan ethic, and many have rejected the belief that appeals to humanity will ever compete with the emotional attachments and the established norms of specific communities in determining human conduct.[2] But the idea that common humanity has profound ethical significance is not entirely friendless in recent moral and political theory. Gaita (2002) has drawn on Simone Weil's writings to defend an ethic of human concerns that is, in some respects, more fundamental than the social moralities that usually shape individual and group behaviour. The central aim of this chapter is to link this idea with the notion of a sociology of global morals with an emancipatory intent. The principal objective is to build on previous endeavours to construct a distinctive mode of comparative sociological analysis that examines the extent to which basic considerations of humanity have not only influenced the conduct of international relations in different historical eras but may yet acquire a central role in bringing unprecedented levels of global connectedness under collective moral and political control.

The chapter begins by summarizing Weil's thesis, noting that it raises significant problems for 'communitarian' arguments which deny that representative moral agents are motivated to act from considerations of humanity. The key contention is that Weil identifies certain humanist dispositions, which have probably existed to some degree in all or most times and places, and which have long contained the possibility of radically enlarging the moral and political boundaries of community. The second part identifies affinities between Weil's doctrine of humanity and critical–theoretical claims that common vulnerabilities to mental and physical suffering provide the most secure foundation for solidarity between strangers. This position has special significance for the task of reconstructing historical materialism and redirecting the course of the critical theory of society. Developing this theme, parts three and four consider the implications of these remarks for a sociology of global morals that analyses the extent to which the most basic forms of human solidarity have influenced international relations in different eras and may yet prove to be decisive in shaping the evolution of the species as a whole.

Universalizable sympathies

Weil maintained that a person stranded in the desert, but possessing ample water, would normally be expected to assist a stranger who was facing death because of thirst. Most moral agents, Weil observed, would assume that considerations of humanity would make rescue 'automatic'; in the circumstances, there would be no request for an explanation of the decision to assist. By contrast, most observers would think an explanation was called for, 'if having enough water in his canteen [the potential rescuer], simply walked past, ignoring the other person's pleas'.[3]

Weil (1952: 6) maintained that the obligation to assist reflected a belief that the dignity of other persons can be respected only through efforts to deal with 'earthly needs'; and on this matter, she proceeded to argue, 'the human conscience has never varied'.[4] The extent to which her theologically grounded empirical claims about human responsiveness to threats to survival can be generalized across human history is an interesting question. It seems reasonable to suppose that the anthropological record reveals great cultural variations with respect to ethical commitments to 'Good Samaritanism'; it may also show that displays of solidarity towards the members of other communities have often been actively discouraged or regarded as morally reprehensible or judged to warrant severe punishment. In many societies, persons in the circumstances that Weil described may have ignored the plight of strangers on the grounds that their ethnicity, colour, enemy status, sacrilegious beliefs or whatever, condemned them to perish. But it will have been noted that Weil did not insist that humanitarian assistance will always be automatic in the desperate conditions she described or believe that other social actors must always be so astonished by the failure to assist as to feel compelled to request an explanation. But if help has been virtually automatic in various encounters with 'outsiders' over the millennia, and if failures to assist have often led to bemusement, astonishment or disgust, then rather more might be said for the ethical importance of considerations of humanity than the critics have recognized.

Weil's argument can be modified in ways that consolidate her claims about the most basic forms of solidarity between strangers. One might ask if it would not seem odd if a person who is facing death because of a lack of water failed to ask or implore a passing stranger to help on the grounds of the invisible ties of common humanity. But here one must also allow for important exceptions. In some societies, such pleas may be regarded as violating cherished social norms, as bringing dishonour to the group, as risking cultural pollution, or some such thing. Unbroken traditions of hostility and warfare may often have led to decisions not to place the self at the mercy of an alien other. In such circumstances, the decision to withhold the request for assistance may not prompt the request for an explanation.

Scepticism about the motivational power of common humanity is weakened significantly if at least some human beings in different historical eras have thought it was right to help a stranger in the circumstances described, if others have endorsed their course of action, and if they have sanctioned the failure to rescue.

Distrust of the ties of humanity is dented if certain basic forms of solidarity with the suffering led at least some moral agents to assist others more or less automatically in different historical eras. Empirical evidence of levels of attachment to Good Samaritanism over time is unavailable, but it does not seem preposterous to speculate that complete strangers have been compelled to act by the ties of humanity in very different times and places. If this is right, and as already noted, then there is more to be said for the ethical significance of shared humanity than 'communitarian' objections to cosmopolitanism have allowed.

Weil's thesis raises several interesting claims about moral agency if it is the case that certain sympathies have been extended to strangers in the circumstances described in many historical epochs. First, the potential rescuer and the endangered do not have to belong to the same moral and political community to participate in the imagined ethical encounter. Second, the ethical exchange does not presuppose the capacity to communicate in the same spoken language. These points will be extended in a moment, but before doing so it is important to stress what the encounter does presume, namely the existence of universally intelligible expressions and gestures, and a shared emotional vocabulary, which make it possible for the members of radically different groups to communicate distress to each other and to respond sympathetically. Given the significance of emotions such as empathy and sympathy for solidarity between strangers, it is worth pausing to note that, from Darwin to Ekman, analysts of the role of emotions in human behaviour have argued that all human beings possess a similar repertoire of facial expressions denoting fear, anger, joy, distress, etc., which ensures intelligibility between groups that are otherwise separated by differences of language and culture (Ekman 2003: ch. 1). Various debates surround the question of whether, or how far, basic emotions such as fear are 'hard-wired', but Weil's argument, which assumes that certain emotional responses to suffering will be automatic, invites consideration of the claim that certain ethical potentialities have long been immanent within a universal vocabulary of moral emotions (Nussbaum 2001).[5]

The ability to communicate distress to another, and capacity to recognize suffering, are clearly essential if the Weilian 'primordial' ethical encounter is to occur, but they are not sufficient conditions. A complete explanation must make reference to the rudimentary emotions of empathy and sympathy, emotions that can be usefully linked with Bentham's thesis about the centrality of sentience for the moral life. In a famous passage on the grounds for being moved by animal suffering, Bentham (1970: 311ff.) maintained that the central question was not whether the animal could speak or reason but whether it could feel pain and had the capacity for suffering. Sympathy for sentient creatures that are all condemned to feel pain and to suffer to some degree was at the heart of morality in Bentham's view.

Just as the decision to assist a non-human animal does not assume the equality of human and non-human species, so the decision to help a stranger from another social group need not rest on a doctrine of the equality of all persons – or rather it need only recognize their equality to a limited extent. Pragmatic considerations that have little or no place for a doctrine of equal rights can be the spur behind assistance; but if the 'Weil thesis' is right, there is often more to help than simple prudential calculations.[6] The main point to make is that the bonds and attachments between strangers may rest entirely on the almost universal experience of being similar to, but not necessarily equal with (or identical to), others, and in being exposed, as part of one's biological heritage, to similar vulnerabilities to mental and physical suffering. It is striking that some of the earliest formulations of the defence of cosmopolitanism in Western moral and political theory grounded the perspective in such universal vulnerabilities of the body (Baldry 1965: 45ff.). This is hardly extraordinary given that mutual recognition of shared mental and physical vulnerability provides the most readily available means of projecting forms of solidarity across the boundaries of community – and across the boundaries that are deemed to exist between human and non-human forms of life.

Earlier, it was noted that the strangers in the 'Weilian condition' need not belong to the same community or speak the same language before they can engage in crucial moral encounters. One might extend the point by adding that no sophisticated 'labour of translation' is required to steer agents towards a Gadamerian fusion of ethical horizons.[7] Nor is any great process of societal rationalization needed in which cultures transcend egocentric or parochial worldviews and embrace highly abstract, post-conventional ethical dispositions – even though it is the case that transcendent religious perspectives have often been the social force that led human beings to project relations of sympathy beyond in-groups.[8] As noted, the preconditions of the ethical encounter described above include certain emotional and expressive capacities that revolve around mutually intelligible concerns about the vulnerabilities of the body. Some such reference to inherent capacities that can bind strangers together has a distinguished presence in the history of Western moral and political thought. It is evident in Aristotle's claim that 'there is . . . a general idea of just and unjust in accordance with nature, as all in a manner divine, even if there are neither communications nor agreement between them' (Aristotle 1959: book 1.13). The capacity for feeling pity for others, he argued, stems from the agent's fears for his or her personal well-being, a position that was defended by Adam Smith (1982: 9) with the correct proviso that the root of the capacity to sympathize with others can be, at one and the same time, the reason for decisions to place the satisfaction of one's relatively minor interests before the welfare of others.

Aristotle's observations about certain intuitive understandings about justice that can bind persons who have neither communicated with each nor entered into a previous pact resonate with the claims made earlier about the most elementary forms of human solidarity. The emphasis here is on how the vulnerabilities of the person and the emotions such as sympathy which can be woven around them – sensitivities that have existed to some degree in all ways of life – create the possibility of 'embodied cosmopolitanism', that is the potentiality for extending rights of moral consideration to all other human beings, and indeed to all creatures that possess the quality of sentience (Linklater 2006b). The emphasis is on the *potentialities* that arise from corporeality or embodiment as, of course, rather more than recognition of this biological legacy must be in place to convert immanent possibilities into binding social practices.

We shall come back to the question of the factors that can intercede between certain basic universal experiences and the structure of moral codes, but some prior remarks about empathy and sympathy may be useful to capture the essential point. As Smith emphasized, certain empathetic dispositions that are based on anxieties about one's own welfare do not guarantee the development of sympathy for others.[9] Empathy can make it easier for the torturer to estimate the victim's likely breaking point, and it may lead to the voyeuristic enjoyment of media spectacles of distant suffering. Sympathy, which all societies must endeavour to inculcate in their members to some degree, has almost always been confined to members of the same 'survival group'.[10] Virtually all social moralities have revolved around insider–outsider distinctions that devalued the suffering of distant strangers and even attached positive value to it. In such conditions, collective help for 'distant strangers' has been far from 'automatic'. Aristotle (1959: book II, section 8; 1995: sections 7.2 and 7.4) observed that a person is more likely to pity another when the victim 'does not deserve it', when the 'evil' involved is of the kind that might afflict oneself or a friend and, crucially, when it 'seems near'. As noted earlier, Smith made a similar point about the unequal moral significance of proximate and distant suffering. Such realities complicate but do not undermine the claim that certain potentialities for supporting embodied cosmopolitanism have existed in all societies, and may have been realized from time to time, albeit fleetingly and exceptionally, in the relations between very different social groups. The interesting question for a sociology of morals is what has determined whether or not these potentialities have been realized, and what has decided how far cosmopolitan sympathies have influenced international relations.

Solidarity and suffering

Largely neglected sociological questions are raised by these observations about the sources and channels of human sympathy, questions that are directly concerned with puzzles about the processes affecting 'the expansion and contraction of the boundaries of community', levels of 'emotional identification' between different societies and the 'scope of moral concern' in international states-systems. These matters have special significance for a mode of sociological investigation that is infused with the normative purposes associated with the Frankfurt School; in particular, they suggest new directions for a critical sociology of world politics with an emancipatory intent. To explain this point more fully, it is necessary to consider how notions of sympathy and compassion have been central to forms of ethical reasoning that challenge Kantian understandings of the relationship between reason and morality of the kind that inform Habermas's conception of critical social theory; it is especially important to consider the rather different approach to ethical reasoning that was advanced by early Frankfurt School reflections on suffering and solidarity; and it is essential to show how these themes provide a new agenda for critical international theory, one that regards the prevalent attitudes to harm, suffering and vulnerability, and the dominant dispositions to cruelty and compassion, in different international states-systems as the principal object of sociological inquiry.

The starting point for this stage in the discussion is that the capacity to acquire sympathies that can be extended to distant persons is universal; this potentiality to extend 'the scope of moral concern' can be regarded as a 'species-power' that is immanent in most if not all social systems. A link can be forged between this contention and the philosophical claim that sympathy belongs among the more 'primitive' moral emotions, a proposition that does not regard sympathy as a natural endowment or biological trait but contends that it is irreducible to more fundamental ethical dispositions. In deliberations of this kind, attention frequently turns to Wittgenstein's remarks on an 'attitude to a soul', which stressed forms of human recognition that have to be instilled in the course of early, routine socialization processes before more complex ethical dispositions and relationships can develop (Wittgenstein 1974: part II, section 4; Gaita 2002: 259ff.). Primitiveness in this context refers to the first stages in human moral development in which children are taught that other persons are independent centres of feeling and experience who can be made to suffer and be harmed in other ways by their actions (Harris 1989; Taylor 2004). Inculcating this awareness of sentience along with recognition of the causal and possibly harmful effects of actions on other sentient creatures is essential for developing respect for the principles of moral responsibility which are intrinsic to every social group. The capacities for empathizing with others, and for acquiring the separate but related moral ability to sympathize with suffering others, are the foundations on which all moral codes rest.

Schopenhauer, whose influence on Horkheimer will be considered later, placed these attitudes towards the soul at the heart of his ethical system, as is evident from an intriguing passage in his writings that reflects on the report of a mother who murdered one child by pouring boiling oil down its throat and another by burying it alive. In the course of analysing the reasons for regarding such behaviour as despicable, he maintained that feelings of revulsion are not a response to the mother's failure to be deterred by the thought of divine sanctions, or to the astonishing disregard for the categorical imperative, but to the fundamental cruelty of the deed and the complete absence of compassion. The steeper the incline between self and other, Schopenhauer (1995: 169, 204–5) added, the more reprehensible such acts are generally regarded. His reflections on such matters did not consider how the 'gradient between self and other' has changed over history or varies in relations between members of the same society as a result of the dominant forms of inclusion and exclusion.[11] Clearly, there are sharp differences in the level of emotional identification between persons, and in the gradient between self and other, in the same society and indeed in the whole history of human societies. Notwithstanding these facts, his emphasis on the significance of revulsion towards certain acts of cruelty for the moral life, and on the lack of compassion, highlighted dimensions of the moral code and related moral emotions that are critical for all functioning social systems.

Schopenhauer was a forceful critic of what has been regarded as Kant's excessive rationalism, which denied that ethical principles can be grounded in the moral emotions. Philosophical inquiries into the relationship between ethics and the emotions are not the subject of this discussion, although it is useful to pause to recall Kant's advice that moral agents should not strive to avoid sites of suffering. Direct encounters with suffering were vital, Kant argued, if agents were to develop moral sensibilities and inclinations that would lead them to do what reason required but might not always accomplish on its own.[12] The core issue here is the nature of ethical motivation. As various analyses of moral codes and the emotional life have revealed, compliance with social norms depends crucially on how far key principles are embodied in the emotional lives of moral agents and have the force of 'second nature'. None of these accounts denies the importance of the fear of external sanctions for agent conformity with moral codes. What all highlight in addition is the role of psychological factors, such as experienced or anticipatory shame or guilt, and feelings of indignation, shock, disgust and so forth in creating harmony between agents' engrained dispositions and the 'external' demands of moral systems. The gap between agent and structure is bridged (but not always successfully) to the extent that ethical responses are embodied and instinctive – that is to the extent that the configuration of the emotions and constitution of central impulses make the agent's compliance with social principles virtually automatic (Barbalet 2002).[13]

Mainstream and critical investigations of world politics are largely guilty of neglecting the psychological and emotional dimensions of social conduct and moral interaction (Crawford 2001). These elements of human behaviour were central preoccupations of Freudian-influenced Frankfurt School theory, and they were critical to how analysts such as Erich Fromm (an associate of the Frankfurt School of Psychoanalysis, which existed alongside the Institute of Social Research) envisaged combining psychological and materialist approaches to the study of society and history (Wiggershaus 1993: 54; see below pp. 188–9). For the purpose of stressing how far Frankfurt School critical theory – and related perspectives in the interwar period – moved the psychological and emotional features of human existence to the forefront of sociological analysis, it is important to recall Schopenhauer's distinctive influence on Horkheimer's reflections on solidarity and suffering and also the place of the idea of 'injurability' in Adorno's ethical reflections on how modern societies should choose between forms of life. All of these preoccupations, it should be added, preserved core elements in Marx's critique of Hegelian idealism – most obviously his claim that social investigation should start with concrete human beings or embodied selves that are required to satisfy basic biological needs that remind them of their origins in, and continuing membership of, the natural world (Marx 1977c). These emphases in Frankfurt School theory are central for the purposes of this chapter not only because they anticipated the recent sociological interest in the body,[14] but also because they foreshadowed parallel efforts to make vulnerability and frailty central to the defence of human rights (Turner 1993).

First-generation Frankfurt School theorists anticipated this last theme by insisting that the critical study of society has a responsibility 'to lend a voice to suffering' (this being a 'condition of all truth') and to 'abolish existing misery' (Adorno 1990: 17–18; Horkheimer 1993: 32). In a parallel with Weil's thesis, Horkheimer argued that 'human solidarity' is best grounded in the 'shared experience of suffering and creaturely finitude'. Schopenhauer's worldly moral theory was a major influence on his attempt to unite 'materialism and morality' (Benhabib 1993: 5).[15] Similar commitments are evident in his claim that the foundation of 'correct solidarity' lies in the fact that human beings are 'finite beings whose community consists of fear of death and suffering' and who can sympathize with each others' 'struggle to improve and lengthen the life of all' (Horkheimer, quoted in Stirk 1992: 178).[16] Adorno's contention that the Holocaust demanded the ethical affirmation of the rights of the 'injurable animal' to receive protection and support defended broadly similar themes.[17] A 'new categorical imperative' was required in his view to ensure that the brutalities of the extermination camps did not occur again (Bernstein 2002: ch. 8). The new imperative would focus on absolute prohibitions rather than on the quest to realize some conception of the good life. Human beings, Adorno (2000: 167ff.) argued, 'may not know' what counts as the 'absolute good', but they have reached some shared understandings about 'inhuman' behaviour and about conceptions of the 'bad life' that should be resisted and opposed.[18]

Such themes have not been at the forefront of attempts to construct a critical theory of international politics – at least, they have not been central to Habermasian-inspired developments. They have been more central to approaches that draw on Honneth's analysis of the 'struggle for recognition' which preserves certain early Frankfurt School preoccupations by stressing the part that 'moral injury' plays in generating social conflicts, whether by inflicting physical pain, humiliating or demeaning others through 'the withdrawal or refusal of recognition' or by denying others a fair share of social resources (Honneth 1995; Hacke 2005).[19] The Habermasian discourse theory of morality has not ignored these themes entirely, but it cannot be said to have stressed them to anything like the same extent.[20]

The next two parts will comment on the Habermasian project of reconstructing historical materialism (and on its possible further reconstruction) but it is useful to pre-empt what is at stake in the discussion by recalling Habermas's specific claim about the cosmopolitan possibilities that were inherent in the first 'speech act' – in the first instances of communicative action that explored the prospects for reaching a shared understanding. The intriguing contention was that the very first speech act contained the promise of the moral and political unity of humankind – alternatively, that the presuppositions of everyday speech, wherever language has been used, raised the possibility of a worldwide communication community in which all persons enjoyed an equal right to advance claims about any decisions that may affect them and also possessed the same entitlement to influence deliberative outcomes. Collective learning processes over many centuries have brought these possibilities to light, and they have made them central to the advanced, 'post-conventional' moral codes and the associated democratic principles of legitimacy that must be included among the achievements of occidental rationalism. But as these ethical possibilities were immanent in the structure of communicative action in previous phases of history, they were available at least in principle to all forms of life.

Many critics have argued that the Habermasian approach to critical social theory rests on an 'excessive rationalism' and a 'limited conception of communication' (Whitebook 1995: 9, 183). Reflecting this concern, one might ask if Weil's claims about the most elementary forms of human solidarity do not suggest a rival conception of the cosmopolitan possibilities that have been immanent in all ways of life. The central issue is whether the very first humanitarian response to the pleas of an 'outsider' did not already contain a vision of universal ethical responsibilities that many ethical codes have developed further, most significantly in the belief that all members of the human race should enjoy the same rights of respect and protection irrespective of citizenship, nationality, race, gender, and so forth. The question then is whether the first displays of sympathy for the stranger did not already embody the immanent possibility of global relations of solidarity formed for the purpose of alleviating or ending unnecessary suffering.

It is not possible to do more than pose these questions here; clearly, further reflections are needed to develop and assess this conjecture and to ascertain whether the 'linguistic turn' in critical social theory failed to capitalize on early Frankfurt School reflections on suffering and solidarity for both normative and sociological purposes. Questions about the normative content of critical theory must be set aside here because the priority is to extend the conception of a sociological project which has been outlined elsewhere, a project that has the task of investigating how far the potentialities for global solidarity that can be derived from basic human concerns about vulnerability and injurability were realized in different states-systems (see Chapters 9 and 10). It is essential to consider Habermas's notion of the reconstruction of historical materialism, and his associated reflections on learning processes in the ethical sphere, before discussing how the links between International Relations and Historical Sociology can be developed further.

Collective learning processes and social evolution

It is widely known that Habermas rejected the historical materialist claim that the labour process explains the evolution of humanity along with its exhausted conviction that the resolution of the main capitalist contradictions requires the transition to universal socialism. The reconstruction of historical materialism elevated the domain of communicative action to a position of equality with the labour process; neither should be privileged, it was argued, in any account of the reproduction of any society or in the broader analysis of the evolution of humanity. An additional contention was that societies have undergone learning processes in the communicative realm that have been as important for the history of the species as the forms of social learning that had given rise to unrivalled mastery of natural forces.

Habermas (1979a: ch. 4) has claimed that the rise of reflective, universalistic ethical perspectives is one of the great accomplishments of occidental rationalism and one of the most significant steps in the development of the species. Collective learning processes replaced mythical narratives with 'rationalized world views' which valued 'argumentative foundations' and which broke through morally parochial ways of life (Habermas 1979a: 105). Abstract ethical systems involved the 'decentration' of worldviews, that is the movement from egotistical moral systems to commitments to the Kantian ideal of thinking from the standpoint of all others. They have been an essential part of long-term learning processes which have enabled the species to realize that consensual efforts to decide universaliz-able ethical principles represent its best hope of freeing global social and political relations from domination and force (Habermas 1979a: chs 3–4).

The claim that there are 'homologies' between ego formation in modern socie-ties and the evolution of humanity as a whole that inform this account of social evolution preserves the early Frankfurt School's specific interest in psychological and psychoanalytical processes.[21] However, the focus on homologies contains few references to the role of collective and individual emotions in social systems – specifically in uniting 'agents' and 'structures' in the manner described earlier.[22] Generally lacking is any recognition of the significance of emotional responses to vulnerability, pain and suffering in understanding long-term patterns of change.[23] The relative silence about these matters underpins the criticism that Habermas's linguistic turn involves the 'decorporealization of Critical Theory' (Whitebook 1996: 300). Honneth (1991: 281) makes a similar claim when he argues that Hab-ermas's approach:

> is directed exclusively to an analysis of rules . . . so that the bodily and physi-cal dimension of social action no longer comes into view. As a result, the hu-man body, whose historical fate both Adorno and Foucault had drawn into the center of the investigation . . . loses all value within a critical social theory.[24]

The lack of interest in corporeality may reflect the influence of Kant's ethical rationalism with its renowned distrust of the instinctual or impulsive.[25] Habermas is explicit that the human compulsion to satisfy the needs that form an important part of its biological legacy has no logical consequences for ethical reasoning; moreover, he insists that any leap from empirical observations about aversions to pain and injury to specific normative claims about how human beings should organize social and political life commits a 'naturalistic fallacy'.[26] No such prob-lems arise, it is argued, for modes of ethical analysis that begin with the nature of communicative action rather than with the vulnerabilities of the body.[27]

There may be a link between Habermas's essentially Kantian ethical position and the neglect of the body and the emotions in his more sociological writings on long-term patterns of change in the modern West (Habermas 1979b). Not that Habermas has been entirely deaf to the influence of emotional or instinctual drives since he has supported including in 'the natural basis of history, the heritage of natural history . . . consisting in an impulse potential that is both libidinal and ag-gressive', although he adds that emotional impulses are never encountered with-out the mediating effect of language and culture. There is explicit recognition here that an inquiry into moral learning which considers 'structures of thought' would be deficient if it neglected the natural 'heritage'. Nevertheless, his writings have not explained how a sociology of collective learning processes should proceed in the light of the fact that natural history 'determines the initial conditions of the reproduction of the human species'.[28]

Towards a sociology of global morals

In a lecture at the launch of the Institute of Psychoanalysis on 16 February 1929, Erich Fromm is reported to have stated that 'the most important psychological and sociological questions' of the era should endeavour to explain the 'connections' between 'the social development of humanity, particularly its economic and technological development, and the development of its mental faculty, particularly the ego-organization of the human being' (Wiggershaus 1993: 55). Fromm (1989) argued for a materialist approach to 'psychological categories' which recognized that every society 'has not only its own economic and political but also its specific libidinous structure' (see also Wiggershaus 1993: 55). Five years later, Horkheimer stressed the importance of integrating psychological approaches into the materialist interpretation of history (McCarthy 1981: 193). Commenting on the Frankfurt School in the 1940s, Wiggershaus (1993: 271) maintains that Horkheimer and Adorno seem to have inclined towards a form of 'biological materialism' in the belief that 'there was a utopian potential in instinctual structures'. Reflecting similar themes, Marcuse later distinguished between 'basic repression' and the 'surplus repression' of the instincts that modern civilization requires. The transition to socialism, he added, would involve not only the reconfiguration of the relations of production but also fundamental changes in the constitution of the human psyche that would include 'a different sensitivity' involving 'different gestures' and 'impulses' and 'an instinctual barrier against cruelty, brutality [and] ugliness' (Marcuse 1972: 29–30). A striking feature of those comments is their commitment to a critical approach to society that analyses the interplay between material structures or forces and the organization of the libidinal and emotional dimensions of individual and collective selves.

Frankfurt School theorists have not been the solitary advocates of the need for 'historical psychology'. By the late 1930s, the aspiration to develop more sophisticated understandings of the connections between the material dimensions of any society and the dominant personality types had already been promoted by Elias's analysis of the 'sociogenetic' and 'psychogenetic' elements of the European 'civilizing process' which gathered pace in the 1500s. Elias's legacy in the shape of figurational sociology as well as Annales histories and the more recent sub-field of emotionology, all have particular importance for the mode of sociological investigation of international politics to which we now turn in conclusion (Burke 1973: 24; Stearns and Stearns 1985; Elias 2000). At the heart of this approach is the suggestion that the most basic forms of solidarity between strangers are grounded in the shared sense of vulnerability to mental and physical suffering and in the related capacity to enlarge the scope of ethical concern to include the members of all other social groups. The main sociological question is how far commitments to embodied cosmopolitanism, which have been possible in all forms of life, emerged from under the shadows of pernicious systems of exclusion to influence the historical development of relations between societies. It is how far these ethical orientations have been central to collective learning processes in different societies of states; it is how far a world historical approach to the human species, one that focuses on how social groups spread to all parts of the world and became more closely interconnected over tens of thousands of years, can profit from analysing the development of moral capacities including the potentiality for the development of cosmopolitan forms of solidarity and sympathy (see Manning 2003). In this perspective, international societies are the key level of analysis because they have been the main steering mechanisms that independent communities have devised for organizing increasing levels of global interconnectedness. As organizers of humanity, they have been the vehicles through which certain universal ethical potentialities could be released and embedded in collective efforts to ensure that the relations between social groups do not cause unnecessary suffering to each other.

It has been suggested that Horkheimer, Adorno, Fromm and others developed a conception of the critical theory of society which aimed to understand the connections between social–structural forces and psychological dynamics, and it has been maintained that Elias's figurational sociology is the main realization of that aspiration. It is fitting that this chapter should end with some brief comments on the significance of Eliasian sociology for Frankfurt School critical theory, beginning with the fact that Elias was a member of the Department of Sociology in Frankfurt in the early 1930s, in the period when Horkheimer, Adorno and Fromm were engaged in developing a critical approach to society that incorporated Freudian insights into sociological analysis. Elias was not a member of the Frankfurt School, nor did he subscribe to partisan social inquiry, although his contention that the ultimate purpose of Sociology is to enable human beings to exercise control over uncontrolled social processes, including the complex forms of interdependence that now exist globally, might be said to share the humanist objectives of the Frankfurt School.[29] It is especially important to stress the affinities between Elias's analysis of the modern West and the sociological directions that members of the Institute of Psychiatry and the Institute of Social Research started to explore in the late 1920s and early 1930s (and to lament the continuing fracturing of that discourse into separate branches of sociology which was initially caused by the rise of Fascism).[30] A sociology of states-systems that draws on Elias's analysis of changing emotional responses to public and private acts of violence and cruelty in Western Europe over five centuries, and on his related examination of how the scope of emotional identification widened in the era in question at least between members of the same bounded communities, can reinvigorate Frankfurt School social inquiry and develop the account of collective learning processes that was at the core of Habermas's account of social evolution. That sociological project must also address Elias's question of whether unprecedented global interconnectedness might yet extend the scope of emotional identification at the level of humanity and increase the sense of moral responsibility for the imperilled in other societies (Mennell 1994; De Swaan 1995; Elias 1996). Finally, it must embrace his question, which was central to the more overtly normative project of Frankfurt School theory, of whether humanity can organize its social and political affairs with the minimum of force, domination and humiliation in its remaining time on earth.

Conclusion

Many thinkers such as Schopenhauer, Weil, Horkheimer and Adorno have placed solidarity with the suffering at the centre of their conceptions of ethical life. Their approach has the merit of highlighting moral sentiments, which have been essential for the reproduction of all forms of life and which may have had some salience in relations with other groups in very different historical eras. The most accessible forms of cosmopolitanism draw on universal capacities for sympathizing with the suffering, but how far embodied cosmopolitanism has shaped different states-systems and has unusual influence in the modern world are matters for a sociological project that can usefully combine Frankfurt School theory with Elias's analysis of civilizing processes. Investigating these questions is critical to understanding how the human race may yet come to organize its political affairs so that all individuals and communities are released from constraints that are not absolutely necessary for the reproduction of society, which are grounded in gross asymmetries of power, in the dominion of sectional interests, in disrespect for other persons or groups, and in forms of fear, distrust and insecurity that are intrinsic to intractable social conflicts. The purpose of a global sociology of morals with an emancipatory intent is to understand how human beings might yet learn to live together without such crippling infestations and afflictions.

Notes

Introduction

1 Andrew Sherratt, quoted in Christian (2004: 393).
2 See Chapter 10.
3 The idea of 'grievability' can be found in Butler (2004).
4 Wight (1966a).
5 Linklater (1990b).
6 Ferguson (1997), Haas (1990) and Keeley (1996).
7 Gallie (1978).
8 Linklater (1990a).
9 Habermas (1996: 515).
10 Linklater (1998).
11 See Linklater (2006a).
12 Elias (1991: 46).

1 'Men and citizens' in the theory of international relations

1 The conflict between the two moralities is evident in the differences between Kantian and Hegelian ethics. See Acton (1970) and Walsh (1969). Hegel (1952: para. 209) brought the two moralities *(moralitat and sittlichkeit* as he called them) into clear opposition as theories of international relations. Reflections on 'communitarian' and 'cosmopolitan' theories of international relations have further investigated the differences between these two conceptions of morality. See Brown (1992).
2 See, for example, the claim that 'the just size of a state should be measured by the strength of its neighbours' in Pufendorf (1934b: 968), an observation that might seem to require a contract of the whole world to divide humanity on a fair basis.
3 Kant's later historical and political writings may represent 'a point of departure' from his earlier accounts of an unchanging humanity. See Raschke (1975: 191–2).
4 'The rays of divine light reveal themselves in a broken form in different peoples, each of whom manifests a new shape and a new conception of the Godhead.' See Treitschke (1915: 127–8).
5 'Historicism claims trans-historical validity for its own thesis, thus refuting it' (Stern 1962: 182).
6 Taylor (1975: 13–29) calls this doctrine 'expressivism'. Its significance for Marx's thought is considered in Taylor (ibid.: 547–52).
7 The materialist dimensions of this argument, as advanced in Marx's thought, inform the reflections on attitudes to harm and suffering in different states-systems which are advanced in the last four chapters of this volume.
8 For further discussion, see Plant (1973). Schiller (1967: letter VI, section 12) offers

the classic summary: 'If the manifold potentialities in man were ever to be developed, there was no other way but to pit them one against the other. This antagonism of faculties and functions is the great instrument of civilization – but it is the only instrument; for as long as it persists, we are only on the way to becoming civilized.'

2 The problem of community in international relations

1 The second and third forms of social learning separate themes that are fused together in Habermas's notion of moral–practical learning.

4 What is a good international citizen?

1 These legal rights are a specific feature of the modern state. True, the Roman empire conferred similar rights on the peoples that it subdued by force, but because of class differences and inequalities it never embraced the idea of 'the equality of all citizens before the law' in the modern sense. For further details, see Garnsey (1974).

2 Aristotle stressed the theme of citizenship as participation rather than the rights of political association and parliamentary representation found in modern democratic states.

3 The stress on vulnerability to harm provides a link between the discussion of citizenship and humanity in Chapter 1 and the argument of Chapters 8–11.

4 The Second World War, for example, led to the development of new industrial roles and responsibilities for women and added to earlier demands for an end to gender inequalities. Also with regard to war, the involvement of African and Asian societies in two world wars helped to accelerate demands for full membership of the society of states. For its part, industrialization has generated the social power that allows state managers to administer societies more effectively but, just as importantly, it has been difficult for states to promote industrialization without fuelling demands for the extension of citizenship rights domestically. There is added reason to think that nineteenth century social theorists were right when they argued that industrialization would create more open societies within an interdependent world economy. Finally, despite the violence that has accompanied state building in most parts of the world, the majority of states in the contemporary world accept the principles of international order that originated in Europe, and most are willing to employ the language of duties to humankind.

5 This theme also challenges the distinction between systemic and reductionist theory in Waltz (1979: chs 2–4). Wight's point that 'principles of legitimacy mark the region of approximation between domestic and international politics' is worth recalling in this context. See Wight (1977: 153).

5 The good international citizen and the crisis in Kosovo

1 'The most pressing foreign policy problem we face is to identify the circumstances in which we should get involved in other people's conflicts.' See Tony Blair, 'Speech to the Economic Club of Chicago', 22 April 1999. The term 'purposes beyond ourselves' can be found in Bull (1973).

2 Statism is found in classical realist writings but also in the 'pluralist' approach as described by Bull (1966a).

3 See Chomsky (1999a) on the double standard of punishing Serbia while tolerating the human rights atrocities of a NATO member – Turkey – in its dealings with the Kurds.

4 Tony Blair set out the following tests of the legitimacy of intervention in his speech to the Economic Club of Chicago in April 1999. First, are we sure of our case? Second, have we exhausted all other options? Third, is the proposed course of action work-

able? Fourth, are we committed to the region for the long term? Fifth, are national interests involved? A sixth test might be suggested, one that has become even more important since the intervention in Iraq. Are others sure of our case, our competence and our motives? I come back to this later.

5 There is no consensus about whether 'collateral damage' in Kosovo was proportionate to NATO's political ends, and deciding whether or not it was proportionate is an almost impossible task. This is not to say that the principle of proportionality is without value, only that it is a grey area.

6 See in particular Articles 53–55 of the Charter of the United Nations, which set out the principles governing 'regional action'.

7 In a recent speech, Havel (1999: 6) argued that it is necessary 'to reconsider whether it is still appropriate, even hypothetically, that in the Security Council one country can outvote the rest of the world'.

8 To illustrate the point, should Turkey be regarded as inside or outside the relevant frontier? A further issue is whether Western Europeans have the right to establish a form of regional exceptionalism without consulting outside powers or needing Security Council approval.

9 But they may not be reassured by the fact that many Western powers believed that Indonesia's consent was required before the UN peacekeeping force could enter East Timor, even though the Indonesian occupation had not been recognized by the UN. See Chomsky (1999b). It might nevertheless be argued that the tension between principle and practice may lead to further change including consistency in the practice of those prepared to take humanitarian action, although realists have noted the difficulties here.

10 The importance of this point has been underlined by the unauthorized use of force against Iraq.

6 Citizenship and sovereignty in the post-Westphalian state

1 For an analysis of cosmopolitan democracy, see Archibugi and Held (1995).

2 As with any other order, Bull argued, the 'neo-medieval' order might well contain the risk of violence amongst other ills, but the main issue is how structures and principles can be put in place which minimize such risks. Bull was strongly disinclined to reflect on alternative forms of political organization on the grounds that moral and political advocacy had a corrupting influence in the social sciences. That, said, the main challenge has become even greater given the complexities involved in balancing liberty and security in multiracial and multifaith societies since '9/11'.

3 A neo-medieval order would emerge 'if modern states were to come to share their authority over citizens, and their ability to command their loyalties, on the one hand with substate or subnational authorities, to such an extent that the concept of sovereignty ceases to the applicable' (Bull 1977: 254).

4 Exceptions to this oversight include the Marxist literature on nationalism and imperialism, and the writings of political theorists such as Rousseau, who underlined the tension between 'man' and 'citizen' by asking whether 'in joining a particular group of men, we have already declared ourselves to be the enemies of the whole human race?' (Forysth *et al.* 1970: 134). Certain questions about the bounded nature of political communities are relevant for all periods of human history. See the discussion on p. 52–4 above. Norbert Elias's comments on the tension between 'man and citizen', on how the bonds between humans have developed over human history and on levels of emotional identification in various eras have special relevance for future research in this area. For details, see Chapter 10.

5 Tilly (1992: 70) points out that the Prussian monarchy's main tax collection agency began life as the Prussian War Commissariat.

6 The argument first arose in the feminist literature, specifically in regard to the

Gilligan/Kohlberg debate. Gilligan argued that Kohlberg's claim that universalistic orientations were the most advanced moral dispositions devalued 'the ethic of care and responsibility'. See Benhabib and Cornell (1987).

7 Kant criticized the theorists involved, Grotius, Pufendorf and Vattel, for taking the view that obligations between citizens were perfect whereas obligations between states were imperfect. But his defence of world citizenship assumed the continuing survival of sovereignty. The duty of hospitality was the essential feature of world citizenship. No institutions were envisaged that would allow the universal kingdom of ends to find expression in a cosmopolitan democracy.

8 A particularly striking example is the discussion in Kymlicka (1989: 137–8) of special citizenship rights that permit indigenous peoples to restrict the mobility, property and voting rights of non-indigenous peoples.

7 Cosmopolitan citizenship

1 Miller (1999: 62–3) argues that republican citizenship consists of the following four themes: equal rights, a corresponding sense of obligation, the willingness to act to protect the interests of other members of the political community and the desire to play an active role in the formal and informal arenas of politics.

2 An example discussed by Shue (1981) is that there is no justification for defending the interests of co-nationals who export hazardous forms of production that have been banned in their own society. In circumstances such as these, insiders and outsiders should have exactly the same moral standing (see also De-Shalit 1998).

3 In particular, Article 7 paragraph 2 of the Statute maintains that the 'official position of any accused person, whether as Head of State or Government or as a responsible Government official, shall not relieve such person of criminal responsibility nor mitigate punishment' (Evans 1994: 393).

4 Article 8 of the Maastricht Treaty maintains that the individual citizens of member states are European citizens with rights and duties 'which do not originate in their respective national parliaments'. But the rights created in this way are the right to vote in, and stand as candidates for, local elections and elections to the European Parliament.

5 An analysis of the effects of globalization on non-European populations in the same period would almost certainly result in a different conclusion.

6 'For the purposes of this argument' is included here because, for various reasons, gender, ethnicity and so forth are relevant when it comes to distributing rights, as Young (1991) and others have argued.

8 Citizenship, humanity and cosmopolitan harm conventions

1 There is no space here to comment in detail on the 'war against terror', but it may suffice to state that the vision of a world in which fewer human beings are burdened with preventable suffering has been dealt a blow from which it will not easily recover. Two other points that connect the current phase of world politics with the study of international relations are worth adding. The first is that the realist will be quick to stress how states can hijack cosmopolitan discourse and harness it to their specific cause. One might note here the rhetorical employment of the idea of 'civilization' against evil. This invites a second observation about how the 'civilizing' role of cosmopolitan harm conventions can become intertwined with the 'decivilizing' role of great power politics which currently includes the relaxation of the global norm prohibiting torture. Some of these themes are considered in more detail in Linklater (2002) and in the note on 'Torture and civilisation' which will appear in the journal *International Relations* in 2007. The terms civilizing and decivilizing processes, and their significance for international relations, are discussed in Chapter 10.

2 Also important is Article 1 of the United Nations General Resolution adopting the Declaration on the Elimination of Violence against Women, which defines violence against women as 'any act of gender-based violence that results in, or is likely to result in, physical, sexual or psychological harm or suffering to women, including threats of such acts, coercion or arbitrary deprivation of liberty, whether occurring in public or private life' (*The United Nations and the Advancement of Women*, New York: United Nations Press, 1996).

9 The problem of harm in world politics

1 This chapter is based on the Martin Wight Memorial Lecture which was delivered at the London School of Economics in November 2001.

2 Wight (1977) and Watson (1992) are the chief legacy of the British Committee's study of historic states-systems.

3 Wight (1977: 23) maintains that a states-system exists when each state ('by "states" we normally mean "sovereign states, political authorities which recognize no superior"') claims 'independence of any political superior' and recognizes 'the validity of the same claim by all the others'.

4 Wight (1977: ch. 1) also distinguishes primary states-systems from secondary states-systems.

5 Wight (1977: 179) argued that 'triangles, like duels, are relationships of conflict, and are resolved by war. The triangle of Russia, China and the United States has not yet been so resolved, but the historical precedents permit no other generalization'. Bull (1991: xvii) underlines the point by maintaining that Wight believed that particular ways are 'avoidable' but war itself is 'inevitable'.

6 The cosmopolitans' goal, he wrote, was one of 'proclaiming a world society of individuals, which over-rides nations or states, diminishing or dismissing this middle link. (They reject) the idea of a society of states and (say) that the only true international society is one of individuals . . . This is the most revolutionary of Revolutionist theories and it implies the total dissolution of international relations'. Cosmopolitanism was understood to be one of three forms of revolutionism. The other two are doctrinal uniformity and doctrinal imperialism. The first, which is attributed to Kant, argues that a world consisting exclusively of republican regimes would be a peaceful world. It favours 'ideological homogeneity'. The second, which is attributed to Stalinism, favours doctrinal unity through the efforts of a great power 'to spread a creed and impose uniformity'. Wight (1991: 40ff) also referred to pacifism or 'inverted revolutionism'.

7 The belief that revolutionism is a divisive force in international society is equally pronounced in Bull's writings – see Bull (1977: 26). This is not to say there was total agreement between Bull and Wight. Bull seems to not have shared Wight's revulsion against progressivist approaches to world politics, which the latter saw as the secular equivalent of eschatological approaches to history. See Bull (1991: xvi).

8 Of course, the period in which Wight wrote hardly encouraged optimism. Like Bull (1977: 240), Wight thought that superpower rivalry, and the two major wars of the twentieth century, revealed that the progressivist or solidarist vision was 'premature'.

9 See also Hoffmann (1990: 23) for the claim that Bull misread Kant 'who was much less cosmopolitan and universalist in his writings on international affairs than Bull suggests'.

10 Both thinkers, it might be added, defended the Stoic idea that the members of the universal community have fundamental duties not to harm one another unnecessarily. See Cicero's claim that 'not only nature, which may be defined as international law, but also the particular laws by which individual peoples are governed similarly ordain that no one is justified in harming another for his own advantage' (Cicero 1967: 144).

11   The 'only restraints on savagery were . . . a dim fear of committing impiety on the part of the conservatives, and prudential calculations on the part of the progressives'. See Wight (1977: 50–1).

12   The definition of harm in the *Oxford English Dictionary* highlights distress and suffering. A broader definition is needed in the light of claims that the dominant forms of industrialization and patterns of consumption will burden future generations with significant costs. In this case the emphasis is not simply on causing pain and suffering but on harming welfare interests. See Feinberg (1984) for the idea of harm as involving 'setbacks' to vital interests.

13   Donelan (1990: ch. 4) argues that the main principles of the rationalist approach to international society can be summarized as the negative duty to minimize injury. See also Jackson (2000: especially ch. 8 and the comments on prudence on p. 154).

14   See Bull (1977: 4–5) on the fact that international society offers its members some security against 'violence resulting in death or bodily harm'.

15   The harm principle is famously defended in Mill's *On Liberty*: 'the only purpose for which power can be rightfully exercised over any member of a civilized community . . . is to prevent harm to others. His own good, either physical or moral, is not a sufficient warrant'. See Mill (1962: 135). The point of the harm principle in Mill's writings is to place limits on government authority and to defend human freedom. The main function of the harm principle in the present argument is to curtail liberties to act as we please and to create moral responsibilities to outsiders. The global harm principle restricts the freedom of some in order to protect the freedom of others. See also Hart (1963).

16   On the claim that a duty of non-maleficence is 'a' but not 'the' foundation of morality, see Warnock (1971: ch. 2 and 80ff.). Warnock also emphasizes benevolence, fairness and the duty of non-deception. Warnock's claims about universality can be found on pp. 147–50 of the same volume. Ross (1930: 21ff.) argues that the duty of non-malificence is the fundamental moral duty.

17   On the need for mutual forbearance in the context of 'human vulnerability', see Hart (1961: ch. 9, section 2).

18   'The driving force behind any future international order must be a belief, however expressed, in the value of individual human beings irrespective of national affinities or allegiance and in a common and mutual obligation to promote their well-being.' See Carr (1945: 144).

19   Wight was too quick to dismiss Marx and Marxism – see Wight (1966a: 25).

20   Feinberg (1984), *Harm to Others*, pp. 227ff., calls this 'public accumulative harm'.

21   See Mason (2001) for a discussion of key theoretical issues and leading international conventions.

22   Donelan (1990: 69–70) addresses the problem of harm in the form of the 'blight of mass tourism' and the 'depletion or pollution of earth, sea and sky', and adds that states compound these injuries by indulging corporations. Liberal states are especially culpable through their 'indiscriminate encouragement of most forms of international traffic, regardless of the nuisance caused'. See also Hurrell (1994).

23   Vincent (1986: 147) cites Chomsky's question, 'Do we really care about the human consequences of our actions?' Connections can also be made with the view that injustice is 'an excess of the harmful and a deficiency of the beneficial, contrary to the rule of fair apportionment'. See Aristotle (1955: book 5, ch. 5).

24   Negligence is 'the failure to take a reasonable precaution against risks of harm'. See Simons (1999: 54).

25   Cruelty is defined as 'indifference to the pain or misery of others' and not just as the 'disposition to inflict suffering'.

26   Jackson (2000) maintains that the pluralist conception of international society 'is the most articulate institutional arrangement that humans have yet come up with in response to their common recognition that they must find a settled and predictable way

to live side by side on a finite planetary space without falling into mutual hostility, conflict, war, oppression, subjugation, slavery, etc'. Arguably, the same sentiment exists in Bull and Watson's claim in *The Expansion of International Society* (1984) that the universal acceptance of the European principle of sovereign equality should be welcomed.

27 It is a short step from Wight's observation (Wight 1977: 34–5) that order in all states-systems has rested on distinctions between 'civilized' and 'uncivilized' peoples to the more specific observation that the democratic peace depends on similar dichotomies with all the dangers that involves.

28 Sznaider (2001) argues that there has been significant progress over the last two centuries in combating cruelty. Also relevant are Thomas (1984), Burke *et al.* (2000) and Gay (1994).

29 I owe this formulation to Ian Clark. Wight (1977: ch. 6) analysed the changing nature of international legitimacy, focusing mainly on the principles that govern membership of the society of states. The point can be extended, as Bull (1983: 127ff.) suggested when he argued that modern international society will have a legitimation problem as long as the majority of the world's peoples who live in the Third World believe it frustrates or does not support their quest to satisfy their basic interests.

30 See Luard (1976: 381) on the distinction between 'the *principles* on which international society [is] based' and 'the *procedures* by which such principles [are] formulated and conflicts resolved' (italics in original).

31 See Richardson (1997) on the tension between the 'liberalism of privilege' and the liberalism that aims for a 'humane and equitable' order.

10 Norbert Elias, the civilizing process and international relations

1 I am grateful to Ian Clark, Toni Erskine, Stephen Mennell and Nick Wheeler for their comments on an earlier version of this chapter.

2 Quoted in Elias (1998a: 235). The comment is derived from Caxton's late fifteenth century *Book of Curtesye* (ibid: 273).

3 See, however, van Benthem van den Bergh (1992) on the significance of Elias's writings for understanding the nuclear age.

4 Elias lived between 1897 and 1990. For biographical details, see Elias (1994), Goudsblom (1990) and Brown (1987).

5 Haferkamp (1987: 546) suggests that Elias's writings from the 1980s onwards placed a greater stress on interstate developments, whereas Mennell (1987) maintains that his work consistently emphasized their significance for the study of the civilizing process.

6 This chapter is not concerned with possible connections between Elias's perspective and constructivism. Several constructivist studies of 'human rights and the use of violence [and] the relationship between humans and nature' have considered the 'normative structures that define modern international society and . . . shape the actions of both individuals and states' (Price and Reus-Smit 1998: 287). What Elias's writings can bring to constructivist and English School analyses of global normative structures is a heightened awareness of how the dominant emotional responses to cruelty and suffering in modern societies influenced, and have been influenced by, the relations between independent political communities over the last few centuries.

7 Elias (1996: 21) suggests that the new term, civility, which gave rise to the idea of civilization, was 'launched' by Erasmus of Rotterdam.

8 Here it is worth recalling that Butterfield and Wight believed that all known societies of states evolved within particular civilizational settings in which notions of moral or religious unity could be harnessed to build order between independent political communities.

9 This is not to imply that Elias influenced Butterfield's thinking about civilizations.

10 The concluding sentence of Wight's lectures at the London School of Economics states that the Grotian or rationalist tradition has been 'a civilizing factor' in world politics (Wight 1991: 268). Other members of the English School have claimed that the normative development of international society depends on the extent to which states are a 'civilizing force' in world politics (Wheeler 1996; Dunne 1998: xiv).

11 On the civilizing function of the balance of power, see van Benthem van den Bergh (1992: 35ff.).

12 Bull's analysis of the incorporation of non-Western peoples into a Western-dominated society of states noted that the former had to adapt their foreign policy behaviour to Western principles of international relations but incorporation could not have occurred 'except as the consequence of processes of cultural change *within* the countries concerned'. See Bull (1984a, italics added).

13 There is a parallel to be drawn here between 'systemic constructivism', as attributed to Wendt, and 'holistic constructivism', as attributed to Kratochwil and Ruggie. The first approach 'accepts the neorealist penchant for systemic theory, while the latter adopts a more encompassing perspective that seeks to incorporate domestic and international phenomena'. See Price and Reus-Smit (1998: 268ff.). Wight's support for such a holistic approach is evident in his belief that principles of international legitimacy are 'the region of approximation between international and domestic politics' (see Wight 1977: 153). Elias's holistic approach to international norms is discussed on pp. 161ff above.

14 The English School's analysis of civility and civilizing processes in international society is the most obvious counterpart to Elias's sociological project, but with the exception of Robertson (1992: 213) interpretations of Elias's work have not attempted to integrate these parallel research projects. Robertson (1992) draws on Bull (1977), Bull and Watson (1984) and Gong (1984).

15 'Animalic needs' refers to the basic physical and psychological needs that all humans beings have as members of the same species.

16 See Mennell (1996b) on applying the notion of the civilizing process to the study of Asian societies, and Mennell and Rundell (1998) on the extent to which broadening the analysis of civilizing processes can reveal how far Eurocentrism pervaded Elias's inquiry.

17 Elias's non-pejorative use of the civilizing process is highlighted in discussions of his primary interest in comprehending long-term patterns of social change that developed in Europe during the fifteenth century. His main aim was to understand the transition from the medieval to the modern world and to comprehend the contrast between the high levels of violence in everyday life during the Middle Ages with the relatively more pacified character of modern Western societies – but, as noted, his perspective has a much broader historical compass which is ultimately concerned with the prospects for the entire human race.

18 van Krieken (1998: 66) argues that Elias rejected theories of social progress but believed that one consequence of their wider rejection was a failure to analyse long-term social developments which meant that 'the baby has been thrown out with the bathwater'. Elias believed that 'overall, humanity was in fact progressing'. But, because the civilizing process was unfinished and unfinishable as well as reversible, Elias had 'an ambiguous attitude to progress' (see van Krieken 1998: 69). Elias believed that 'the conscious, planned concern with improvement of the social order and human living conditions has never been greater than it is today'. But civilizing tendencies are 'always linked to counter-trends' which may finally gain the 'upper hand' (Elias, as quoted in van Krieken 1998: 69–70). See also Elias (1997).

19 On the face of it, this claim suggests that ethical comparisons between different phases of human history are pointless. On the other hand, Elias (1978: 154) maintained that 'there has been a progressive reduction in inequality between and within countries since the end of the eighteenth century', but not one that was 'consciously planned'.

Elias (1996: 25) argued that the 'power gradient' between men and women, parents and children, the European societies and the former colonies and, 'with qualifications', between the rulers and the ruled decreased during the twentieth century in the modern West. Elias's comparisons between ancient and modern attitudes to genocide are also relevant in this context (see pp. 172ff., 202ff. in this book).

20 Modern societies are different from Greek city-states but 'in a period of incessant violence in interstate affairs, these internalized defences against impulses to violence inevitably remain unstable and brittle' (Elias 1996: 133).

21 As Dunning and Mennell state in their preface to Elias (1996: xv), *The Civilizing Process* was 'written against the background of the Third Reich in Elias's country of birth'. They quote the following statement from that work: 'The armour of civilized conduct would crumble very rapidly if, through a change in society, the degree of insecurity that existed earlier were to break in upon us again, and if danger became as incalculable as once it was. Corresponding fears would soon burst the limits set to them today.' This is one of several examples of Elias's almost Burkeian belief in the fragility of the civilizing process and its dependence on stable monopolies of power.

22 This is not the place to compare Elias and Bauman on the Holocaust. On this subject, see Tester (1997: 77–80) and Smith (2001: ch. 6).

23 Debates about how much the German population knew about the Holocaust (and approved of it) need not detain us here. Relevant works include the controversial thesis of Goldhagen (1996) and the recent work by Gellately (2001).

24 See Elias (1987a) on why the civilizing process involved high levels of personal detachment from society.

25 Elias did not regard such phenomena as incompatible with his general theme about the lowering of the threshold of repugnance towards public acts of cruelty in modern societies – and there is no reason why he should have done. It is important to add that he argued that modern societies made new forms of bureaucratized violence possible; it did not make them inevitable. To understand the course of German history in the first part of the twentieth century it was necessary to take many forces into account including the power of militarist attitudes and, of course, anti-Semitism. See Elias (1996) on the multiple forces that led to genocide. How far Nazi Germany illustrated the pathological dimensions of the civilizing process or revealed how far Germany was out of step with developments in Britain and France need not detain us.

26 Elias (1996: 460) resisted reducing civilization to 'the non-violent coexistence of humans' and stressed that more 'positive characteristics' were involved. Elsewhere, Elias (1994: 140) refers to the capacity to think 'from the standpoint of the multiplicity of people', a theme defended by Kant (see Bohman 1997). An interesting question is how far the stress on detachment can be reconciled with the emphasis on increased emotional identification between members of the same society, but we cannot consider this here. A related issue is whether advances in mutual identification between human beings as such can overcome detachment from distant suffering. For a discussion of such matters, see Cohen (2001), Moeller (1999), Sontag (2003) and Linklater (2006b).

27 Elias was indebted to Huizinga (1955: ch. 1), which is problematical, but we cannot go on to discuss this here. For intriguing discussions of punishment that are relevant to this account of placing violence behind the scenes, see Garland (1990) and Sarat (2001). Garland (ibid.: 223) notes that, for Elias, violence moved behind the scenes, as opposed to being eliminated, and its public reappearance therefore could not be discounted.

28 See Elias (2000: 161, 170) on the fact that civilization has subdued the 'joy in killing and destruction' in war. This theme was central to the sociology of sport which Elias developed with Eric Dunning. In a comment on foxhunting, Elias (1996: 163) claimed that 'one can see [the] growing internalization of the social prohibition against violence and the advance in the threshold of revulsion against violence, especially against

killing and even against seeing it done, if one considers that, in its heyday, the ritual of English fox-hunting, which prohibited any direct human participation in the killing, represented a civilizing spurt. It was an advance in people's revulsion against doing violence, while today, in accordance with the continued advance of the threshold of sensitivity, not a few people find even this representative of an earlier civilizing spurt distasteful and would like to see it abolished'. Elias adds that 'increasing restraints upon the use of physical force and particularly upon killing . . . can be observed as symptoms of a civilizing spurt' in many other spheres of human activity. See also Dunning (1986: 229–30).

29   The literature on the Holocaust is significant here, not least Lifton (2000) as noted in Fletcher (1997: 196).

30   Elias's general thesis finds support from different quarters. See Sznaider (2001: 4) on the 'broad social movement' of moral change and refinement in the nineteenth century as exemplified by 'campaigns of compassion', which included the struggle to abolish slavery and torture, to promote prison and hospital reform, to improve the lives of children and to abolish cruelty towards animals. Sznaider (ibid.: 9) adds that 'public compassion was initially the fight against cruelty, understood as the unjustifiable affliction of pain. Modern humanitarianism protests against such suffering and pain.' Sznaider (ibid.: 81) takes issue with Foucault's account of modernity on the grounds that it underestimates the importance of humanitarian movements in modern societies and the significance of bottom-up struggles for freedom from violence as against top-down impositions of discipline and control. Of course, Foucault argued that the humanitarianism that Sznaider describes gave rise to new forms of power and control, whereas Elias believed that long-term changes in the emotional life of the members of modern societies could not be reduced to the play of power but constrained its exercise to some extent. Their narratives are complementary in many ways – by arguing that modern societies no longer celebrate (or require) public acts of violence but rely on higher levels of self-monitoring and self-control, by claiming that they have placed the distasteful behind the scenes (to prisons and asylums according to Foucault) and by stressing that such 'civilizing' traits do not lay 'decivilizing processes' to rest. For the reasons Sznaider gives, Elias's discussion of the effects of changing emotional responses to cruelty and suffering has an advantage over Foucault's narrative. Other writings that consider the significance of changing attitudes to cruelty in modern societies include Thomas (1984), Gay (1994) and Burke *et al.* (2000). Garland (1990) and Smith (2001) provide a useful account of Elias's and Foucault's interpretations of Western modernity.

31   On changing attitudes towards violence to animals, including violent sport, see Elias and Dunning (1986). On the movement of attitudes towards violence to women, see Elias (1996: 176). For a discussion of the changing relationship between parents and children in Western modernity, see Elias (1998c: 190ff.). On this last topic the following comment is especially interesting: 'In ancient Greece and Rome we hear time and time again of infants thrown onto dungheaps or in rivers . . . Until the late nineteenth century there was no law against infanticide. Public opinion in antiquity also regarded the killing of infants or the sale of children – if they were pretty, to brothels, otherwise as slaves – as self-evident. The threshold of sensibility among people in antiquity – like those of Europeans in the Middle Ages and the early modern period – was quite different from that of the present day, particularly in relation to the use of physical violence. People assumed that they were violent to each other, they were attuned to it. No one noticed that children required special treatment' (Elias 1998c: 192–3). See also Elias (1998c: 207) on the fact that the 'heightening of the taboos against violence in relations between parents and children . . . is one of many examples of the complexity of the civilizing movement in our time'. Consideration of the disputes about such matters must be deferred for now.

32 See Sznaider (2001: 36, 53) on how nineteenth century 'campaigns of compassion' eroded supposedly natural rights to use violence in the family domain.

33 See Elias (2000: 402) for the claim that what changes in history 'is the way in which people are bonded to each other'. Elias (1996: 160) refers to 'the integrating tendency [which is] also a disintegrating tendency, at least as long as humanity as a whole is not [the] effective frame of reference'. This is a central theme in Elias's emphasis on one of the main processes in human history, which is the development of monopolies of power over increasingly larger areas of the planet (see Mennell 1990). Elias (2000: 254) maintains: 'We may surmise that with continuing integration even larger units will gradually be assembled under a stable government and internally pacified, and that they in their turn will turn their weapons outwards against human aggregates of the same size until, with a further integration, a still greater reduction of distances, they too gradually grow together and world society is pacified.' Throughout this process, one witnesses the 'quite different bonding of individuals' (Elias 2000: 255). Mennell (1990: 364) notes Elias's pessimism about the future of world society. For a different approach that develops Elias's writings, see van Benthem van den Bergh (1992: ch. 6 and p. 35ff.) on how the balance of power, great power responsibility and the global nuclear regime can act as 'the functional equivalent for a central monopoly of violence' and underpin 'pacification processes' in world politics.

34 See also Elias (2001b: 82) on the continuing danger of catastrophic interstate war. He adds that 'free competition between states' in the absence of 'a monopoly mechanism . . . plays a decisive role' in 'the drift towards war'. It is suggested in Elias (1996: 3–4) that it is 'possible that today humankind is approaching the end of elimination contests in the form of wars, but one cannot yet be certain of that'. Mennell (1990: 364) notes that Elias believed that there was no case in human history in which the gradual destruction of the smaller powers did not result in violent conflict between the remaining great powers. There is a parallel here with Wight (1977: ch. 1).

35 In connection with the threat of nuclear war, Elias (1992: 163) argued that 'the danger is that the present civilizing spurt has not reached the state where individual self-restraint takes precedence over restraint by others.' See also Elias (1996: 143) on the need for 'a common code of norms' as opposed to a global monopoly of power. An interesting question for Elias is how far the increasing interdependence of the human species, which has been caused by the rise of larger monopolies of power and the revolution in transport and communications, will further extend the self-constraints that developed in the course of the civilizing process. On this point, see Elias (1987a: lxxii) and Mennell (1998:101ff). Useful connections can be developed between Elias's perspective and studies of the role that global regimes have played in securing advances in the level of national self-restraint (see Morgan 2003).

36 At this point it is worth noting Elias's conviction that one of the central purposes of Sociology is to cast light on the possibilities for expanding human control over previously unplanned social processes: 'So far, the civilizing of human beings and the standards of civilization have developed completely unplanned and in a haphazard manner. It is necessary to form a theory so that, in the future, we may be able to judge more closely what kind of restraints are required for complicated societies to function and what type of restraints have been merely built into us to bolster up the authority of certain ruling groups.' See Elias (1978: 153–4; 1998d: 145). Parallels with Frankfurt School critical theory may suggest themselves, on which subject see Bogner (1987) and also Chapter 11. In *The Loneliness of the Dying*, Elias (2001b: 7, 81–2) states that the inhabitants of modern societies enjoy very high levels of protection from sudden death but they have still to bring several unplanned social processes under their collective control, war being an obvious example. Mennell (1998: 66, 171) notes that Elias was interested in immanent social developments but not in partisan inquiry.

37 This leads Haferkamp (1987) to argue that Elias cannot explain modern concerns

about human rights, apartheid and genocide, but he did take account of global civilizing processes, as Goudsblom (1990), Mennell (1987, 1990) and others contend.

38   Mennell (1990: 367) notes that nuclear weapons had a civilizing effect on the superpowers by requiring self-restraint on their part. For a more extensive discussion of
this theme, see van Benthem van den Bergh (1992). van Vree (1999: especially ch. 8)
offers an Eliasian account of international relations which stresses the development of
'meeting behaviour' and its effect on pacifying 'the struggle for power, prestige and
wealth . . . at continental and global levels'.

39   The aristocratic ethical code 'tempered' the use of violence and deception in the relations between princes to some extent. See Elias (1996: 139).

40   On the subject of Germany, Elias (1996: 179) stressed that one cannot 'understand the
development of Germany' without discussing its 'position in the interstate framework
and correspondingly in the power and status hierarchies of states. It is impossible here
to separate interstate and intra-state lines of development; from a sociological standpoint, intra-state and interstate structures are inseparable even though the sociological
tradition up till now has involved a concentration mainly, and quite often exclusively,
on the former. The development of Germany shows particularly clearly how *processes
within and between states are indissolubly interwoven*' (italics added). See Elias's
references to the fact that his own work began to expand 'the field of vision' from 'the
level of intra-state relationships to that of humankind' in Goudsblom and Mennell
(1998: 256, 259), and the related discussion in Elias (1991: 138ff.). On the obsolescence of the 'theoretical distinction' between endogenous accounts of social change
and foreign policy or external relations, see Elias (1978: 168).

41   Elias (1987b: 266, 244) refers to his interest in 'long-term social processes' which
involve, 'in the last resort, the development of humanity' understood as the 'totality
of human societies'.

42   It was important to remember not only 'spontaneous repugnance' towards the Nazi era
but also the subsequent decision by the victorious powers to readmit Germany into the
society of states (Elias 1996: 16, 445; see also Mennell 1998: 57ff.).

43   Crawford's discussion of the collapse of the moral defence of colonialism shows
how Western attitudes to cruelty and suffering in the colonies changed over several
centuries. She analyses the efforts of moral and religious reformers to highlight the cruelty of forced labour and slavery and to publicize the injustices of colonial exploitation.
Reformers succeeded in changing emotional responses to cruelty towards subordinated
peoples. They challenged notions of 'European superiority' which legitimized violence in
the minds of the colonizers; they 'harnessed the emotions of embarrassment and shame'
to challenge domination; and they called for greater emotional identification with, and
compassion for, the victims of imperial rule (Crawford 2002: 387ff.). Crawford does
not discuss Elias's account of Western modernity but her analysis is compatible with
an Eliasian account of the long-term processes of change that affected the organization
of humanity. Crawford's analysis of the importance of emotions or 'passions' in world
politics is also important (see Crawford 2001).

44   In *Quest for Excitement*, Elias and Dunning (1986: 144) note that, although the records
are incomplete, 'the wholescale massacre of enemies' occurred frequently in antiquity
and may have 'aroused pity' but not 'widespread condemnation'. Recent literature
suggests a more complex picture. Shipley (1995) argues that 'annihilation was rare
and usually exemplary' given the Greeks' over-riding interest in exacting tribute from
defeated enemies. For supporting discussions, see Bauslaugh (1991), Dillon and Garland (1994, especially ch. 12), Garlan (1976), Hanson (1998: 117), Kern (1999) and
Kozak (2001a, 2001b). Important conceptual issues also arise here. Elias's comment
about the frequency of genocide in the Ancient World is more plausible if genocide
is taken to mean either the partial or the complete destruction of a people, to follow
the definition given in the United Nations Convention on Genocide. Katz (1994) dis-

cusses the conceptual issues and adds that mass violence in classical antiquity did not constitute genocide in the broader sense of the term.

45 Elias (1996: 51) maintains that in 'all warrior societies (including, for example, Ancient Athens), proving oneself in physical combat against other people, being victorious over them, and if necessary murdering them, played an integral part in establishing a man's standing. The present-day military tradition seeks to limit training in the use of physical violence as far as possible to violence against people who do not belong to one's own state-society.'

46 See Wight (1977: 51) on Thucydides' efforts to show that the constraints on war were 'minimal', and Konstan (2001) on the limited role of pity in the Ancient World more generally.

47 To illustrate, Evans's (1997) study of the development of capital punishment in Germany takes issue with Elias's observations about higher levels of cruelty in early modern European societies.

48 Hans-Peter Duerr's critique of Elias as discussed by van Krieken (1998: 119–24) is worth noting as it asks 'whether human psychology today is so different from that of earlier historical epochs'. A related issue is whether Elias exaggerated the contrasts between the violence of the Middle Ages and the Ancient World and relatively more pacified modern societies.

49 Elias does not refer to states-systems as such. He noted that political communities 'form part of another less highly organized, less well-integrated system' such as the 'balance of power system' in the modern world. He added that 'whatever form it may take, that system in the hierarchy of systems which constitutes the highest level of integration and organized power is also the system which has the highest capacity to regulate its own course' (see Elias 1987a: 30). The question which will be explored in future work is how far collective learning processes in international societies contributed to global agreements about the need to reduce various forms of unjustifiable harm as far as possible. We can call this the sociology of global civilizing processes.

50 This develops the argument in Chapter 9.

51 This is the most complex and controversial of the forms of harm described above. Legal systems have taken different positions on the extent to which individuals should be punished for failing to rescue others. As Feinberg (1984) explains, the Anglo-American legal tradition is generally more tolerant of 'Bad Samaritanism' than its continental European counterparts. Turning to international relations, the complexities arise in dramatic fashion if we ask whether the failure to intervene to prevent genocide can be deemed to be harmful. Some deny that failures to rescue constitute harm; others argue that inaction in the face of human suffering, assuming the possibility of acting without great personal cost, harms others by prolonging suffering and by indicating that it is immaterial whether or not the other survives. Arguably, the failure to rescue causes harm for these reasons. For further discussion, see Linklater (2006a).

52 Questions about the appropriate methodology for realizing these purposes must be left for another occasion. The growing literature on the role of emotions in social life, and especially Stearns and Stearns's (1985) discussion of 'emotionology', is especially important – see also the pioneering work of Lucien Fevbre in Burke (1973), Elias (1987b) on emotions and long-term patterns of change, and the rich discussion in De Swaan (1995). Stearns and Stearns define emotionology as the study of 'the attitudes or standards that society or a definable group within a society, maintains towards basic emotions and their appropriate expression'. The sociology of states-systems outlined here has a specific interest in 'standards' governing emotional responses to human suffering, particularly cruelty and compassion. The focus is on dominant understandings of permissible and proscribed forms of harm (see Chapter 8), as expressed in the dominant standards of legitimacy in international relations (Wight 1977: ch. 6).

53 Elias (2001a: 164–5) discusses the possibility that the species may be entering an era in which 'it will no longer be individual states but unions of states which will serve mankind as the dominant social unit'. Elias immediately added that 'the immense process of integration' which the species is undergoing could easily give way to a 'dominant disintegration process'. See also Elias (ibid.: 218). Goudsblom (1990: 172) emphasizes Elias's interest in organizations such as Amnesty International.

54 For more recent discussions of this theme, see Cohen (2001), Moeller (1999) and Sontag (2003).

55 Other comments on the growth of a sense of personal responsibility 'for the fate of others far beyond the frontiers of their own country or continent' can be found in Elias (2001b: 167, 232). But see also Elias (2001b: 202–3).

56 'If one remembers that we, too still live at an early stage in the development of humanity, one should probably think of it as humankind's prehistory where humans are still unable to understand and to control the social dynamics which [threaten] to drive rulers of different states towards settling their conflicts through the use of force', Elias (1992: 156). The observation indicates that Elias's analysis of the civilizing process is designed to cast light on the ability of the human race to control increasing global interconnections and to pacify world society.

11 Towards a sociology of global morals with an 'emancipatory intent'

1 I am grateful to Toni Erskine and Stephen Mennell for their comments on an earlier draft of this chapter.

2 See David Hume's claim that 'there is no such passion in human minds, as the love of mankind, merely as such' in Hume (1969: 533) and the reservations about cosmopolitan motivation in Walzer (2002).

3 See also Gaita (2002). Similar sentiments are present in Weil's claim that: 'To no matter whom the question may be put in general terms, nobody is of the opinion that any man is innocent if, possessing food himself in abundance and finding someone on his doorstep three parts dead from hunger, he brushes past without giving him anything'. See Weil (1952: 6).

4 Weil here maintains that this obligation is 'eternal'.

5 Nussbaum (2001: 169) maintains that 'biology and common circumstances . . . make it extremely unlikely that the emotional repertoires of two societies will be entirely opaque to one another'.

6 Gaita (2002: 276) notes that a slave owner might assist a slave in desperate circumstances, but the desire to protect another slave-owner's property, rather than human solidarity, may prompt an act of rescue.

7 The idea of a form of universality that requires a complex labour of translation can be found in Butler (2002).

8 On occidental rationalism and societal rationalization, see Habermas (1984).

9 Smith (1982: 136–7) maintains that a person may be unable to sleep at night knowing that his or her small finger will be removed the following day; but the same person will sleep peacefully even though he or she knows that countless distant strangers face the most awful calamities – presuming, Smith added, that the person 'never sees them'.

10 Or sympathy has been confined to some members of the survival group because forms of stigmatization blocked its universal expression within the same society.

11 These were crucial themes in the writings of Norbert Elias.

12 Kant denied that an ethic could be grounded in the emotions, and indeed he expressed a preference for 'cold-blooded goodness' over the 'warmth of affection' precisely because the former was 'more reliable'. See Cunningham (2001: 222). Oakley (1992: 109ff.) stresses that recent Kantians have been less cautious about emotions such as compassion because of their importance for developing a sense of 'connectedness'

with other persons, not that this theme was wholly alien to Kant, as we have seen. Exposure to the poor, the sick and imprisoned could produce 'the pain of compassion', an impulse that had been created by nature 'for effecting what the representation of duty might not accomplish by itself' (quoted in Cunningham 2001: 77, 213).

13 Interesting issues are raised here about how the emotions mark the point at which the 'cultural' and the 'somatic' intersect. See Harre and Parrott (1996: introduction).

14 Embodiment was central to Elias's analysis of the civilizing process which was first set out in the 1930s. Its significance for the Frankfurt School and for the critical sociology of world politics is considered on pp. 184ff.

15 See Bronner (1994: 332–5) on the importance of such themes in Frankfurt School theory more generally.

16 Vulnerability did not merely underpin solidarity with 'the community of men lost in the universe' – see Horkheimer (1974: 75). Schopenhauer's defence of a post-anthropocentric ethic was reflected in Horkheimer's claim that the idea of vulnerability should underpin compassion for all sentient creatures and 'solidarity with life in general' (Horkheimer 1993: 36; see also Schopenhauer 1995: 175ff.). For broadly similar views, see Adorno (2000: 145) on the insights that can be learnt from Schopenhauer's 'crankiness'.

17 The expression, 'injurable animal', can be fond in Bernstein (2000: 122).

18 Whether Adorno overwrote this ethical argument is a question that goes beyond this discussion. Suffice it to add that his comments about an ethic that starts with the condition of frailty and vulnerability finds sympathy in many different areas of philosophical analysis. For comments on parallel themes in recent moral and political theory, see Linklater (2006a). The rejection of what O'Neill (1996: 165–6) calls the practice of placing 'the principle of injury' at the centre of social life can be traced back to the European Enlightenment. Taylor (1989) situates this within the broad cultural shift which supported 'the affirmation of ordinary life' and the parallel rejection of sacred suffering. Horkheimer's later reflections on theology and suffering (see Habermas 1993) invite the comment that several major faith traditions have regarded the capacity for suffering, and the potential for sympathy with the distressed, as the most natural point of solidarity between strangers. See Bowker (1970).

19 See also Honneth, 'Mutual recognition as a key for a universal ethics', at www.unesco.or.kr/.

20 With respect to exploitation, Habermas (1979a: 164) distinguishes between 'bodily harm (hunger, exhaustion, illness), personal injury (degradation, servitude, fear), and finally spiritual desperation (loneliness, emptiness) – to which in turn there correspond various hopes – for well-being and security, freedom and dignity, happiness and fulfillment'.

21 See the discussion of psychoanalytical theory in Habermas (1972: chs 10–12) and the references to 'cognitive developmental psychology' in Habermas (1979a: 100; see also ch. 2, 'Moral development and ego identity').

22 Some critics regard this oversight as a weakness in Habermas's position, but not one that his approach is incapable of correcting. See Crossley (1998).

23 Habermas (1979a: ch. 3). See also the references to the significance of 'affective expressions' in the evolutionary movement from primates to hominids on p. 134, and the more central concern with the development of 'structures of thought' which is expressed on p. 149 of the same work.

24 What has been lost, it might be argued, is the 'underground history' that concerns the body and 'the fate of the human instincts and passions which are displaced and distorted by civilization'. See Adorno and Horkheimer (1972: 231).

25 Contrasts can be drawn between broadly Kantian moral perspectives that privileged reason over the emotions and various conceptions of a sentimental ethic that support the emancipation of positive moral emotions.

26 See, for example, the following claim in Habermas (1979a: 176): 'In living, the

organisms themselves make an evaluation to the effect that self-maintenance is preferable to the destruction of the system, reproduction of life to death, health to the risks of sickness.' But from the 'descriptive statement that living systems prefer certain states to others' nothing follows ethically from the standpoint of observers.

27 See the following claim in Habermas (1979a: 177): 'For a living being that maintains itself in the structures of ordinary language communication, the validity basis of speech has the binding force of universal and unavoidable – in this sense transcendental – presuppositions. The *theoretician* does not have the same possibility of choice in relation to the validity claims immanent in speech as he does in relation to the basic biological value of health' (italics in original).

28 See Habermas (1972: 256, 285).

29 Elias moved to Frankfurt University when Karl Mannheim was appointed to the Chair of Sociology in 1929. For further details, see Bogner (1987) and Wiggershaus (1993). See also Rojek (2004).

30 It is idle to speculate – but irresistible nonetheless – about how critical social theory might have developed if Adorno's discussions with Elias had continued beyond the 1930s so that Horkheimer and Adorno's *The Dialectic of Enlightenment* had engaged directly with *The Civilising Process* (the former was first published in 1944, the latter in 1939). It is equally tempting to speculate about how an explicit engagement with Frankfurt School critical theory might have shaped Elias's own project and the fate of European Sociology more generally.

References

Acton, H.B. (1970) *Kant's Moral Philosophy*. London: Macmillan.

Adorno, Theodor (1990) *Negative Dialectics*. London: Routledge.

Adorno, Theodor (2000) *Problems of Moral Philosophy*. Cambridge: Polity Press.

Adorno, Theodor and Max Horkheimer (1972) *Dialectic of Enlightenment*. New York: Herder and Herder.

Akehurst, Michael B. (1992) *A Modern Introduction to International Law*. London: Routledge.

Annan, Kofi (1999) 'Two concepts of sovereignty', *The Economist,* 18–24 September.

Apel, Karl-Otto (1979) 'The conflicts of our time and the problem of political ethics', in Fred Dallmayr (ed.) *From Contract to Community*. New York: Marcel Dekker.

Apel, Karl-Otto (1980) *Towards a Transformation of Philosophy*. London: Routledge and Kegan Paul.

Archibugi, Danielle (1995) 'Immanuel Kant, cosmopolitan law and peace', *European Journal of International Relations* 1(3): 429–56.

Archibugi, Danielle (1998) 'Principles of cosmopolitan democracy', in Danielle Archibugi, David Held and Martin Kohler (eds) *Re-Imagining Political Community: Studies in Cosmopolitan Democracy*. Cambridge: Polity Press.

Archibugi, Danielle and David Held (eds) (1995) *Cosmopolitan Democracy: An Agenda for a New World Order*. Cambridge: Polity Press.

Archibugi, Danielle, David Held and Martin Kohler (eds) (1998) *Re-imagining Political Community: Studies in Cosmopolitan Democracy*. Cambridge: Polity Press.

Arendt, Hannah (1973) *Men in Dark Times*. Harmondsworth: Penguin.

Arendt, Hannah (1994) *Eichmann in Jerusalem*. Harmondsworth: Penguin.

Aristotle (1955) *Ethics*. Harmondsworth: Penguin.

Aristotle (1959) *The 'Art' of Rhetoric*. London: William Heinemann.

Aristotle (1960) *The Politics*. Oxford: Clarendon Press.

Aristotle (1995) *Poetics*. Harmondsworth: Penguin.

Arneson, Richard (1998) 'The priority of the right over the good rides again', in Paul Kelly (ed.) *Impartiality, Neutrality and Justice: Re-reading Brian Barry's Justice as Impartiality*. Edinburgh: Edinburgh University Press.

Aron, Raymond (1966) *Peace and War: A Theory of International Relations*. London: Weidenfeld and Nicholson.

Ashley, Richard K. (1981) 'Political realism and human interests', *International Studies Quarterly* 25(2): 204–46.

Ashley, Richard K. (1984) 'The poverty of neo-realism', *International Organization* 38(2): 225–86.

Ashley, Richard K. and R.B.J. Walker (1990) 'Reading dissidence/writing the discipline: crisis and the question of sovereignty in international studies', *International Studies Quarterly* 34(3): 337–26.

Bain, William (2006) 'In praise of folly: international administration and the corruption of humanity', *International Affairs* 82(3): 525–38.

Baldry, H.C. (1965) *The Unity of Mankind in Greek Thought.* Cambridge: Cambridge University Press.

Balibar, Etienne (1988) 'Propositions on citizenship', *Ethics* 98(4): 723–30.

Bankowski, Zenon and Emilios Christodoulidis (1999) 'Citizenship bound and citizenship unbound', in Kimberly Hutchings and Roland Dannreuther (eds) *Cosmopolitan Citizenship.* London: Macmillan.

Barbalet, Jack (1988) *Citizenship: Rights, Struggle and Class Inequality.* Milton Keynes: Open University.

Barbalet, Jack (2002) 'Introduction: why emotions are crucial', in Jack Barbalet (ed.) *Emotions and Sociology.* Oxford: Blackwell.

Barnett, Victoria J. (2000) *Bystanders: Conscience and Complicity During the Holocaust.* London: Praeger.

Barry, Brian (1973) *The Liberal Theory of Justice: A Critical Examination of the Principal Doctrines in A Theory of Justice by John Rawls.* Oxford: Clarendon Press.

Barry, Brian (1998) 'Something in the disputation not unpleasant', in Paul Kelly (ed.) *Impartiality, Neutrality and Justice: Re-reading Brian Barry's Justice as Impartiality.* Edinburgh: Edinburgh University Press.

Bauman, Zygmunt (1989) *Modernity and the Holocaust.* Cambridge: Polity Press.

Bauslaugh, Robert A. (1991) *The Concept of Neutrality in Classical Greece.* Berkeley, CA: University of California Press.

Beck, Ulrich (1992) *Risk Society: Towards a New Modernity.* London: Sage.

Beitz, Charles (1979) *Political Theory and International Relations.* Princeton, NJ: Princeton University Press.

Beitz, Charles (1994) 'Cosmopolitan liberalism and the states system', in Chris Brown (ed.) *Political Restructuring in Europe: Ethical Perspectives.* London: Routledge.

Benhabib, Seyla (1993) *Situating the Self: Gender, Community and Postmodernism in Contemporary Ethics.* Cambridge: Polity Press.

Benhabib, Seyla and Drucilla Cornell (eds) (1987) *Feminism as Critique: Essays on the Politics of Gender in Late Capitalist Societies.* Cambridge: Polity Press.

Bentham, Jeremy (1970) *The Principles of Morals and Legislation.* Date Darien, CT: Hafner.

van Benthem van den Bergh, Godfried (1992) *The Nuclear Revolution and the End of the Cold War: Forced Restraint.* Basingstoke: Macmillan.

Berlin, Isaiah (1976) *Vico and Herder: Two Studies in the History of Ideas.* London: Hogarth Press.

Bernstein, J.M. (2000) 'After Auschwitz: trauma and the grammar of ethics', in Robert Fine and Charles Turner (eds) *Social Theory after the Holocaust.* Liverpool: Liverpool University Press.

Bernstein, J.M. (2002) *Adorno: Disenchantment and Ethics.* Cambridge: Cambridge University Press.

Bernstein, Richard J. (1986) *Philosophical Profiles: Essays in a Pragmatic Mode.* Philadelphia, PA: University of Pennsylvania Press.

Bernstein, Richard. J. (1988) 'Fred Dallmayr's critique of Habermas', *Political Theory* 16(4): 580–93.

Biro, G. (1994) 'Minority rights in Eastern and Central Europe and the role of international institutions', in Jeffrey Laurenti (ed.) *Search for Moorings: East Central Europe in the International System*. Thousand Oaks, CA: Sage.

Blair, Tony (1999) 'Speech to the Economic Club of Chicago', 22 April, available at www.pm.gov.uk.

Blundell, Mary W. (1989) *Helping Friends and Harming Enemies: A Study in Sophocles and Greek Ethics*. Cambridge: Cambridge University Press.

Bodin, Jean (1967) *Six Books on the Commonwealth*. London: Blackwell.

Bogner, A. (1987) 'Elias and the Frankfurt School', *Theory, Culture and Society* 4(2–3): 249–85.

Bohman, James (1997) 'The public spheres of the world citizen', in James Bohman and Matthias Lutz-Bachmann (eds) *Perpetual Peace: Essays on Kant's Cosmopolitan Ideal*. London: MIT Press.

Boli, John and George M. Thomas (eds) (1999) *Constructing World Culture: International Nongovernmental Organisations since 1875*. Stanford, CA: Stanford University Press.

Borkenau, Franz (1942) *Socialism, National or International*. London: Labour Book Service.

Bowker, John (1970) *Problems of Suffering in the World's Religions*. Cambridge: Cambridge University Press.

Bredvold, Louis I. and Ralph G. Ross (eds) (1970) *The Philosophy of Edmund Burke* (a selection of his speeches and writings). Ann Arbor, MI: University of Michigan Press.

Brewin, Christopher (1988) 'Liberal states and international obligations', *Millennium* 17(2): 321–38.

Brewin, Christopher (1994) 'Society as a kind of community: problems in creating a new order of citizen in Europe from Ataturk to the Treaty of Maastricht', mimeo, University of Keele, Staffordshire.

Bronner, Stephen E. (1994) *Of Critical Theory and its Theorists*. Oxford: Blackwell.

Brown, Chris (1988) 'The modern requirement? Reflections on normative international theory in a post-Western world', *Millennium* 17(2): 339–48.

Brown, Chris (1992) *International Relations Theory: New Normative Approaches*. Hemel Hempstead: Harvester Wheatsheaf.

Brown, R. (1987) 'Norbert Elias at Leicester: some reflections', *Theory, Culture and Society* 4(2–3): 533–9.

Bull, Hedley (1966a) 'The Grotian conception of international society', in Herbert Butterfield and Martin Wight (eds) *Diplomatic Investigations: Essays in the Theory of International Politics*. London: Unwin.

Bull, Hedley (1966b) 'International theory: the case for a classical approach', *World Politics* 18(3): 361–77.

Bull, Hedley (1973) 'Foreign policy of Australia', *Proceedings of the Australian Institute of Political Science Summer School*. Sydney: Angus and Robertson.

Bull, Hedley (1977) *The Anarchical Society: A Study of Order in World Politics*. London: Macmillan.

Bull, Hedley (1979) 'The state's positive role in world affairs', *Daedalus* 108(4): 111–23.

Bull, Hedley (1982) 'The West and South Africa', *Daedalus* 111(2): 255–70.

Bull, Hedley (1983) 'The international anarchy in the 1980s', *Australian Outlook* 37(3): 127–31.

Bull, Hedley (1984a) *Justice and International Relations*. (The Hagey Lectures), University of Waterloo: Ontario.

Bull, Hedley (ed.) (1984b) *Intervention in World Politics*. Oxford: Clarendon Press.

Bull, Hedley (1991) 'Martin Wight and the theory of international relations', in Martin Wight, *International Theory: The Three Traditions*, edited by Gabrielle Wight and Brian Porter. Leicester: Leicester University Press.

Bull, Hedley and Adam Watson (eds) (1984) *The Expansion of International Society.* Oxford: Oxford University Press.

Bull, Hedley, Benedict Kingsbury and Adam Roberts (eds) (1990) *Hugo Grotius and International Relations*, Oxford: Clarendon Press.

Bullock, Alan and Maurice Shock (eds) (1956) *The Liberal Tradition: From Fox to Keynes*. Oxford: Clarendon Press.

Burke, Peter (ed.) (1973) *A New Kind of History: From the Writings of Lucien Febvre*. London: Routledge and Kegan Paul.

Burke Peter, Brian Harrison and Paul Slack (eds) (2000) *Civil Histories: Essays Presented to Sir Keith Thomas*. Oxford: Oxford University Press.

Bury, John B. (1955) *The Idea of Progress*. New York: Dover Publications.

Butler, Judith (2002) 'Universality in culture', in Martha Nussbaum, *For Love of Country?* Boston, MA: Beacon Press.

Butler, Judith (2004) *Precarious Life: The Powers of Mourning and Violence*. London: Verso.

Butterfield, Herbert (1953) *Christianity, Diplomacy and War.* London: Epworth Press.

Buzan, Barry and Richard Little (2000) *International Systems in World History: Remaking the Study of International Relations*. Oxford: Oxford University Press.

Camilleri, Joseph and Jim Falk (1992) *The End of Sovereignty? The Politics of a Shrinking and Fragmenting World*. Aldershot: Elgar.

Carlyle, A.J. (1930) *A History of Medieval Political Theory in the West: Volume One*. Edinburgh: William Blackwood.

Carr, Edward Hallett (1945) *Nationalism and After*. London: Macmillan.

Carr, Edward Hallett (2001) *The Twenty Years' Crisis, 1919–1939: An Introduction to the Study of International Relations* (edited by M. Cox). London: Palgrave.

Cavanagh, J. (1997) 'The global resistance to sweatshops', in Andrew Ross (ed.) *No Sweat: Fashion, Free Trade and the Rights of Garment Workers*. London: Verso.

Chabbot, Colette (1999) 'Development INGOs', in John Boli and George M. Thomas (eds) *Constructing World Politics: International Nongovernmental Organisations since 1875*. Stanford, CA: Stanford University Press.

Chomsky, Noam (1999a) *The New Military Humanism: Lessons from Kosovo*. Monroe, ME: Common Courage Press.

Chomsky, Noam (1999b) 'Sovereignty and world order', lecture delivered at Kansas State University, 20 September.

Christian, David (2004) *Maps of Time: An Introduction to Big History.* Berkeley, CA: University of California Press.

Christoff, Peter (1996) 'Ecological citizens and ecologically guided democracy', in Brian Doherty and Marius De Geus (eds) *Democracy and Green Political Thought: Sustainability, Rights and Citizenship*. London: Routledge.

Cicero (1967) *On Obligation* (introduction and notes by J. Higginbotham). London: Faber and Faber.

Clark, Ian (1989) *The Hierarchy of States: Reform and Resistance in the International Order*. Cambridge: Cambridge University Press.

Cohen, Jean (1990) 'Discourse ethics and civil society', in David Rasmussen (ed.) *Universalism vs Communitarianism*. Cambridge, MA: MIT Press.

Cohen, Stanley (2001) *States of Denial: Knowing about Atrocities and Suffering*. Cambridge: Polity Press.

Colletti, Lucio (1972) *From Rousseau to Lenin: Studies in Ideology and Society*. New York: Monthly Review Press.

Colletti, Lucio (1973) *Marxism and Hegel*. London: Verso.

Connolly, William (1992) 'Democracy and territoriality', in Marjorie Ringrose and Adam J. Lerner (eds) *Reimagining the Nation*. Buckingham: Open University Press.

Corrigan, Peter and Derek Sayer (1985) *The Great Arch: English State Formation as Cultural Revolution*. Oxford: Basil Blackwell.

Cox, Robert W. (1981) 'Social forces, states and world orders: beyond international relations theory', *Millennium* 10(2): 126–55.

Cox, Robert W. (1983) 'Gramsci, hegemony and international relations: an essay in method', *Millennium* 12(2): 162–75.

Cox, Robert W. (1989) 'Production, the state and change in world order', in Ernst-Otto Czempiel and James Rosenau (eds) *Global Change and Theoretical Challenges: Approaches to World Politics*. Lexington, MA: Lexington Books.

Crawford, Neta C. (2001) 'The passions of world politics: propositions on emotions and emotional relationships', *International Security* 24(4): 116–56.

Crawford, Neta C. (2002) *Argument and Change in World Politics: Ethics, Decolonization and Humanitarian Intervention*. Cambridge: Cambridge University Press.

Crossley, Nick (1998) 'Emotion and communicative action: Habermas, linguistic philosophy and existentialism', in G. Bendelow and S.J. Williams (eds) *Emotions in Social Life: Critical Themes and Contemporary Issues*. London: Routledge.

Cunningham, Anthony (2001) *The Heart of What Matters: The Role for Literature in Moral Philosophy*. Berkeley, CA: University of California Press.

Davies, Rees (1989) 'Frontier arrangements in fragmented societies: Ireland and Wales', in Robert T. Bartlett and Angus Mackay (eds) *Medieval Frontier Societies*. Oxford: Clarendon Press.

Denemark, Robert A., Jonathan Friedman, Barry K. Gills and George Modelski (eds) (2000) *World System History*. London: Routledge.

De-Shalit, Avner (1998) 'Transnational and international exploitation', *Political Studies* 46(4): 693–708.

De Swaan, Abram (1995) 'Widening circles of identification: emotional concerns in sociogenetic perspective', *Theory, Culture and Society* 12(2): 25–39.

Der Derian, James and Michael J. Shapiro (eds) (1979) *International/Intertextual Relations: Post-Modern Readings of World Politics*. Lexington, MA: Lexington Books.

Derrida, Jacques (1992) *The Other Heading: Reflections on Today's Europe*. Bloomington, IN: Indiana University Press.

Deutsch, Karl (1970) *Political Community at the International Level*. New York: Archon Books.

Devetak, Richard (1995) 'Incomplete states: the theory and practice of statecraft', in John Macmillan and Andrew Linklater (eds) *Boundaries in Question: New Directions in International Relations*. London: Frances Pinter.

Dews, Peter (1987) *Logics of Disintegration: Post-Structuralist Thought and the Claims of Critical Theory*. London: Verso.

Dibblin, Jane (1988) *Day of Two Suns: US Nuclear Testing and the Pacific Islanders*. London: Virago.

Dillon, Matthew and Lynda Garland (eds) (1994) *Ancient Greece: Social and Historical Documents from Archaic Times to the Death of Socrates*. London: Routledge.

Donelan, Michael D. (1990) *Elements of International Political Theory*. Oxford: Clarendon Press.

Doyle, Michael (1983) 'Kant, liberal legacies and foreign affairs: Parts I and II', *Philosophy and Public Affairs* 12(3): 205–34 and 12(4): 323–53.

Dower, Nigel (2000) 'The idea of global citizenship', *Global Society* 14(4): 553–67.

Dunne, Timothy J. (1998) *Inventing International Society: A History of the English School*. Basingstoke: Macmillan.

Dunning, Eric (1986) 'Social bonding and violence in sport', in Norbert Elias and Eric Dunning, *The Quest for Excitement: Sport and Leisure in the Civilizing Process*. Oxford: Basil Blackwell.

Ekman, P. (2003) *Emotions Revealed: Understanding Face and Feelings*. London: Weidenfeld and Nicholson.

Elias, Norbert (1978) *What is Sociology?* New York: Columbia University Press.

Elias, Norbert (1987a) *Involvement and Detachment*. Oxford: Basil Blackwell.

Elias, Norbert (1987b) 'On human beings and their emotions: a process-sociological essay', *Theory, Culture and Society* 4(2–3): 339–61.

Elias, Norbert (1991) *The Symbol Theory*. London: Sage.

Elias, Norbert (1992) *Time: An Essay*. Oxford: Basil Blackwell.

Elias, Norbert (1994) *Reflections on a Life*. Cambridge: Polity Press.

Elias, Norbert (1995) 'Technization and civilization', *Theory, Culture and Society* 12(3): 18–41.

Elias, Norbert (1996) *The Germans: Power Struggles and the Development of Habitus in the Nineteenth and Twentieth Centuries*. Cambridge: Polity Press.

Elias, Norbert (1997) 'Toward a theory of social processes: an introduction', *British Journal of Sociology* 48(3): 355–83.

Elias, Norbert (1998a) 'Informalization and the civilizing process', in Johan Goudsblom and Stephen Mennell (eds) *The Norbert Elias Reader*. Oxford: Basil Blackwell.

Elias, Norbert (1998b) 'An outline of *The Civilizing Process*', in Johan Goudsblom and Stephen Mennell (eds) *The Norbert Elias Reader*. Oxford: Basil Blackwell.

Elias, Norbert (1998c) 'The civilizing of parents', in Johan Goudsblom and Stephen Mennell (eds) *The Norbert Elias Reader*. Oxford: Basil Blackwell.

Elias, Norbert (1998d) 'An interview in Amsterdam', in Johan Goudsblom and Stephen Mennell (eds) *The Norbert Elias Reader*. Oxford: Basil Blackwell.

Elias, Norbert (1998e) 'The breakdown of civilization', in Johan Goudsblom and Stephen Mennell (eds) *The Norbert Elias Reader*. Oxford: Basil Blackwell.

Elias, Norbert (1998f) 'The expulsion of the Huguenots from France', in Johan Goudsblom and Stephen Mennell (eds) *The Norbert Elias Reader*. Oxford: Basil Blackwell.

Elias, Norbert (2000) *The Civilizing Process: Sociogenetic and Psychogenetic Investigations*. Oxford: Basil Blackwell.

Elias, Norbert (2001a) *The Society of Individuals*. London: Continuum.

Elias, Norbert (2001b) *The Loneliness of the Dying*. London: Continuum.

Elias, Norbert and Eric Dunning (1986) *Quest for Excitement: Sport and Leisure in the Civilizing Process*. Oxford: Blackwell.

Elias, Norbert and John L. Scotson (1994) *The Established and the Outsiders: A Sociological Enquiry into Community Problems*. London: Sage.

Engels, Friedrich (1969) 'Principles of Communism', in Friedrich Engels, *Selected Works*. Moscow: Progress Publishers.

Evans, Senator Gareth (1989a) 'Making Australian foreign policy', Melbourne: Australian Fabian Society.

Evans, Senator Gareth (1989b) 'Human rights and Australian foreign policy', an address to the National Annual General Meeting of Amnesty International, Sydney, 19 May.

Evans, Gareth and Bruce Grant (1991) *Australia's Foreign Relations in the World of the 1990s*. Melbourne: Melbourne University Press.

Evans, Michael (1975) *Karl Marx*. London: Allen and Unwin.

Evans, Michael D. (1994) *International Law Documents*, 2nd edn. London: Blackstone Press.

Evans, Richard J. (1997) *Rituals of Retribution: Capital Punishment in Germany, 1600–1987*. London: Penguin.

Falk, Richard (1983) 'On the recent further decline of international law', in Anthony R. Blackshield (ed.) *Legal Change: Essays in Honour of Julius Stone*. Sydney: Butterworths.

Falk, Richard (1990) 'Evasions of sovereignty', in R.B.J. Walker and S. Mendlowitz (eds) *Contending Sovereignties: Redefining Political Community*. Boulder, CO: Lynne Rienner.

Falk, Richard (1994) 'The making of global citizenship', in Bart Van Steenbergen (ed.) *The Condition of Citizenship*. London: Sage.

Falk, Richard (1998) 'The United Nations and cosmopolitan democracy: bad dream, utopian fantasy, political project', in Danielle Archibugi, David Held and Martin Kohler (eds) *Re-imagining Political Community: Studies in Cosmopolitan Democracy*. Cambridge: Polity Press.

Feinberg, Joel (1984) *Harm to Others: The Moral Limits of the Criminal Law*. Oxford: Oxford University Press.

Ferguson, R. Brian (1997) 'Violence and war in prehistory', in D.L. Martin and D.W. Frayer (eds) *Troubled Times: Violence and Warfare in the Past*. Amsterdam: Gordon and Breach.

Fichte, Johann Gottlieb (1869) *The Science of Rights*. Philadelphia, PA: J.B. Lippincott.

Filmer, Robert (1949) *Patriarcha and Other Political Works* (edited with an introduction by Peter Laslett). New York: Macmillan.

Finer, Samuel (1997) *A History of Government*. Oxford: Clarendon Press.

Finnemore, Martha (1999) 'Rules of war and wars of rules: the International Red Cross and the restraint of state violence', in John Boli and George M. Thomas (eds) *Constructing World Culture: International Nongovernmental Organisations since 1875*. Stanford, CA: Stanford University Press.

Fletcher, Jonathan (1997) *Violence and Civilization: An Introduction to the Work of Norbert Elias*. Cambridge: Polity Press.

Forsyth, Murray, H.M.A. Keens-Soper and P. Savigear (eds) (1970) *Theories of International Relations: Selected Texts from Gentili to Treitschke*. London: Allen and Unwin.

Foucault, Michel (1979) *Discipline and Punish: The Birth of the Prison*. Harmondsworth: Penguin.

Frazer, Elizabeth and Nicola Lacey (1993) *The Politics of Community: A Feminist Critique of the Liberal–Communitarian Debate*. Hemel Hempstead: Harvester.

Fromm, Erich (1989) 'Politics and psychoanalysis', in Stephen E. Bronner and D.M. Kellner (eds) *Critical Theory and Society*. London: Routledge.

Gaita, Raimond (2002) *A Common Humanity: Thinking about Love and Truth and Justice*. London: Routledge.

Gallie, W. Bryce (1978) *Philosophers of Peace and War*. Cambridge: Cambridge University Press.

Gamble, Andrew (1999) 'Marxism after communism: beyond realism and historicism', *Review of International Studies* 25(4): 127–44.

Garlan, Yvon (1976) *War in the Ancient World: A Social History*. London: Chatto and Windus.

Garland, David (1990) *Punishment and Modern Society: A Study in Social Theory*. Oxford: Clarendon Press.

Garnsey, Peter (1974) 'Legal privilege in the Roman Empire', in Moses I. Finley (ed.) *Studies in Ancient History*. London: Routledge and Kegan Paul.

Gay, Peter (1994) *The Cultivation of Hatred: The Bourgeois Experience*. London: Harper Collins.

Gellately, Robert (2001) *Backing Hitler: Consent and Coercion in Nazi Germany*. Oxford: Oxford University Press.

Gellner, Ernest (1983) *Nations and Nationalism*. New York: Cornell University Press.

George, Jim (1994) *Discourses of Global Politics: A Critical (Re)Introduction to International Relations*. Boulder, CO: Lynne Rienner.

Geras, Norman (1999) 'The view from everywhere', *Review of International Studies* 25(1): 157–63.

Giddens, Anthony (1985) *The Nation-State and Violence*. Cambridge: Polity Press.

Gill, Stephen (1995) 'Globalization, market civilisation and disciplinary neoliberalism', *Millennium* 24(3): 399–423.

Gilligan, Carol (1993) *In a Different Voice*. Cambridge, MA: Harvard University Press.

Goldgeier, James M. and Michael McFaul (1992) 'A tale of two worlds: core and periphery in the post-Cold War era', *International Organisation* 46(2): 467–91.

Goldhagen, Daniel J. (1996) *Hitler's Willing Executioners: Ordinary Germans and the Holocaust*. London: Little Brown.

Gong, Gerrit (1984) *The Standard of Civilization in International Society*. Oxford: Clarendon Press.

Goodin, Robert E. (1985) *Protecting the Vulnerable: A Reanalysis of our Social Responsibilities*. London: University of Chicago Press.

Goudsblom, Johan (1990) 'Norbert Elias, 1897–1990', *Theory, Culture and Society* 7(4): 169–74.

Goudsblom, Johan and Stephen Mennell (eds) (1998) *The Norbert Elias Reader*. Oxford: Basil Blackwell.

Green, Thomas Hill (1916) *Prolegomena to Ethics*. Oxford: Clarendon Press.

Green, Thomas Hill (1966) *Lectures on the Principles of Political Obligation*. London: Longmans.

Haas, Jonathan (1990) *The Anthropology of War*. Cambridge: Cambridge University Press.

Habermas, Jurgen (1972) *Knowledge and Human Interests*. Boston, MA: Beacon Press.

Habermas, Jurgen (1979a) *Communication and the Evolution of Society*. London: Heinemann.

Habermas, Jurgen (1979b) 'History and evolution', *Telos* 39: 5–44.

Habermas, Jurgen (1984) *The Theory of Communicative Action*, Vol.1, *Reason and the Rationalisation of Society*. Boston, MA: Beacon Press.

Habermas, Jurgen (1985) 'A philosophical–political profile', *New Left Review* 151: 75–105.

Habermas, Jurgen (1989) *The Theory of Communicative Action,* Vol. 2, *The Critique of Functionalist Reason.* Cambridge: Polity Press.

Habermas, Jurgen (1990) *Moral Consciousness and Communicative Action.* Cambridge: Polity Press.

Habermas, Jurgen (1993) 'Reflections on the development of Horkheimer's work', in Seyla Benhabib, Wolfgang Bonß and John McCole (eds) *On Max Horkheimer: New Perspectives.* Cambridge: MIT Press.

Habermas, Jurgen (1994) *The Past as Future.* Cambridge: Polity Press.

Habermas, Jurgen (1996) *Between Facts and Norms: Contributions to a Discourse Theory of Law and Democracy.* Cambridge: Polity Press.

Habermas, Jurgen (1997) 'Kant's idea of perpetual peace, with the benefit of two hundred year's hindsight', in James Bohman and Matthias Lutz-Bachmann (eds) *Perpetual Peace: Essays on Kant's Cosmopolitan Ideal.* London: MIT Press.

Hacke, Jurgen (2005) 'The Frankfurt School and international relations: on the centrality of recognition', *Review of International Studies* 31(1): 181–94.

Haferkamp, Hans (1987) 'From the intra-state to the inter-state civilizing process?' *Theory, Culture and Society* 4(2–3): 545–57.

Halliday, Fred (1994) *Rethinking International Relations.* London: Palgrave.

Hanke, Lewis (1955) *Aristotle and the American Indians.* Chicago: Henry Regnery and Co.

Hanson, Victor (1998) *Warfare and Agriculture in Ancient Greece.* London: University of California Press.

Harre, Rom and W. Gerrod Parrott (eds) (1996) *The Emotions: Social Cultural and Biological Dimensions.* London: Sage.

Harris, D. (1987) *Justifying Social Welfare: The New Right versus the Old Left.* Oxford: Basil Blackwell.

Harris, Paul L. (1989) *Children and Emotion: The Development of Psychological Understanding.* Oxford: Blackwell.

Hart, H.L.A. (1961) *The Concept of Law.* Oxford: Oxford University Press.

Hart, H.L.A. (1963) *Law, Morality and Society.* Oxford: Oxford University Press.

Havel, Vaclav (1999) 'Speech on Kosovo', *The New York Review of Books,* 10 June.

Heater, Derek (1990) *Citizenship: The Civic Ideal in World History, Politics and Education.* London: Longman Press.

Heater, Derek (1996) *World Citizenship and Government: Cosmopolitan Ideas in the History of Western Political Thought.* Basingstoke: Macmillan.

Hegel, G.W.F. (1952) *The Philosophy of Right.* Oxford: Clarendon Press.

Hegel, G.W.F. (1956) *The Philosophy of History.* New York: Dover Publications.

Held, David (1993) 'Democracy: from city states to a cosmopolitan order', in David Held (ed.) *Prospects for Democracy: North, South, East, West.* Cambridge: Polity Press.

Held, David (1995) *Democracy and the Global Order: From the Modern State to Cosmopolitan Governance.* Cambridge: Polity Press.

Hirst, Paul and Graeme Thompson (1995) 'Globalisation and the future of the nation-state', *Economy and Society* 24(3): 408–42.

Hobden, Steve (1998) *International Relations and Historical Sociology.* London: Routledge.

Hobden, Steve and John Hobson (eds) (2002) *Historical Sociology of International Relations.* Cambridge: Cambridge University Press.

Hobhouse, Leonard T. (1906) *Morals in Evolution.* New York: Henry Holt and Co.

Hobsbawm, Eric (1964) Introduction to *Marx's Pre-capitalist Economic Formations*. London: Wishart.

Hoffmann, Stanley (1960) *Contemporary Theory in International Relations*. Westport, CT: Greenwood.

Hoffmann, Stanley (1965) 'Rousseau on war and peace', in S. Hoffmann, *The State of War: Essays on the Theory and Practice of International Politics*. London: Pall Mall Press.

Hoffmann, Stanley (1990) 'International society', in J.D.B. Miller and R.J. Vincent (eds) *Order and Violence: Hedley Bull and International Relations*. Oxford: Clarendon Press.

Hollis, Martin and Steve Smith (1990) *Explaining and Understanding International Relations*. Oxford: Clarendon Press.

Honderich, Ted (1980) 'Our omissions and their violence', in Ted Honderich, *Violence for Equality: Inquiries into Political Philosophy*. Harmondsworth: Pelican.

Honneth, Axel (1991) *Critique of Power: Reflective Stages in a Critical Social Theory*. London: MIT Press.

Honneth, Axel (1995) *The Struggle for Recognition: The Moral Grammar of Social Conflicts*. Cambridge: Polity Press.

Honneth, Axel 'Mutual recognition as a key for a universal ethics', available at www.unesco.or.kr/.

Horkheimer, Max (1974) 'Schopenhauer today', in Max Horkheimer, *Critique of Instrumental Reason*. New York: Seabury.

Horkheimer, Max (1978) 'Traditional and critical theory', in Paul Connerton (ed.) *Critical Sociology: Selected Readings*. Harmondsworth: Penguin.

Horkheimer, Max (1993) 'Materialism and morality', in Max Horkheimer, *Between Philosophy and Social Science: Selected Early Writings*. Cambridge: MIT Press.

Hoy, David C. (1986) *Foucault: A Critical Reader*. Oxford: Blackwell.

Huizinga, Johan (1955) *The Waning of the Middle Ages*. Harmondsworth: Penguin.

Hume, David (1969) *A Treatise of Human Nature*. Harmondsworth: Penguin.

Hurrell, Andrew (1994) 'A crisis of ecological viability? Global environmental change and the nation-state', *Political Studies*, 42(special issue): 146–65.

Ignatieff, Michael (1991) 'Citizenship and moral narcissism', in Geoff Andrews (ed.) *Citizenship*. London: Lawrence and Wishart.

Jackson, Robert (2000) *The Global Covenant: Human Conduct in a World of States*. Oxford: Oxford University Press.

James, Alan (1986) *Sovereign Statehood: The Basis of International Society*. London: Allen and Unwin.

Johansen, Robert C. (1980) *The National Interest and the Human Interest: An Analysis of U.S. Foreign Policy*. Princeton, NJ: Princeton University Press.

Kalberg, Stephen (1994) *Max Weber's Comparative Historical Sociology*. Cambridge: Polity Press.

Kaldor, Mary (1999) *New and Old Wars: Organized Violence in a Global Era*. Cambridge: Polity Press.

Kant, Immanuel (1963) *Conjectural Beginning of Human History*, in Lewis W. Beck (ed.) *Kant on History*. Indianapolis, IN: Bobbs-Merrill.

Kant, Immanuel (1964) *The Metaphysical Principles of Virtue*. New York: Bobbs-Merrill.

Kant, Immanuel (1970a) *Idea for a Universal History from a Cosmo-political Point of View*, in M.G. Forsyth, H.M.A. Keens-Soper and P. Savigear (eds) *The Theory of International Relations: Selected Texts from Gentili to Treitschke*. London: Allen and Unwin.

Kant, Immanuel (1970b) 'Perpetual peace', in M. Forsyth, H.M.A. Keens-Soper and P. Savigear (eds) *The Theory of International Relations: Selected Texts from Gentili to Treitschke.* London: Allen and Unwin.

Kant, Immanuel (1970c) 'Idea for a universal history with a cosmopolitan purpose', in H. Reiss (ed.) *Kant's Political Writings.* Cambridge: Cambridge University Press.

Katz, Steven T. (1994) *The Holocaust in Historical Context, Volume One, The Holocaust and Mass Death in the Modern Age.* Oxford: Oxford University Press.

Keeley, Lawrence H. (1996) *War Before Civilization: The Myth of the Peaceful Savage.* Oxford: Oxford University Press.

Keenan, Tom (1987) 'The paradox of knowledge and power: reading Foucault on a bias', *Political Theory* 15(1): 5–37.

Keohane, Robert O. and Joseph S. Nye (1989) *Power and Interdependence.* Glenview, IL: Scott, Foresman and Co.

Kern, Paul B. (1999) *Ancient Siege Warfare.* London: Souvenir Press.

King, Desmond S. (1987) *The New Right: Politics, Markets and Citizenship.* Basingstoke: Macmillan.

Kissinger, Henry (1979) *White House Years.* London: Weidenfeld and Nicholson.

Konstan, David (2001) *Pity Transformed.* London: Duckworth.

Kozak, Nancy (2001a) 'Moderating power: a thucydidean perspective', *Review of International Studies* 27(1): 27–49.

Kozak, Nancy (2001b) 'Between anarchy and tyranny: excellence and the pursuit of power and peace in Ancient Greece', *Review of International Studies* 27(special issue): 91–118.

van Krieken, Robert (1998) *Norbert Elias.* London: Routledge.

Kutz, Charles (2000) *Complicity: Ethics and Law for a Collective Age.* Cambridge: Cambridge University Press.

Kyle, Donald G. (1998) *Spectacles of Death in Ancient Rome.* London: Routledge.

Kymlicka, Will (1989) *Liberalism, Community and Culture.* Oxford: Oxford University Press.

Kymlicka, Will (1995) *Multicultural Citizenship: A Liberal Theory of Minority Rights.* Oxford: Clarendon Press.

Lifton, Robert J. (2000) *The Nazi Doctors: Medical Killing and the Psychology of Genocide.* New York: Basic Books.

Linklater, Andrew (1990a) *Beyond Realism and Marxism: Critical Theory and International Relations.* London: Macmillan.

Linklater, Andrew (1990b) *Men and Citizens in the Theory of International Relations*, 2nd edn. London: Macmillan.

Linklater, Andrew (1992) 'The question of the next stage: a critical–theoretical point of view', *Millennium* 21(1): 77–98.

Linklater, Andrew (1994) 'Neo-realism in theory and practice', in Ken Booth and Steve Smith (eds) *International Political Theory Today.* Cambridge: Polity Press.

Linklater, Andrew (1995) 'Political community', in Alex Danchev (ed.) *Fin De Siecle: The Meaning of the Twentieth Century.* London: Tauris Academic Publishing.

Linklater, Andrew (1998) *The Transformation of Political Community: Ethical Foundations of the Post-Westphalian Era.* Cambridge: Polity Press.

Linklater, Andrew (1999) 'Cosmopolitan citizenship', in Kimberly Hutchings and Roland Dannreuther (eds) *Cosmopolitan Citizenship.* London: Macmillan.

Linklater, Andrew (2002) 'Unnecessary suffering', in Ken Booth and Timothy J. Dunne (eds) *Worlds in Collision: Terror and the Global Order.* London: Palgrave.

Linklater, Andrew (2005) 'A European civilising process?', in Christopher J. Hill and Michael Smith (eds) *International Relations and the European Union*. Oxford: Oxford University Press.

Linklater, Andrew (2006a) 'The harm principle and global ethics', *Global Society* 20(3): 329–43.

Linklater, Andrew (2006b) 'Distant suffering and cosmopolitan obligation', *International Politics* 44(1): 19–36.

Linklater, Andrew and Hidemi Suganami (2006) *The English School of International Relations: A Contemporary Reassessment*. Cambridge: Cambridge University Press.

Lovejoy, Arthur O. (1941) 'The meaning of romanticism for the historian of ideas', *Journal of the History of Ideas* 2(3): 257–78.

Luard, Evan (1976) *Types of International Society*. London: Free Press.

Lyotard, Jean-Francois (1993) 'The other's rights', in Stephen Shute and Susan Hurley (eds) *On Human Rights: The Oxford Amnesty Lectures*. New York: Oxford University Press.

McCarthy, Thomas (1981) *The Critical Theory of Jurgen Habermas*. London: MIT Press.

McCarthy, Thomas (1990) 'The critique of impure reason: Foucault and the Frankfurt School', *Political Theory* 18(3): 437–69.

McCarthy, Thomas (1997) 'On the idea of a reasonable law of peoples', in James Bohman and Matthias Lutz-Bachmann (eds) *Perpetual Peace: Essays on Kant's Cosmopolitan Ideal*. London: MIT Press.

Macaulay, Lord (1880) 'Notes on the Indian penal code', in Lord Macaulay, *Miscellaneous Works of Lord Macaulay*. New York: Harper.

MacIntyre, Alasdair (1984) *Is Patriotism a Virtue?* Lawrence, KN: University of Kansas.

Mann, Michael (1986) *The Sources of Social Power, Vol. One, A History of Power from the Beginning to 1760*. Cambridge: Cambridge University Press.

Mann, Michael (1987) 'Ruling class strategies and citizenship', *Sociology* 21(3): 339–43.

Mann, Michael (1993) *The Sources of Social Power, Vol. Two, The Rise of Classes and Nation-States, 1760–1914*. Cambridge: Cambridge University Press.

Manning, Patrick (2003) *Navigating World History: Historians Create a Global Past*. Basingstoke: Palgrave Macmillan.

Marcuse, Herbert (1969) *Reason and Revolution*. London: Routledge and Kegan Paul.

Marcuse, Herbert (1972) *An Essay on Liberation*. Harmondsworth: Pelican.

Marshall, T.H. (1973) *Class, Citizenship and Social Development*. Westport, CT: Greenwood Press.

Marx, Karl (1977a) *Theses on Feuerbach*, in David McLellan (ed.) *Karl Marx: Selected Writings*. Oxford: Oxford University Press.

Marx, Karl (1977b) *The Eighteenth Brumaire of Louis Bonaparte*, in David McLellan (ed.) *Karl Marx: Selected Writings*. Oxford: Oxford University Press.

Marx, Karl (1977c) *The German Ideology*, in David McLellan (ed.) *Karl Marx: Selected Writings*. Oxford: Oxford University Press.

Mason, Michael (2001) 'Transnational environmental obligations: locating new spaces of accountability in a post-Westphalian order', *Transactions of the Institute of British Geographers* 26(4): 407–29.

Meinecke, Friedrich (1970) *Cosmopolitanism and the National State*. Princeton, NJ: Princeton University Press.

Mennell, Stephen (1987) 'Comment on Haferkamp', *Theory, Culture and Society* 4(2–3): 559–61.

Mennell, Stephen (1990) 'The globalization of human society as a very long-term social process: Elias's theory', *Theory, Culture and Society* 7(2–3): 359–71.

Mennell, Stephen (1994) 'The formation of we-images: a process theory', in C. Calhoun (ed.) *Social Theory and the Politics of Identity*. Oxford: Blackwell.

Mennell, Stephen (1996a) 'Civilizing and decivilizing processes', in Johan Goudsblom, Eric L. Jones, and Stephen Mennell, *The Course of Human History: Economic Growth, Social Process and Civilization*. London: M.E. Sharpe.

Mennell, Stephen (1996b) 'Asia and Europe: comparing civilizing processes', in Johan Goudsblom, Eric L. Jones, and Stephen Mennell, *The Course of Human History: Economic Growth, Social Process and Civilization*. London: M.E. Sharpe.

Mennell, Stephen (1998) *Norbert Elias: An Introduction*. Dublin: University College Dublin Press.

Mennell, Stephen and John Rundell (eds) (1998) *Classical Readings in Culture and Civilization*. London: Routledge.

Mill, John Stuart (1962) *On Liberty*, in J.S. Mill, *Utilitarianism* (edited by Mary Warnock). London: Collins.

Miller, David (1988) 'The ethical significance of nationality', *Ethics* 98(4): 647–62.

Miller, David (1989) *Market, State and Community: Theoretical Foundations of Market Socialism*. Oxford: Clarendon Press.

Miller, David (1999) 'Bounded citizenship', in Kimberly Hutchings and Roland Dannreuther (eds) *Cosmopolitan Citizenship*. London: Macmillan.

Mitrany, David (1960) *A Working Peace System*. Chicago, IL: Quadrant Books.

Moeller, Susan D. (1999) *Compassion Fatigue: How the Media Sell Disease, Famine, War and Death*. London: Routledge.

Morgan, Catherine A. (2003) 'The figurational imagination and international relations', *Figurations: Newsletter of the Norbert Elias Foundation*, 20: 3–5 (published by University College Dublin).

Morgenthau, Hans (1973) *Politics Among Nations: The Struggle for Power and Peace*. New York: Alfred A. Knopf.

Moss, Jeremy (ed.) (1998) *The Later Foucault: Politics and Philosophy*. London: Sage.

Mueller, John (1989) *Retreat from Doomsday: The Obsolescence of Major War*. New York: Basic Books.

Murphy, Jeffrie G. (1970) *Kant: The Philosophy of Right*. London: Macmillan.

Murphy, Raymond (1988) *Social Closure: The Theory of Monopolisation and Closure*. Oxford: Oxford University Press.

Nagel, Thomas (1986) *The View from Nowhere*. Oxford: Oxford University Press.

Neff, Stephen C. (1999) 'International law and the critique of cosmopolitan citizenship', in Kimberly Hutchings and Roland Dannreuther (eds) *Cosmopolitan Citizenship*. London: Macmillan.

Nelson, Benjamin (1971) 'Note on the notion of civilization by Emile Durkheim and Marcel Mauss', *Social Research* 38(4): 808–13.

Nelson, Benjamin (1973) 'Civilizational complexes and inter-civilizational relations', *Sociological Analysis* 34(2): 79–105.

Nussbaum, Martha (1997) 'Kant and cosmopolitanism', in James Bohman and Matthias Lutz-Bachmann (eds) *Perpetual Peace: Essays on Kant's Cosmopolitan Ideal*. London: MIT Press.

Nussbaum, Martha (2001) *Upheavals of Thought: The Intelligence of Emotions*. Cambridge: Cambridge University Press.

Nussbaum, Martha (2002) 'Patriotism and cosmopolitanism', in Martha Nussbaum, *For Love of Country?* Boston: Beacon Press.

Oakley, Justin (1992) *Morality and the Emotions.* London: Routledge.

O'Brien, George D. (1975) *Hegel on Reason and History.* Chicago: University of Chicago Press.

O'Malley J. (ed.) (1970) *Marx's Critique of Hegel's Philosophy of Right.* Cambridge: Cambridge University Press.

O'Neill, Onora (1988) 'Ethical reasoning and ideological pluralism', *Ethics* 98(4): 705–22.

O'Neill, Onora (1989) 'Justice, gender and international boundaries', *British Journal of Political Science* 20(4): 439–59.

O'Neill, Onora (1991) 'Transnational justice', in David Held (ed.) *Political Theory Today.* Cambridge: Polity Press.

O'Neill, Onora (1996) *Towards Justice and Virtue: A Constructive Account of Practical Reason.* Cambridge: Cambridge University Press.

O'Neill, Onora (2000) *Bounds of Justice.* Cambridge: Cambridge University Press.

Parekh, Bhikkhu (1991) 'British citizenship and cultural difference', in Geoff Andrews (ed.) *Citizenship.* London: Lawrence and Wishart.

Phillips, A. (1991) 'Citizenship and feminist theory', in Geoff Andrews (ed.) *Citizenship.* London: Lawrence and Wishart.

Plant, Raymond (1973) *Hegel.* London: George Allen and Unwin.

Pogge, Thomas (2002) *World Poverty and Human Rights.* Cambridge: Polity.

Preuss, Ulrich K. (1998) 'Citizenship in the European Union: a paradigm for transnational democracy?', in Danielle Archibugi, David Held and Martin Kohler (eds) *Re-imagining Political Community: Studies in Cosmopolitan Democracy.* Cambridge: Polity Press.

Price, Richard and Chris Reus-Smit (1998) 'Dangerous liaisons? Critical international theory and constructivism', *European Journal of International Relations* 4(3): 259–94.

von Pufendorf, Samuel (1927) *The Two Books on the Duty of Man and Citizen According to the Natural Law.* Washington, DC: Carnegie Institution of Washington.

von Pufendorf, Samuel (1934a) *The Two Books of the Elements of Universal Jurisprudence.* Oxford: Clarendon Press.

von Pufendorf, Samuel (1934b) *The Law of Nature and Nations: Eight Books.* New York: Carnegie Endowment for International Peace.

Rabinow, Paul (1986) *The Foucault Reader.* Harmondsworth: Penguin.

Rae, Heather (2002) *State Identities and the Homogenisation of Peoples.* Cambridge: Cambridge University Press.

Raschke, Carl A. (1975) *Moral Action, God and History in the Thought of Immanuel Kant*, University of Montana Dissertation Series No.5. Missoula, MT: University of Montana.

Ray, James L. (1989) 'The abolition of slavery and the end of war', *International Organisation* 43(3): 405–39.

Reus-Smit, Christian (1999) *The Moral Purpose of the State: Culture, Social Identity and Institutional Rationality in international Politics.* Princeton, NJ: Princeton University Press.

Richardson, James (1997) 'Contending liberalisms', *European Journal of International Relations* 3(1): 5–33.

Roberts, Adam (1993) 'Humanitarian war: military intervention and human rights', *International Affairs* 69(3): 429–49.

Robertson, Roland (1992) 'Civilization and the civilizing process: Elias, globalization and analytic synthesis', *Theory, Culture and Society* 9(1): 211–27.

Rojek, Chris (2004) 'An anatomy of the Leicester School of Sociology: an interview with Eric Dunning', *Journal of Classical Sociology* 4(3): 337–59.

Rorty, Richard (1989) *Contingency, Irony and Solidarity*. Cambridge: Cambridge University Press.

Rosecrance, Richard (1986) *The Rise of the Trading State: Commerce and Conquest in the Modern World*. New York: Basic Books.

Rosenberg, Justin (1994) *The Empire of Civil Society: A Critique of the Realist Theory of International Relations*. London: Verso.

Ross, W. David (1930) *The Right and the Good*. Oxford: Clarendon Press.

Rousseau, Jean-Jacques (1968) *A Discourse on the Origin of Inequality, The Social Contract and Discourses* (edited by G.D.H. Cole). London: Everyman.

Rousseau, Jean-Jacques (1970) 'Abstract of the Abbé de Saint-Pierre's project for perpetual peace', in M.G. Forsyth, H.M.A. Keens-Soper and P. Savigear (eds) *The Theory of International Relations: Selected Texts from Gentili to Treitschke*. London: Unwin University Books.

Rowe, Christopher and Malcolm Schofield (eds) (2000) *Cambridge History of Greek and Roman Political Thought*. Cambridge: Cambridge University Press.

Rowse, Tim (1998) *White Flour, White Power: From Rations to Citizenship in Central Australia*. Cambridge: Cambridge University Press.

Ruggie, John (1983) 'Continuity and transformation in the world polity: towards a neorealist synthesis', *World Politics* 35(1): 261–85.

Sadowski, Yahya (1998) *The Myth of Global Chaos*. Washington, DC: Brookings Institution Press.

Sarat, Austin (ed.) (2001) *Pain, Death and the Law*. Ann Arbor, MI: University of Michigan Press.

Scheff, Thomas (1994) *Bloody Revenge: Emotions, Nationalism and War*. Boulder, CO: Westview Press.

Schelling, Thomas C. (1966) *Arms and Influence*. London: Yale University Press.

Schiller, Friedrich (1967) *Letters on the Aesthetic Education of Man*. Oxford: Clarendon Press.

Schnabel, Albert and Ramesh Thakur (eds) (2000) *Kosovo and the Challenge of Humanitarian Intervention: Selective Indignation, Collective Action and International Citizenship*. Tokyo: United Nations University Press.

Scholte, Jan-Aart (1993) *International Relations of Social Change*. Buckingham: Open University Press.

Schopenhauer, Arthur (1995) *On the Basis of Morality*. Oxford: Berghahn.

Shapcott, Richard (1994) 'Conversation and coexistence: Gadamer and the interpretation of international society', *Millennium* 23(1): 57–83.

Sharp, Paul (2001) 'The English School, Herbert Butterfield and diplomacy', paper presented to the *International Studies Association Annual Conference*, New Orleans, LA, 24–27 March.

Sharp, Paul (2003) 'Herbert Butterfield, the English School and the civilizing virtues of diplomacy', *International Affairs* 79(4): 855–78.

Shaw, Martin (1991) *Post-Military Society: Militarism, Demilitarization and War at the End of the Twentieth Century*. Cambridge: Polity Press.

Shipley, Graham (1995) 'The limits of war', in John Rich and Graham Shipley (eds) *War and Society in the Greek World*. London: Routledge.

Shiva, Vandina (2000) 'Ecological balance in an era of globalization', in Paul Wapner and L. Edwin J. Ruiz (eds) *Principled World Politics: The Challenge of Normative International Relations*. Oxford: Rowman and Littlefield.

Shklar, Judith (1984) *Ordinary Vices*. London: Harvard University Press.

Shue, Henry (1988) 'Mediating ethics', *Ethics* 98(4): 687–704.

Shue, Henry (1981) 'Exporting hazards', in Peter G. Brown and Henry Shue (eds) *Boundaries: National Autonomy and its Limits*. Towota, NJ: Rowman and Littlefield.

Simons, Kenneth W. (1999) 'Negligence', in Ellen Frankel Paul, Fred D. Miller and Jeffrey Paul (eds) *Responsibility*. Cambridge: Cambridge University Press.

Skocpol, Theda (1979) *States and Social Revolutions*. Cambridge: Cambridge University Press.

Smith, Adam (1982) *Theory of Moral Sentiments*. Indianapolis, IN: Liberty Fund.

Smith, Dennis (2001) *Norbert Elias and Modern Social Theory*. London: Sage.

Snowden, Frank M. (1983). *Beyond Color Prejudice: The Ancient View of Blacks*. Cambridge, MA: Harvard University Press.

Sontag, Susan (2003) *Regarding the Pain of Others*. London: Hamish Hamilton.

Spierenburg, Peter (1991) *The Broken Spell: A Cultural and Anthropological History of Preindustrial Europe*. New Brunswick, NJ: Rutgers University Press.

Stearns, Peter N. and Carol Z. Stearns (1985) 'Emotionology: clarifying the history of the emotions and emotional standards', *American Historical Review* 90(4): 813–36.

Sterling, Richard W. (1958) *Ethics in a World of Power: The Political Ideas of Meinecke*. Princeton, NJ: Princeton University Press.

Stern, Alfred (1962) *Philosophy of History and the Problem of Values*. The Hague: Mouton and Co.

Stevens, Christine (1994) *White Man's Dreaming: Killipaninna Mission 1866–1915*. Melbourne: Oxford University Press.

Stirk, Peter M.R. (1992) *Max Horkheimer: A New Interpretation*. Hemel Hempstead: Harvester Wheatsheaf.

Suganami, Hidemi (1989) *The Domestic Analogy and World Order Proposals*. Cambridge: Cambridge University Press.

Sznaider, Natan (2001) *The Compassionate Society: Care and Cruelty in Modern Society*. Oxford: Rowman and Littlefield.

Taylor, Charles (1975) *Hegel*. Cambridge: Cambridge University Press.

Taylor, Charles (1985) 'Connolly, Foucault, and truth', *Political Theory* 13(3): 377–85.

Taylor, Charles (1994) *Multiculturalism and the Politics of Recognition*. Princeton, NJ: Princeton University Press.

Taylor, Charles (1989) *Sources of the Self: The Making of Modernity*. Cambridge: Cambridge University Press.

Taylor, Craig (2004) *Sympathy: A Philosophical Analysis*. London: Routledge.

Tester, Keith (1997) *Moral Culture*. London: Sage.

Thakur, Ramesh and William Maley (1999) 'The Ottowa Convention on Landmines: a landmark humanitarian treaty in arms control?', *Global Governance* 5(3): 273–301.

Thomas, Caroline (1999) 'Where is the Third World now?' *Review of International Studies* 25(special issue): 225–44.

Thomas, Keith (1984) *Man and the Natural World: Changing Attitudes in England, 1500–1800*. Harmondsworth: Penguin.

Thomas, Ward (2001) *The Ethics of Destruction: Norms and Force in International Relations*. London: Cornell University Press.

Tilly, Charles (1992) *Coercion, Capital and European States AD 900–1992*. Oxford: Basil Blackwell.

Todorov, Tzvetan (1984) The *Conquest of America*. New York: Harper and Row.

Toynbee, Arnold (1978) *Mankind and Mother Earth*. London: Paladin.

Treitschke, Heinrich von (1915) *'Die Politik': The Political Thought of Heinrich von Treitschke* (edited by H.W.C. Davis) London: Constable.

Tronto, Joan (1993) *Moral Boundaries: A Political Argument for an Ethic of Care*. London: Routledge.

Turner, Bryan S. (ed.) (1986) *Citizenship and Social Theory*. London: Sage.

Turner, Bryan S. (1993) 'Outline of a theory of human rights', *Sociology* 27(3): 489–512.

Ullman, Walter (1961) *Principles of Government and Politics in the Middle Ages*. London: Methuen.

Van Steenbergen, Bart (1994) 'Towards a global ecological citizenship', in Bart Van Steenbergen (ed.) *The Condition of Citizenship*. London: Sage.

de Vattel, Emmerich (1916) *The Law of Nations, or the Principles of Natural Law Applied to the Conduct and to the Affairs of Nations and of Sovereigns*. Washington: Carnegie Institution of Washington.

de Vattel, Emmerich (1964) *The Law of Nations; or, Principles of the Law of Nature, applied to the Conduct and Affairs of Nations and Sovereigns*. New York: Wildy.

Verkamp, Bernard J. (1993) *The Moral Treatment of Returning Warriors in Early Medieval and Modern Times*. Scranton, PA: University of Scranton Press.

Vincent, R. John (1986) *Human Rights and International Relations*. Cambridge: Cambridge University Press.

Vincent, R. John (1990). 'Grotius, human rights and intervention', in Hedley Bull, Benedict Kingsbury and Adam Roberts (eds) *Hugo Grotius and International Relations*. Oxford: Clarendon Press.

Vincent, John, and Peter Wilson (1993) 'Beyond non-intervention', in Mark Hoffman and Ian Forbes (eds) *Political Theory, International Relations and the Ethics of Intervention*. London: Macmillan.

van Vree, Wilbert (1999) *Meetings, Manners and Civilization: The Development of Modern Meeting Behaviour*. London: Leicester University Press.

Walker, R.B.J. (1988) *One World, Many Worlds: Struggles for a Just World Peace*. Boulder, CO: Lynne Rienner.

Walker, R.B.J. (1993) *Inside/Outside: International Relations as Political Theory*. Cambridge: Cambridge University Press.

Walsh, W.H. (1969) *Hegelian Ethics*. London: Macmillan.

Walsh, W.H. (1972) 'Open and closed morality', in Bhikkhu Parekh and Robert Berki (eds) *The Morality of Politics*. London: George Allen and Unwin.

Waltz, Kenneth N. (1959) *Man, the State and War: A Theoretical Analysis*. New York: Columbia University Press.

Waltz, Kenneth N. (1979) *Theory of International Politics*. Reading, MA: Addison Wesley.

Walzer, Michael (1970) 'Prisoners of war. Does the fight continue after the battle?', in Michael Walzer, *Obligations: Essays on Disobedience, War and Citizenship*. Cambridge, MA: Harvard University Press.

Walzer, Michael (1980) *Just and Unjust Wars: A Moral Argument with Historical Illustrations*. Harmondsworth: Pelican.

Walzer, Michael (1995) *Spheres of Justice: A Defence of Pluralism and Equality*. Oxford: Blackwell.

Walzer, Michael (2002) 'Spheres of affection', in Martha Nussbaum, *For Love of Country?* Boston, MA: Beacon Press.

Warnock, Geoffrey (1971) *The Object of Morality.* London: Methuen.

Watson, Adam (1992) *The Evolution of International Society.* London: Routledge.

Weil, Simone (1952) *The Need for Roots: Prelude to a Declaration of Duties Towards Mankind.* London: Routledge and Kegan Paul.

Wendt, Alexander (1987) 'The agent–structure problem in international relations theory', *International Organization* 41(3): 335–70.

Wendt, Alexander (1992) 'Anarchy is what states make of it: the social construction of power politics', *International Organization* 46(2): 391–425.

Wertheimer, Alan (1996) *Exploitation.* Princeton, NJ: Princeton University Press.

Wheeler, Nicholas J. (1996) 'Guardian angel or global gangster: the ethical claims of international society revisited', *Political Studies* 44(1): 123–35.

Wheeler, Nicholas J. (1997) 'Humanitarian intervention and world politics', in John Baylis and Steve Smith (eds) *The Globalisation of World Politics: An Introduction to International Relations.* Oxford: Oxford University Press.

Wheeler, Nicholas J. (2000a) 'Humanitarian vigilantes or legal entrepreneurs: enforcing human rights in international society', *Critical Review of International Social and Political Philosophy* 3(1) 139–62.

Wheeler, Nicholas J. (2000b) *Saving Strangers: Humanitarian Intervention in International Society.* Oxford: Oxford University Press.

Wheeler, Nicholas J. (2002) 'Dying for enduring freedom: accepting responsibility for civilian casualties in the war against terrorism', *International Relations* 16(2): 205–25.

Wheeler, Nicholas J. and Timothy J. Dunne (1998) 'Good international citizenship: a Third Way for British foreign policy', *International Affairs* 74(4): 847–70.

White, Stephen K. (1991) *Political Theory and Post-Modernism.* Cambridge: Cambridge University Press.

Whitebook, Joel (1995) *Perversion and Utopia: A Study in Psychoanalysis and Critical Theory.* London: MIT Press.

Whitebook, Joel (1996) 'Fantasy and critique: some thoughts on Freud and the Frankfurt School', in David M. Rasmussen (ed.) *The Handbook of Critical Theory.* Oxford: Blackwell.

Wiggershaus, Rolf (1993) *The Frankfurt School: Its History, Theories and Political Significance.* Cambridge: Polity Press.

Wight, Martin (1966a) 'Why is there no international theory?', in Martin Wight and Herbert Butterfield (eds) *Diplomatic Investigations: Essays in the Theory of International Politics.* London: George Allen and Unwin.

Wight, Martin (1966b) 'Western values in international relations', in Martin Wight and Herbert Butterfield (eds) *Diplomatic Investigations: Essays in the Theory of International Politics.* London: George Allen and Unwin.

Wight, Martin (1977) *Systems of States.* Leicester: University of Leicester Press.

Wight, Martin (1978) *Power Politics.* Leicester: University of Leicester Press.

Wight, Martin (1991) *International Theory: The Three Traditions.* Leicester: University of Leicester Press.

Williams, Howard and Ken Booth (1996) 'Kant: theorist beyond limits', in Ian Clark and Iver B. Neumann (eds) *Classical Theories of International Relations.* Basingstoke: Macmillan.

Williams, Raymond (1976) *Keywords: A Vocabulary of Culture and Society.* Glasgow: Fontana.

Wise, Mark and Richard Gibb (1993) *Single Market to Social Europe: The European Community in the 1990s*. London: Longman.

Wittgenstein, Ludwig (1974) *Philosophical Investigations*. Oxford: Basil Blackwell.

Wright, Andrew (1990) 'The good citizen', *New Statesman and Society*, 18 May: 31–2.

Young, Iris Marion (1991) *Justice and the Politics of Difference*. Princeton, NJ: Princeton University Press.

Zolo, Danilo (1997) *Cosmopolis: Prospects for World Government*. Cambridge: Polity Press.

Index